EARLY TWENTIETH

Lighting Fixtures

featuring:

GAS & ELECTRIC
CEILING, WALL, TABLE
&
ART GLASS FIXTURES

SELECTIONS FROM THE
R. WILLIAMSON
LAMP CATALOG

JO ANN THOMAS

COLLECTOR BOOKS
A Division of Schroeder Publishing Co., Inc.

The current values in this book should be used only as a guide. They are not intended to set prices, which vary from one section of the country to another. Auction prices as well as dealer prices vary greatly and are affected by condition and demand. Neither the author nor the publisher assumes responsibility for any losses which might be incurred as a result of consulting this guide.

Cover Design: Beth Summers

Searching For A Publisher?

We are always looking for knowledgeable people considered experts within their fields. If you feel that there is a real need for a book on your collectible subject and have a large comprehensive collection, contact Collector Books.

Collector Books
P.O. Box 3009
Paducah, KY 42002-3009

INTRODUCTION

Thanks to those who called, wrote, or hollered for a reprint of this book. I would especially like to thank Lisa Stroup at Collector Books for being so gracious and patient, and others on the staff for revitalizing a nearly twenty-year-old book — and its author.

The antique lighting field has seen many changes since 1980. The restoration of vintage houses and commercial buildings has increased the interest in and demand for antique lighting dramatically. But, the interest and demand haven't stopped there. Builders and decorators of new homes and buildings, recognizing the beauty, charm, and diversity, have become enthusiastic admirers of antique lighting.

Besides revising the prices to reflect today's values, I have added several pages to give more information. When pricing or buying, one must always take into consideration the area where purchased, condition, and supply and demand. If it is not possible to find old shades, there are some reproduction shades being made.

ABOUT PRICING

Of prime consideration when buying old fixtures or lamps that are not completely restored — usually referred to as "in the rough" or "as is" condition — should be that while the initial cost may be less than a completely restored piece, the cost of restoration as well as finding someone to do the restoring could well bring the overall price up equal to or even above the price of a piece already restored. Also bear in mind that depending on the style and type of shade or shades used, the overall price of a fixture or lamp can and will vary greatly. For this reason the fixtures in this book are priced without shades except where the shade or shades are made as an integral part of the overall unit, e.g., wood and art glass dome fixtures.

MANUFACTURERS OF AND DEALERS IN
ELECTRICAL SUPPLIES AND ACCESSORIES
— GLASSWARE —
HOLOPHANE
— TEPLITZ —
BENT ART GLASS
— BRASS AND IRON FITTINGS —
MISSION LAMPS AND MISCELLANEOUS GOODS

CATALOGUE NO. 15

ILLUSTRATING

ELECTRIC AND COMBINATION FIXTURES

ART GLASS DOMES

MANUFACTURED BY

R. WILLIAMSON & Co.

WASHINGTON & JEFFERSON STS.

CHICAGO, ILLS. U.S.A.

TO THE TRADE

ATALOGUE 15 is no doubt the most complete of its kind illustrating an up-to-date variety of designs in electric and combination chandeliers and lighting effects. We have endeavored to compile this catalogue in the most practical form so as to make it very convenient in furnishing estimates on complete installations. You will note that all trimmings are listed separately under their respective stock numbers and at per each price, enabling you to figure on any changes that may be necessary in meeting the requirements.

Our art glass studio is complete in every detail which places us in a position to furnish artistic effects as well as making to order art glass shades and domes according to designs furnished.

We guarantee all fixtures to be perfect in material and construction and will make good any unnecessary expense you are put to through any fault of ours.

Will furnish special designs upon application, giving us full information as to about what is required.

Soliciting your many inquiries, we remain,

Respectfully,

R. WILLIAMSON & COMPANY

TO FACILITATE CORRESPONDENCE BY TELEGRAPH THE FOL-
LOWING TELEGRAPH CODE MAY BE USED

REMEMBER

In using the telegraph code, that we will always reply in the code. Furthermore, if we have reason to believe that you have a copy of our catalogue, that we will use code in telegraphing you, regardless of whether or not you have used it in your inquiry.

When ordering goods or asking for quotations by telegraph or telephone always confirm same by letter, marking same "comfirming."

QUESTIONS	ANSWERS
MAN—At what price can you furnish?	PEACH—We will furnish you at........
LADY—At what price and how soon can you furnish?	PEAR—We can ship at once at the net price of.........
BOY—When can you ship?	PLUM—Can ship to-day.
GIRL—Have you shipped order of........?	APPLE—Can ship to-morrow.
BABY—When will you ship order of.......?	PRUNE—Can ship in three days.
WOMAN—How soon can you furnish special designs for ....?	ORANGE—Can ship in one week.
CHILD—Have you in stock? If not, how soon can you ship?	QUINCE—Not in stock, can furnish in...days.
	CHERRY—Your order was shipped..........
PAPA—Can you ship at once upon receipt of order?	MELON—Can furnish designs in......days.
AUNT—Can you furnish electric fixtures No ....in combination and at what price?	GRAPE—Our representative will be there in ......days, in the meantime write full particulars.
UNCLE—Can you furnish combination fixture No......in electric only and at what price?	LEMON—Can furnish goods of any description or make.
COUSIN—Will you send your representative here to figure on large contract?	STRAWBERRY—Will furnish estimate upon receipt of architect's designs.
NEPHEW—Will you furnish fixtures selected from other catalogues?	FIGS—See catalogue, Plate....
NIECE—Will you estimate on special work from architect's designs?	DATES—We are mailing you quotations to-day.
MAID—Did you receive letter of......as we have no reply?	CITRON—We have no letter from you.
SERVANT—What can you substitute in place of.........so you can ship at once?	OLIVE—We have based quotations on immediate acceptance.

DESCRIPTION

Poplar—One light Bracket.
Elm—Two light Bracket.
Fir—Three light Bracket.
Hemlock—Four light Bracket.
Chestnut—Five light Bracket.
Sycamore—One light Fixture.
Cypress—Two light Chandelier.
Ash—Three light Chandelier.
Walnut—Four light Chandelier.
Spruce—Five light Chandelier.
Birch—Six light Chandelier.
Pine—Eight light Chandelier.
Oak—Ten light Chandelier.
Maple—Twelve light Chandelier.
Willow—Fourteen light Chandelier.
Ebony—Sixteen light Chandelier.
Cedar—Eighteen light Chandelier.
Beech—Twenty light Chandelier.
Hickory—Twenty-two light Chandelier.
Mahogany—Twenty-four light Chandelier.

NOTE

We have based the number of lights on electric only; for combination fixtures this same rule applies. Catalogue number describes article.

SPECIFICATION

Celery—Wired as explained in catalogue.
Corn—Not wired as explained in catalogue
Beans—Not wired, *with* insulating joints.
Peas—With glassware as shown, no sockets
Turnip—Without glassware.

Tomato—With blank insulated joints.
Squash—Complete as shown, no lamps.
Lentils—Assembled ready to hang.
Rice—Regular length as in catalogue.
Rose—Rich Gilt and Satin.
Tulip—Brushed Brass.
Lilac—Old Brass.
Daisy—Oxidized Copper.
Peony—Mottled Copper.
Dahlia—Statuary Bronze.
Carnation—Verd Antique.
Calla—Butler's Silver.

INSTRUCTIONS

Mama—If you cannot fill order in full, ship all you can and let balance follow as soon as possible.

Brother—Send by freight, draft attached to bill of lading, through......Bank.

Sister—Send by express, C. O. D.

Wife—Furnish designs at once for building (Describe kind of building.)

Husband—Get goods ready and hold for shiping instructions.

House—Ship by Adams Express.

Home—Ship by American Express.

Barn—Ship by National Express.

Lot—Ship by United States Express.

Cellar—Ship by Pacific Express.

Yard—Ship by Wells Fargo Express.

Water—Ship by boat.

Stop—Wait receipt of letter before proceeding with order.

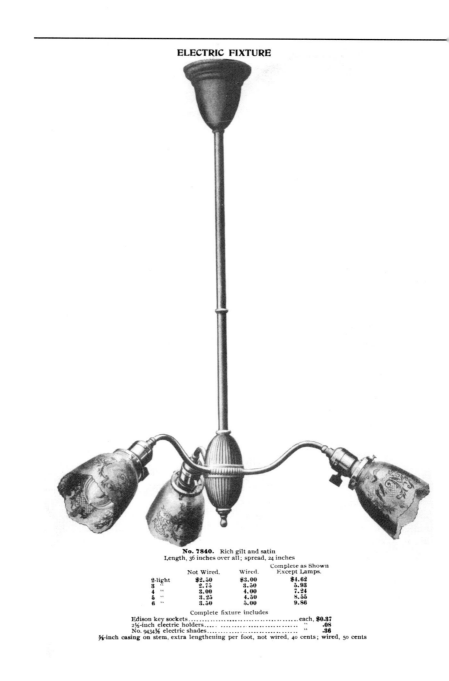

No. 7840. Rich gilt and satin
Length, 36 inches over all; spread, 24 inches

	Not Wired.	Wired.	Complete as Shown Except Lamps.
2-light	$2.50	$3.00	$4.62
3 "	2.75	3.50	5.93
4 "	3.00	4.00	7.24
5 "	3.25	4.50	8.55
6 "	3.50	5.00	9.86

Complete fixture includes

Edison key sockets.................................each, $0.37
2½-inch electric holders.... .... " .08
No. 9434½ electric shades............................. " .36
¾-inch casing on stem, extra lengthening per foot, not wired, 40 cents; wired, 50 cents

ELECTRIC FIXTURE

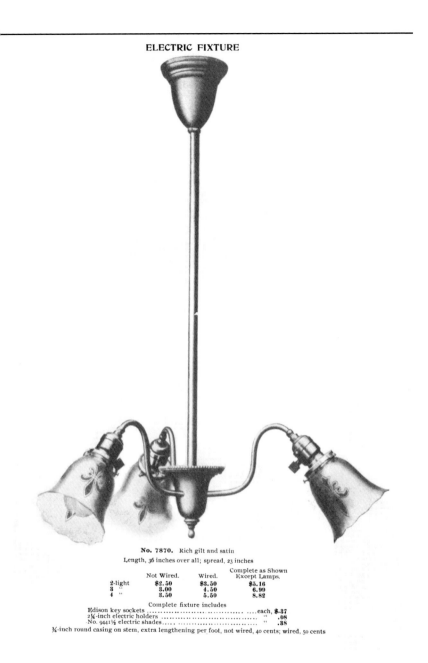

No. 7870. Rich gilt and satin

Length, 36 inches over all; spread, 23 inches

	Not Wired.	Wired.	Complete as Shown Except Lamps.
2-light	**$2.50**	**$3.50**	**$5.16**
3 "	3.00	4.50	6.99
4 "	3.50	5.50	8.82

Complete fixture includes

Edison key sockets ....each, **$.37**
2¼-inch electric holders .... " **.08**
No. 9441½ electric shades..... .... " **.38**

¾-inch round casing on stem, extra lengthening per foot, not wired, 40 cents; wired, 50 cents

ELECTRIC FIXTURE

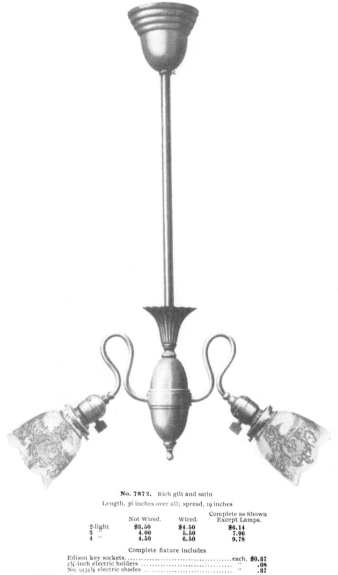

No. 7872. Rich gilt and satin

Length, 36 inches over all; spread, 19 inches

	Not Wired.	Wired.	Complete as Shown Except Lamps.
2-light	$3.50	$4.50	$6.14
3 "	4.00	5.50	7.96
4 "	4.50	6.50	9.78

Complete fixture includes

Edison key sockets...each,	**$0.37**
2¼-inch electric holders .... "	**.08**
No. 9134½ electric shades.. .... "	**.37**

¾-inch casing on stem, extra lengthening per foot, not wired, 40 cents; wired, 50 cents

ELECTRIC FIXTURE

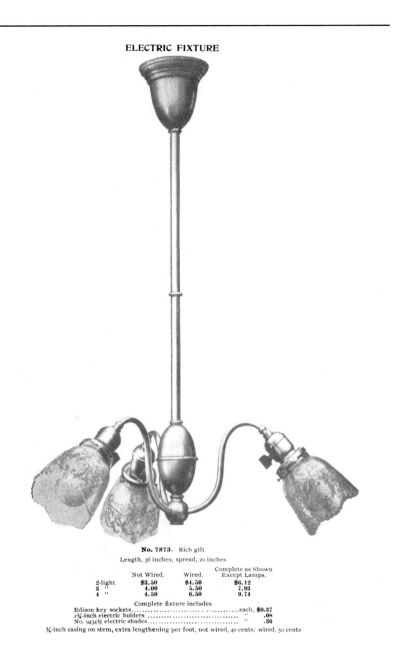

No. 7873. Rich gilt

Length, 36 inches; spread, 20 inches

	Not Wired.	Wired.	Complete as Shown Except Lamps.
2-light	**$3.50**	**$4.50**	**$6.12**
3 "	**4.00**	**5.50**	**7.93**
4 "	**4.50**	**6.50**	**9.74**

Complete fixture includes

Edison key sockets..each, **$0.37**
2¼-inch electric holders .... " **.08**
No. 9434½ electric shades..................................... " **.36**

¾-inch casing on stem, extra lengthening per foot, not wired, 40 cents; wired, 50 cents

ELECTRIC FIXTURE

No. 7874.   Rich gilt and satin

Length, 36 inches over all; spread, 22 inches

	Not Wired.	Wired.	Complete as Shown Except Lamp.
2-light	$3.75	$4.75	$6.37
3 "	4.25	5.75	8.18
4 "	4.75	6.75	9.99

Complete fixture includes

Edison key sockets..each, $0.37
2¼-inch electric holders ....   "   .08
No. 9134½ electric shades...............................   "   .36

¼-inch casing on stem, extra lengthening per foot, not wired, 40 cents; wired, 50 cents

ELECTRIC FIXTURE

No. 7875. Rich gilt and satin
Length, 36 inches over all; spread, 22 inches

	Not Wired.	Wired.	Complete as Shown Except Lamps.
2-light	$3.85	$4.85	$ 6.51
3 "	4.35	5.85	8.34
4 "	4.85	6.85	10.17
5 "	5.35	7.85	12.00
6 "	5.85	8.85	13.83

Complete fixture includes

Edison key sockets ....each, $0.37
2¼-inch electric holders................................... " .08
No. 1906¼ electric shades .... " 38

¾-inch casing on stem, extra lengthing per foot, not wired, 40 cents; wired, 50 cents

ELECTRIC FIXTURE

No. 7876. Rich gilt and satin

Length, 36 inches over all; spread, 24 inches

	Not Wired.	Wired.	Complete as Shown Except Lamps.
2-light	$4.00	$5.00	$ 6.66
3 "	4.75	6.25	8.74
4 "	5.50	7.50	10.82

Complete fixture includes

Edison key sockets	each,	$0.37
2¼-inch electric holders	"	.08
No. 1906½ electric shades	"	.38

¾-inch casing on stem, extra lengthening per foot, not wired, 40 cents; wired, 50 cents

ELECTRIC FIXTURE

No. 7877. Rich gilt and satin

Length, 36 inches ; spread, 22 inches

	Not Wired.	Wired.	Complete as Shown Except Lamps.
2-light	**$4.50**	**$5.50**	**$ 7.24**
3 "	5.00	6.50	9.11
4 "	5.50	7.50	10.88

Complete fixture includes

Edison key sockets	each,	**$0.37**
2¼-inch electric holders	"	.08
No. 6566½ electric shades........	"	.42

¾-inch casing on stem, extra lengthening per foot, not wired, 40 cents; wired, 50 cents

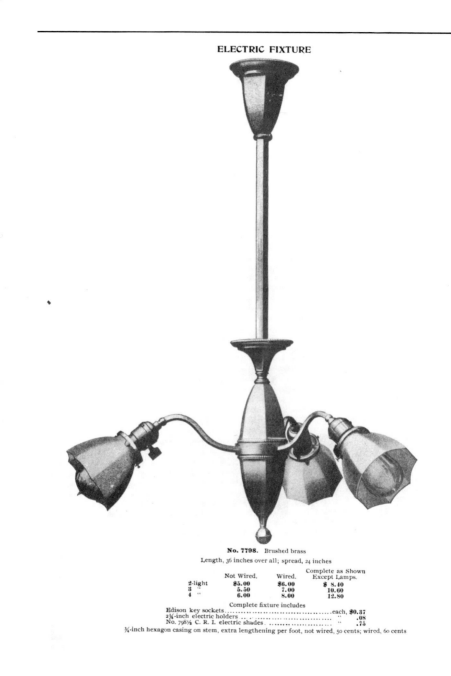

No. 7798. Brushed brass

Length, 36 inches over all; spread, 24 inches

	Not Wired.	Wired.	Complete as Shown Except Lamps.
2-light	$5.00	$6.00	$ 8.40
3 "	5.50	7.00	10.60
4 "	6.00	8.00	12.80

Complete fixture includes

Edison key sockets..each, $0.37
2¼-inch electric holders .... "   .08
No. 7981⁄4 C. R. I. electric shades .... "   .75

¾-inch hexagon casing on stem, extra lengthening per foot, not wired, 50 cents; wired, 60 cents

ELECTRIC FIXTURE

No. 7878. Rich gilt and satin

Length, 36 inches over all; spread, 22 inches

	Not Wired.	Wired.	Complete as Shown Except Lamps.
2-light	$5.25	$6.25	$ 8.49
3 "	6.25	7.75	11.11
4 "	7.25	9.25	13.73
5 "	8.25	10.75	16.35

Complete fixture includes

Edison key sockets.................................each,	$0.37
2¼-inch electric holders .... "	.08
No. 9178½ electric shades .... "	.67

¾-inch casing on stem, extra lengthening per foot, not wired, 40 cents; wired, 50 cents

ELECTRIC FIXTURE

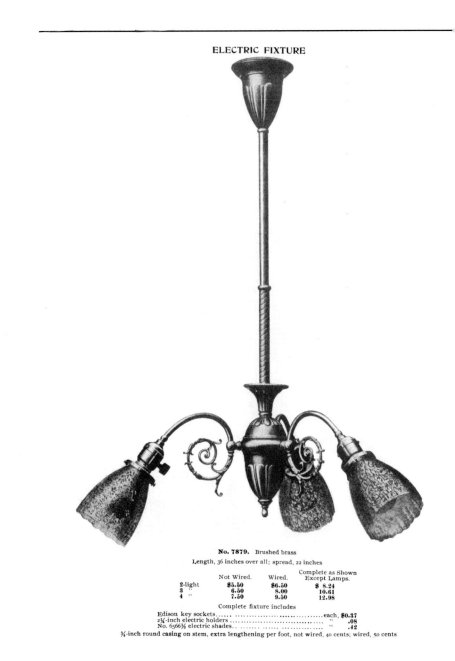

No. 7879. Brushed brass

Length, 36 inches over all; spread, 22 inches

	Not Wired.	Wired.	Complete as Shown Except Lamps.
2-light	$5.50	$6.50	$ 8.24
3 "	6.50	8.00	10.61
4 "	7.50	9.50	12.98

Complete fixture includes

Edison key sockets......................................each, $0.37
2¼-inch electric holders .... " .08
No. 6566½ electric shades.................................. " .42

¾-inch round casing on stem, extra lengthening per foot, not wired, 40 cents; wired, 50 cents

ELECTRIC FIXTURE

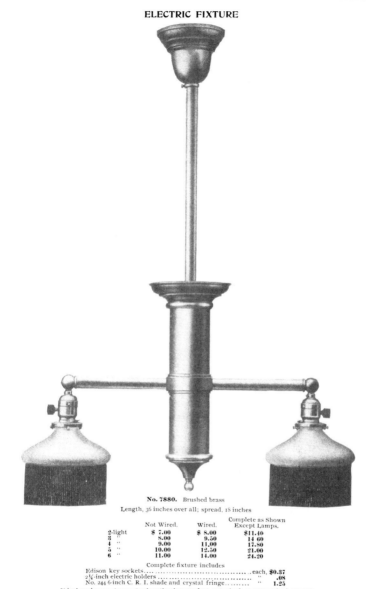

No. 7880. Brushed brass

Length, 36 inches over all; spread, 18 inches

	Not Wired.	Wired.	Complete as Shown Except Lamps.
2-light	$ 7.00	$ 8.00	$11.40
3 "	8.00	9.50	14.60
4 "	9.00	11.00	17.80
5 "	10.00	12.50	21.00
6 "	11.00	14.00	24.20

Complete fixture includes

Edison key sockets....................................each, **$0.37**
2¼-inch electric holders .... " **.08**
No. 244 6-inch C. R. I. shade and crystal fringe......... " **1.25**

⅜-inch casing on stem, extra lengthening per foot, not wired, 45 cents; wired, 55 cents

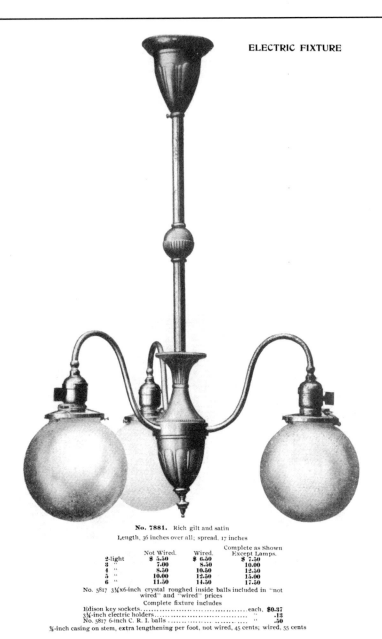

No. 7881. Rich gilt and satin

Length, 36 inches over all; spread, 17 inches

	Not Wired.	Wired.	Complete as Shown Except Lamps.
2-light	$ 5.50	$ 6.50	$ 7.50
3 "	7.00	8.50	10.00
4 "	8.50	10.50	12.50
5 "	10.00	12.50	15.00
6 "	11.50	14.50	17.50

No. 5817 3¼x6-inch crystal roughed inside balls included in "not wired" and "wired" prices

Complete fixture includes

Edison key sockets	each,	**$0.37**
3¼-inch electric holders	"	.13
No. 5817 6-inch C. R. I. balls	"	.50

⅝-inch casing on stem, extra lengthening per foot, not wired, 45 cents; wired, 55 cents

ELECTRIC FIXTURE

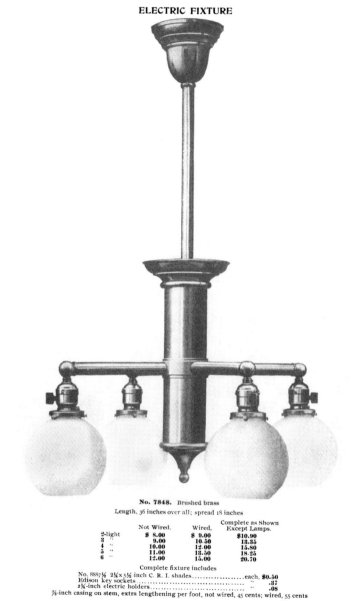

No. 7848. Brushed brass

Length, 36 inches over all; spread 18 inches

	Not Wired.	Wired.	Complete as Shown Except Lamps.
2-light	$ 8.00	$ 9.00	$10.90
3 "	9.00	10.50	13.35
4 "	10.00	12.00	15.80
5 "	11.00	13.50	18.25
6 "	12.00	15.00	20.70

Complete fixture includes

No. 8887½ 2¼ x 5½ inch C. R. I. shades...................each, **$0.50**
Edison key sockets .... "   .37
2¼-inch electric holders................................. "   .08
⅞-inch casing on stem, extra lengthening per foot, not wired, 45 cents; wired, 55 cents

No. 7882. Brushed Brass
Length, 36 inches over all; spread, 12 inches

	Not Wired.	Wired,	Complete as Shown Except Lamps.
2-light	$7.00	$ 8.00	$12.40
3 "	7.75	9.25	15.85
4 "	8.25	10.25	19.05
5 "	9.00	11.50	22.50
6 "	9.75	12.75	25.95
Extra chain, per foot	1.13	1.25	

Complete fixture includes

Edison key sockets........................ ....each, $0.37
2¼-inch electric holders........................... " .08
No. 7588 Teplitz shades.......................... " 1.75

No. 6977. Verd antique
Length, 36 inches over all; spread, 6 inches

	Not Wired.	Wired with Silk Cord.	Complete as Shown Except Lamps
1-light	$15.00	$16.00	$16.34
Extra chain, per foot	.75	.95	

No. 404G solid venetian colored grapes, in blue, purple, amber and yellow, included in "not wired" and "wired" prices.

Complete fixture includes
Edison keyless sockets.......................each, $ 0.34
No. 404G yellow, purple, amber or blue..... " 12.00

ELECTRIC FIXTURE

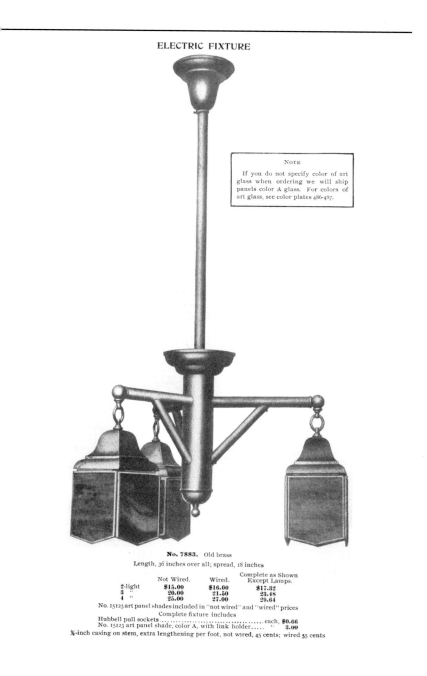

NOTE

If you do not specify color of art glass when ordering we will ship panels color A glass. For colors of art glass, see color plates 486-487.

No. 7883. Old brass

Length, 36 inches over all; spread, 18 inches

	Not Wired.	Wired.	Complete as Shown Except Lamps.
2-light	$15.00	$16.00	$17.32
3 "	20.00	21.50	23.48
4 "	25.00	27.00	29.64

No. 15123 art panel shades included in "not wired" and "wired" prices

Complete fixture includes

Hubbell pull sockets...............................each, $0.66
No. 15123 art panel shade, color A, with link holder,.... " 3.00
⅞-inch casing on stem, extra lengthening per foot, not wired, 45 cents; wired 55 cents

ELECTRIC FIXTURE

No. 7784. Brushed brass

Length, 36 inches over all; spread, 22 inches

	Not wired.	Wired.	Complete as Shown Except Lamps.
2-light	$ 7.50	$ 8.50	$10.30
4 "	10.00	12.00	15.60

Complete fixture includes

Edison key sockets..each, **$0.37**
2¼-inch electric holders................................. " **.08**
No. 9321½ C. R. I. shades .... " **.45**

¾-inch casing on stem, extra lengthening per foot, not wired, 40 cents; wired, 50 cents

ELECTRIC FIXTURE

No. 7885. Brushed brass
Length, 36 inches; spread, 20 inches

	Not wired.	Wired.	Complete as Shown Except Lamps.
2-light	**$19.50**	**$20.50**	**$21.82**
4 "	**30.50**	**32.50**	**35.14**
Extra chain, 0556—per foot	**2.50**	**2.70**	

No. 15124 shades and bead fringe included in "not wired" and "wired" prices

Complete fixture includes

Hubbell pull sockets .... each, **$0.66**
No. 15124 shade and 5-inch green fringe................ "   **2.00**

For color of fringe see plate 485

No. 7533. Brushed brass

Length, 14 inches over all; spread, 15 inches

	Not Wired.	Wired.	Complete as Shown Except Lamps.
2-light	$18.00	$19.00	$23.50
4 "	28.00	30.00	39.00

Complete fixture includes

Edison key sockets..each, $0.37
3¼-inch electric holders................................... " .13
No. 1911 3¾x8-inch engraved stalactites...... .... " 1.75

No. 7886. Brushed brass
Length, 36 inches over all; spread, 14 inches

	Not Wired.	Wired.	Complete as Shown Except Lamps.
2-light	$22.00	$23.00	$24.80
4 "	32.00	34.00	37.60

Complete fixture includes

Edison key sockets..each, $0.37
2¼-inch electric holders.. " .08
No. 9321¼ C. R. I. electric shades................................. " .45

¾-inch casing on stem, extra lengthening per foot, not wired, 75 cents; wired, 85 cents

ELECTRIC FIXTURE

No. 7887. Burnished gilt

Length, 42 inches over all; spread, 18 inches

	Not Wired.	Wired.	Complete as Shown Except Lamps.
2-light	**$32.00**	**$33.00**	**$33.74**
3 "	39.00	40.50	41.61
4 "	46.00	48.00	49.48
5 "	53.00	55.50	57.35

3¼ x6-inch No. 423 straw opalescent balls and cast holders included in "not wired" and "wired" prices

Complete fixture includes

Edison key sockets	..................each,	**$0.37**
No. 423 6-inch S. O. balls	.... "	.75
3¼-inch cast holders	.... "	.75

⅝-inch casing on stem, extra lengthening, per foot, not wired, 45 cents; wired, 55 cents

No. 7888. Old brass

Length, 36 inches over all; spread, 20 inches

	Not Wired.	Wired.	Complete as Shown Except Lamps.
No. 7888. 2-light (2 arms, no lt. on bottom)	$ 9.50	$10.50	$11.25
No. 7888½. 3-light (2 arms, 1 lt. on bottom)	11.50	13.00	14.11
No. 7888. 3-light (3 arms, no lt. on bottom)	12.25	13.75	14.86
No. 7888½. 4-light (3 arms, 1 lt. on bottom)	14.25	16.25	17.73
No. 7888. 4-light (4 arms, no lt. on bottom)	15.00	17.00	18.48
No. 7888½. 5-light (4 arms, 1 lt. on bottom)	17.00	19.50	21.35
No. 7888. 5-light (5 arms, no lt. on bottom)	17.75	20.25	22.10
No. 7888½. 6-light (5 arms, 1 lt. on bottom)	19.75	22.75	24.97
No. 7888. 6-light (6 arms, no lt. on bottom)	20.50	23.50	25.72

No. 5817 3¾x6-inch balls on arms and 7-inch on bottom with 3¾-inch fancy spun holders, included in "not wired" and "wired" prices

Complete fixture includes

Edison key sockets	each,	$0.37
No. 5817 3¾x6-inch C. R. I. balls	"	.50
No. 5817 3¾x7-inch C. R. I. balls	"	.63
3¾-inch fancy spun holder	"	1.00

1-inch casing on stem, **extra** lengthening per foot, not wired 45 cents; wired, 55 cents

ELECTRIC DINING ROOM FIXTURE

No. 7812. Brushed brass

Length, 36 inches over all; spread, 22 inches

	Not Wired.	Wired.	Complete as Shown Except Lamps.
3-light	$5.00	$6.50	$ 9.27
4 "	5.50	7.50	11.47
5 "	6.00	8.50	13.67
6 "	6.50	9.50	15.87

No. 433 3¼x10-inch C. R. I. dome included in "not wired" and "wired" prices

Complete fixture includes

Edison key sockets...each,		$0.37
2¼-inch electric holders...................................	"	.08
No. 798½ C. R. I. shades..................................	"	.75
No. 433 3¼x10-inch C. R. I. dome......................	"	1.00

⅝-inch casing on stem, extra lengthening per foot, not wired, 40 cents; wired, 50 cents

ELECTRIC FIXTURE

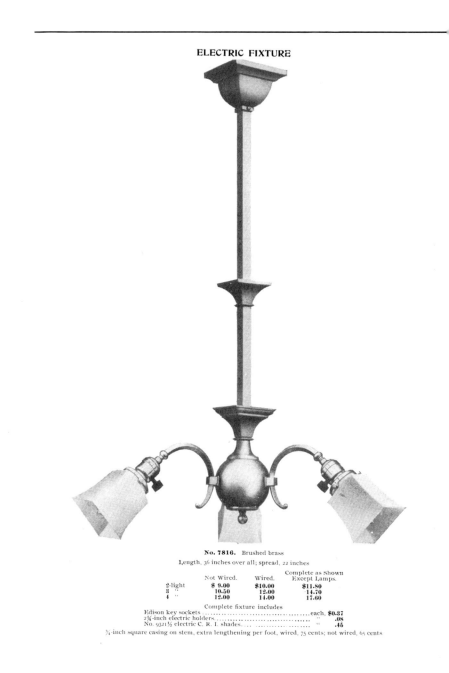

No. 7816. Brushed brass

Length, 36 inches over all; spread, 22 inches

	Not Wired.	Wired.	Complete as Shown Except Lamps.
2-light	$ 9.00	$10.00	$11.80
3 "	10.50	12.00	14.70
4 "	12.00	14.00	17.60

Complete fixture includes

Edison key sockets ....each, **$0.37**
2¼-inch electric holders... " .08
No. 9321½ electric C. R. I. shades.... .... " .45

¾-inch square casing on stem, extra lengthening per foot, wired, 75 cents; not wired, 65 cents

ELECTRIC FIXTURE

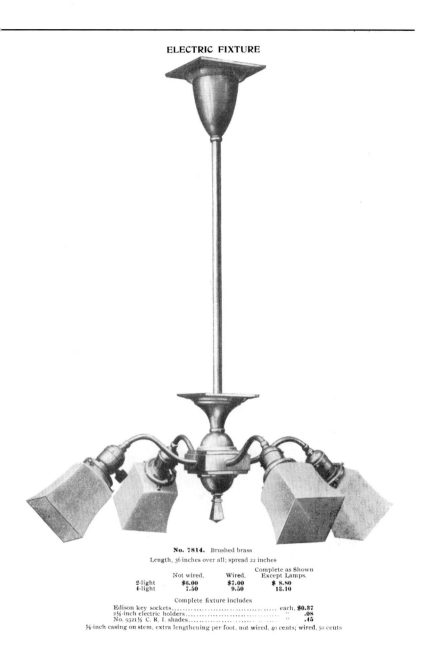

No. 7814. Brushed brass

Length, 36 inches over all; spread 22 inches

	Not wired.	Wired.	Complete as Shown Except Lamps.
2-light	**$6.00**	**$7.00**	**$ 8.80**
4-light	**7.50**	**9.50**	**13.10**

Complete fixture includes

Edison key sockets..................................... each, **$0.37**
2½-inch electric holders.............................. " **.08**
No. 9321½ C. R. I. shades............................ " **.45**
⅝-inch casing on stem, extra lengthening per foot, not wired, 40 cents; wired, 50 cents

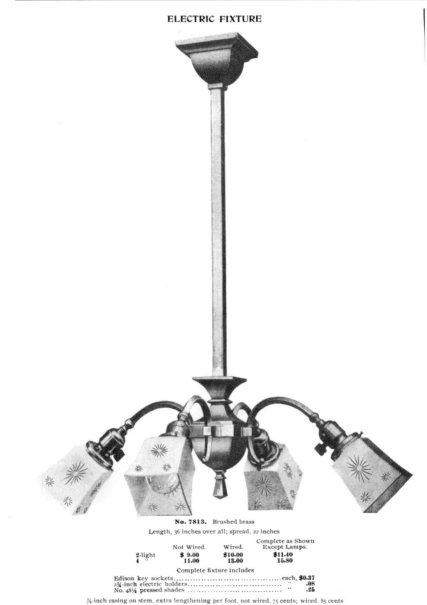

No. 7813. Brushed brass

Length, 36 inches over all; spread, 22 inches

	Not Wired.	Wired.	Complete as Shown Except Lamps.
2-light	$ 9.00	$10.00	$11.40
4 "	11.00	13.00	15.80

Complete fixture includes

Edison key sockets	each,	$0.37
2¼-inch electric holders	"	.08
No. 48½ pressed shades	"	.25

⅞-inch casing on stem, extra lengthening per foot, not wired, 75 cents; wired, 85 cents

ELECTRIC FIXTURE

No. 7811. Brushed brass

Length, 36 inches over all; spread, 18 inches

	Not Wired.	Wired.	Complete as Shown Except Lamps.
2-light	**$11.00**	**$12.00**	**$13.80**
4 "	**13.00**	**15.00**	**18.60**

Complete fixture includes

Edison key sockets...each,	**$0.37**
2¼-inch electric holders................................... "	**.08**
No. 94 C. R. I. shades .... "	**.45**

⅞-inch squre casing on stem, extra lengthening per foot, not wired. 75 cents; wired, 85 cents

No. 7889. Rich gilt
Length, 36 inches over all; spread, 20 inches

	Not Wired.	Wired.	Complete as Shown Except Lamps.
3-light	$5.50	$ 6.75	$ 9.07
4 "	6.00	7.75	10.90
5 "	6.50	9.00	12.98
6 "	7.00	10.00	14.81

No. 430 3¼x10-inch crystal roughed inside dome included in "not wired" and "wired" prices
Complete fixture includes

Edison key sockets (on arms)..............................each,		$0.37
2¼-inch electric holders (on arms)......................	"	.08
Hubbell pull sockets (under dome)......................	"	.66
No. 5671½ electric shades................................	"	.38
No. 430 3¼x10-inch C. R. I. dome	"	1.13

⅞-inch round casing on stem, extra lengthening per foot, not wired, 45 cents; wired, 55 cents

ELECTRIC DINING ROOM FIXTURE

No. 7890. Rich gilt and satin

Length, 36 inches over all; spread, 18 inches

	Not Wired.	Wired.	Complete as Shown Except Lamps.
3-light	$ 8.00	$ 9.50	$10.87
4 "	9.50	11.50	13.37
5 "	11.00	13.50	15.87
6 "	12.50	15.50	18.37

No. 5817 3¼x6-inch C. R. I. balls and No. 430 3¼x10-inch C. R. I. dome included in "not wired" and "wired" prices.

Complete fixture includes

Edison key sockets (on arms and under dome)........each,	**$0.37**
3¼-inch electric holders (on arms) .... "	.13
No. 5817 6-inch C. R. I. balls .... "	.50
No. 430 3¼x10-inch C. R. I. dome .... "	1.13

⅞-inch round casing on stem, extra lengthening per foot, not wired, 45 cents; wired, 55 cents

ELECTRIC DINING ROOM FIXTURE

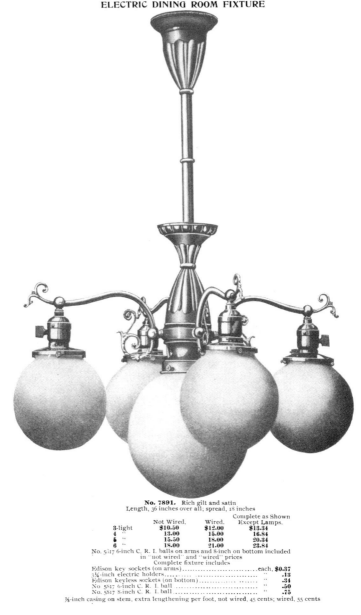

No. 7891. Rich gilt and satin
Length, 36 inches over all; spread, 18 inches

	Not Wired.	Wired.	Complete as Shown Except Lamps.
3-light	$10.50	$12.00	$13.34
4 "	13.00	15.00	16.84
5 "	15.50	18.00	20.34
6 "	18.00	21.00	23.84

No. 5817 6-inch C. R. I. balls on arms and 8-inch on bottom included
in "not wired" and "wired" prices
Complete fixture includes

Edison key sockets (on arms)..........................each,	**$0.37**
3¼-inch electric holders.............................. "	.13
Edison keyless sockets (on bottom)................ "	.34
No 5817 6-inch C. R. I. ball .... "	.50
No. 5817 8-inch C. R. I. ball .... "	.75

¾-inch casing on stem, extra lengthening per foot, not wired, 45 cents; wired, 55 cents

ELECTRIC DINING ROOM FIXTURE

No. 7847. Old brass
Length, 36 inches over all; spread, 18 inches

	Not wired.	Wired.	Complete as Shown Except Lamps.
3-light	$13.75	$15.25	$19.16
4 "	15.15	17.15	22.70
5 "	16.50	19.00	26.18
6 "	17.90	20.90	29.71

No. 15134 3¼x10-inch square art glass shade, color L, with 3-inch bead fringe only, included in "not wired" and "wired" prices

Complete fixture includes

Edison key sockets (on arms)	each,	$0.37
Hubbell pull sockets (under dome)	"	.66
3¼-inch electric holders	"	.13
No. 15134 10-inch art dome and fringe only	"	6.00
No. 4013 C. R. I. ball, hexagon	"	1.13

¼-inch hexagon casing on stem, extra lengthening per foot, not wired, 50 cents; wired, 60 cents

ELECTRIC DINING ROOM FIXTURE

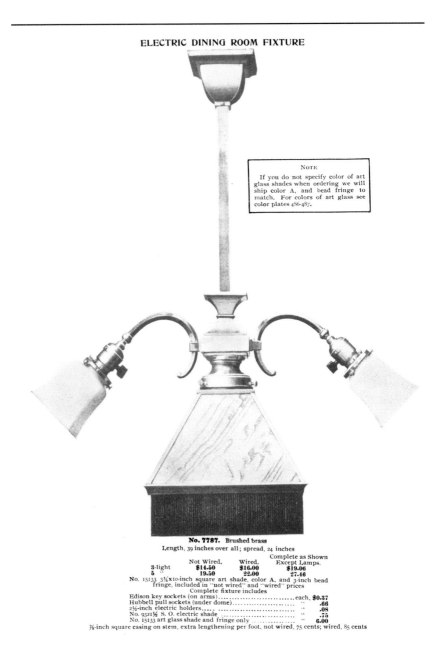

NOTE

If you do not specify color of art glass shades when ordering we will ship color A, and bead fringe to match. For colors of art glass see color plates 486-487.

No. 7787. Brushed brass

Length, 39 inches over all; spread, 24 inches

	Not Wired.	Wired.	Complete as Shown Except Lamps.
3-light	**$14.50**	**$16.00**	**$19.06**
5 "	19.50	22.00	27.46

No. 15133 3¼x10-inch square art shade, color A, and 3-inch bead fringe, included in "not wired" and "wired" prices

Complete fixture includes

Edison key sockets (on arms)	each,	**$0.37**
Hubbell pull sockets (under dome)	"	**.66**
2½-inch electric holders	"	**.08**
No. 9321½ S. O. electric shade	"	**.75**
No. 15133 art glass shade and fringe only	"	**6.00**

⅞-inch square casing on stem, extra lengthening per foot, not wired, 75 cents; wired, 85 cents

No. 7708. Brushed brass
Length, 42 inches over all; spread, 16-inch shade

	Not Wired.	Wired.	Complete as Shown Except Lamps.
2-light	$27.00	$28.00	$28.68
3 "	27.50	29.00	30.02
4 "	28.00	30.00	31.36

16-inch art gass shade, color F, and 6-inch beaded fringe to match included in "not wired" and "wired" prices. For color of glass see color plates 486-487.
Complete fixture includes
Edison keyless sockets.............................each, **$0.34**
⅝-inch casing on stem, extra lengthening per foot, not wired, 45 cents; wired, 55 cents

---

NOTE

If you do not specify color of art glass shade when ordering we ship same color as listed on fixture. For colors of art glass see color plates 486-487.

No. 7817. Brushed brass
Length, 48 inches over all; spread, 16-inch shade

	Not Wired.	Wired.	Complete as Shown Except Lamps.
4-light	**$18.00**	**$20.00**	**$21.36**

Cast crown holder, 16-inch art glass shade, color K, 4-inch bead fringe to match included in "not wired" and "wired" prices.
Complete fixture includes
Edison keyless sockets.....................each, **$0.34**
⅝-inch casing on stem, extra lengthening per foot, not wired, 75 cents; wired, 85 cents

39

ELECTRIC DOME FIXTURES

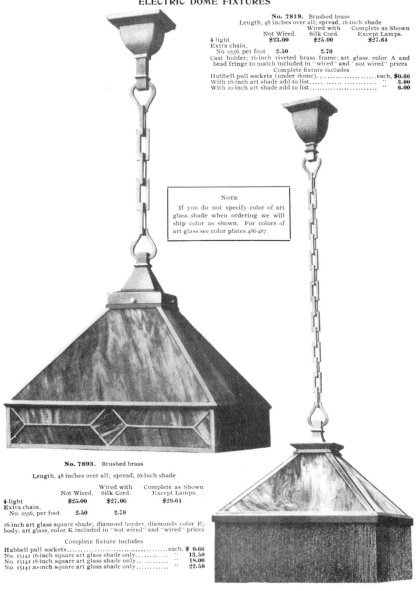

No. 7819. Brushed brass

Length, 48 inches over all; spread, 16-inch shade

	Not Wired.	Wired with Silk Cord.	Complete as Shown Except Lamps.
4-light	**$23.00**	**$25.00**	**$27.64**
Extra chain, No. 0556, per foot	2.50	2.70	

Cast holder; 16-inch riveted brass frame; art glass, color A and bead fringe to match included in "wired" and "not wired" prices

Complete fixture includes

Hubbell pull sockets (under dome)	each,	**$0.66**
With 18-inch art shade add to list	"	**3.00**
With 20-inch art shade add to list	"	**6.00**

NOTE

If you do not specify color of art glass shade when ordering we will ship color as shown. For colors of art glass see color plates 486-487.

No. 7893. Brushed brass

Length, 48 inches over all; spread, 16-inch shade

	Not Wired.	Wired with Silk Cord.	Complete as Shown Except Lamps.
4-light	**$25.00**	**$27.00**	**$29.64**
Extra chain, No. 0556, per foot	2.50	2.70	

16-inch art glass square shade; diamond border, diamonds color E; body, art glass, color K included in "not wired" and "wired" prices

Complete fixture includes

Hubbell pull sockets	each,	**$ 0.66**
No. 15142 16-inch square art glass shade only	"	**13.50**
No. 15142 18-inch square art glass shade only	"	**18.00**
No. 15142 20-inch square art glass shade only	"	**22.50**

ELECTRIC DINING ROOM FIXTURE

NOTE

If you do not specify color of art shade when ordering we will ship color **L** with bead fringe to match. For art glass colors see color plates 486-487.

No. 7850. Brushed brass
Length, 42 inches over all; spread, 21 inches

	Not Wired.	Wired.	Complete as Shown Except Lamps.
3-light (2 arms)	$23.50	$25.00	$27.46
5 " 4 "	28.50	31.00	35.26

4-inch cast holder; 4x16-in., No. 15139, square art glass shade, color **L**;
4-in. bead fringe to match included in "not wired" and "wired" prices
Complete fixture includes

No. 15139 4x16-inch square art shade and fringe........each,	**$12.00**	
Edison key sockets (on arms)......................	"	.37
Hubbell pull sockets (under dome)....................	"	.66
2½-inch electric holders.............................	"	.08
No. 94 crystal roughed inside shades................	"	.45

⅞-inch casing on stem, extra lengthening per foot, not wired, 45 cents; wired, 55 cents

ELECTRIC DINING ROOM FIXTURE

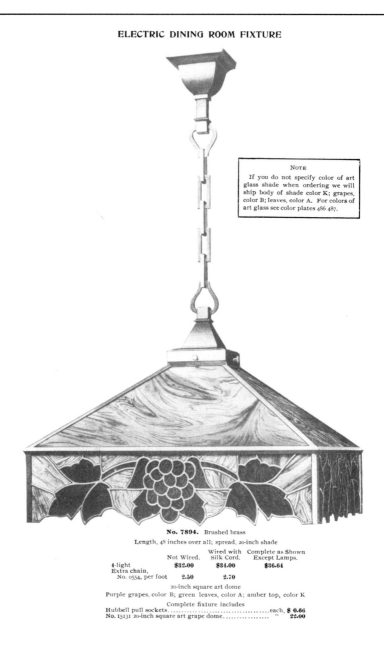

No. 7894. Brushed brass

Length, 48 inches over all; spread, 20-inch shade

	Not Wired.	Wired with Silk Cord.	Complete as Shown Except Lamps.
4-light	**$32.00**	**$34.00**	**$36.64**
Extra chain, No. 0554, per foot	**2.50**	**2.70**	

20-inch square art dome

Purple grapes, color B; green leaves, color A; amber top, color K

Complete fixture includes

Hubbell pull sockets.....................................each, **$ 0.66**
No. 15131 20-inch square art grape dome................. " **22.00**

ELECTRIC DINING ROOM FIXTURE

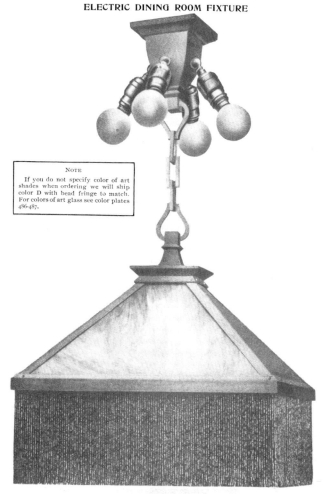

> **NOTE**
>
> If you do not specify color of art shades when ordering we will ship color D with bead fringe to match. For colors of art glass see color plates 486-487.

No. 7818. Brushed brass

Length, 48 inches over all; spread, 16-inch shade

	Not Wired.	Wired with Silk Cord.	Complete as Shown Except Lamps.
6-lights (2 lts. under dome)	$25.50	$27.50	$30.18
8 " 4 " "	26.00	28.50	32.50
Extra chain, No. 0554, per foot	2.50	2.70	

With No. 15130 16-inch riveted brass frame, art glass color D, 6-inch beaded fringe to match, included in "wired" and "not wired" prices

Complete fixture includes

Edison keyless sockets (on canopy) ....each, **$0.34**

Hubbell pull sockets (under dome)...................... " **.66**

With 18-inch shade add **$3.00** to list

With 20-inch shade add **6.00** to list

NOTE

If you do not specify color of art glass shade when ordering we will ship body of shade color L, and border, color E. For colors of art glass see color plates 486-487.

No. 7863. Brushed brass
Length, 48 inches over all; spread, 24-inch shade

	Not Wired.	Wired.	Complete as Shown Except Lamps.
4-light	$60.00	$62.00	$64.64
5 "	60.50	63.00	66.30
6 "	61.00	64.00	67.96
Extra chain, per foot	5.75	6.00	

24-inch art glass shade, body of shade, color L,; border, color E. The wiring is run through inside of chain and is entirely concealed. A special "Williamson" feature.

Complete fixture includes

Hubbell pull sockets........ ....each, $ 0.66
No. 15126 6x24-inch shade only.......................... " **39.00**

ELECTRIC DINING ROOM FIXTURE

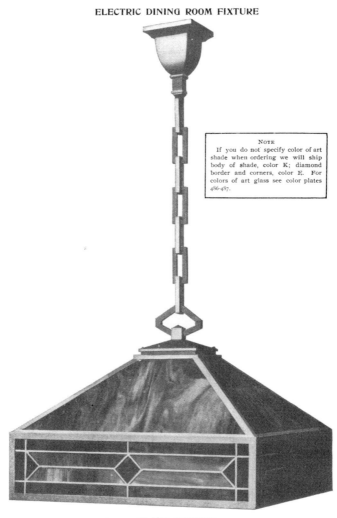

NOTE

If you do not specify color of art shade when ordering we will ship body of shade, color K; diamond border and corners, color E. For colors of art glass see color plates 486-487.

No. 7932. Brushed brass

Length, 48 inches over all; spread, 20-inch shade

	Not Wired.	Wired with Silk Cord.	Complete as Shown Except Lamps.
4-light	$43.00	$45.00	$47.64
5 "	43.50	46.00	49.30
6 "	44.00	47.00	50.96
Extra chain,			
No. 6554, per foot	3.70	3.90	

20-inch square art shade, diamond border, color E; yellow top, color K, and center green border, color L; ruby corners, color E included in "not wired" and "wired" prices.

Complete fixture includes

Hubbell pull sockets................................each, $0.66

NOTE

If you do not specify color of art shade when ordering we will ship shade color J, with 5-inch cut bead fringe to match. For colors of art glass see color plates 456 487.

No. 7895. Brushed brass

Length, 42 inches over all; spread, 24-inch shade

	Not Wired.	Wired with Silk Cord.	Complete as Shown Except Lamps.
4-light	$73.00	$75.00	$77.64
5 "	73.50	76.00	79.30
6 "	74.00	77.00	80.96
Extra chain, No. 0559, per foot	2.25	2.45	

24-inch bent art dome, color J, and 5-inch cut beaded fringe to match, included in "not wired" and "wired" prices.

Complete fixture includes

Hubbell pull sockets...............................each, $0.66

ELECTRIC DINING ROOM FIXTURE

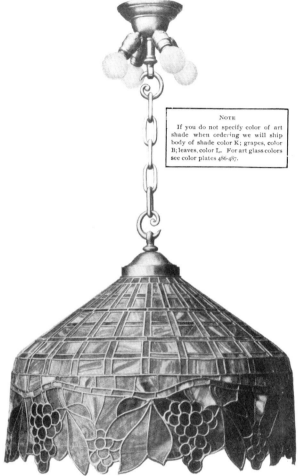

NOTE

If you do not specify color of art shade when ordering we will ship body of shade color K; grapes, color B; leaves, color L. For art glass colors see color plates 486-487.

No. 7896. Brushed brass

Length, 48 inches over all; spread, 24-inch shade

	Not Wired.	Wired with Silk Cord	Complete as Shown Except Lamps.
8-light	**$120.00**	**$124.00**	**$129.28**
Extra chain, No. 0559, per foot	**2.25**	**2.45**	

24-inch art dome with grape border, body of shade color K; grapes, color B; leaves, color L; with 6-inch holder

Complete fixture includes

Hubbell pull sockets (under dome) ....each, $		**0.66**
Edison keyless sockets (on canopy)................. "		**.34**
No. 15128 6x24-inch art shade....................... "		**105.00**

47

No. 7917. Brushed brass

Length, 48 inches over all; spread, top plate and cast band, 21x21 inches

	Not Wired.	Wired with Silk Cord.	Complete as Shown Except Lamps.
8-light	**$129.50**	**$133.50**	**$136.25**

Extra lengthening requiring 8 chains. No. 0557. per foot, not wired, **$15.36**; wired with silk cord, **$17.20**

With socket cover holders and No. 15136 art shades, color K, square cast band with art glass, color K, body border, color E, included in "not wired" and "wired" prices. For colors of art glass see color plates 486-487.

Complete fixture includes

Art shades No. 15136.................................each, **$5.00**
Edison keyless sockets........................ " .34

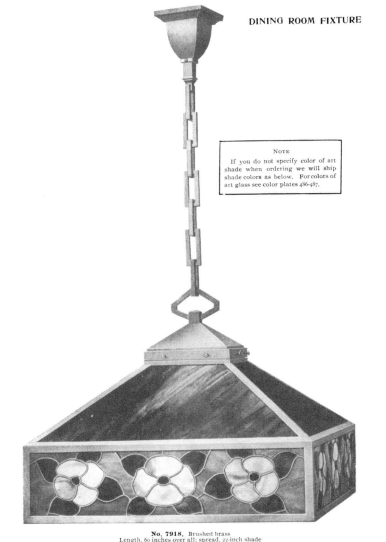

DINING ROOM FIXTURE

NOTE

If you do not specify color of art shade when ordering we will ship shade colors as below. For colors of art glass see color plates 486-487.

No. 7918, Brushed brass
Length, 60 inches over all; spread, 22-inch shade

	Not Wired.	Wired with Silk Cord.	Complete as Shown Except Lamps.
2-light	$47.50	$49.50	$50.82
3 "	47.75	50.00	51.98
4 "	48.00	50.50	53.14
5 "	48.25	51.00	54.30
6 "	48.50	51.50	55.46

Extra chain.
No. 0555, per foot   3.00   3.20

With 22-inch square art shade; with 6-inch holder; background, color F; roses, color G; leaves, color C. For art glass colors see color plates 486-487.

Complete fixture includes

Hubbell pull sockets.............................each, $ 0.66
No. 15127 6x22-inch art shade only.................... " 85.00

NOTE

If you do not specify color of art shade when ordering we will ship shade colors as below. For colors of art glass see color plates 486-487.

No. 7920. Brushed brass
Length, 60 inches over all; spread, 24-inch shade

	Not Wired.	Wired with Silk Cord.	Complete as Shown Except Lamps.
3-light	**$150.00**	**$152.00**	**$153.98**
4 "	150.25	152.50	155.14
5 "	150.50	153.50	156.80
6 "	150.75	154.00	157.96
Extra chain, per foot	3.25	3.45	

With 24-inch bent art dome; color top neck of shade, color L,; background, color K; roses and buds, color G; leaves, color F.

Complete fixture includes
Hubbell pull sockets.....................................each, **$0.66**

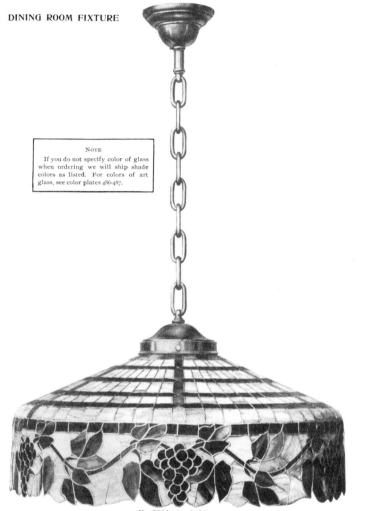

NOTE

If you do not specify color of glass when ordering we will ship shade colors as listed. For colors of art glass, see color plates 486-487.

No. 7921. Brushed brass
Length, 60 inches over all; spread, 26-inch shade

	Not Wired.	Wired with Silk Cord.	Complete as Shown Except Lamps.
3-light	**$125.00**	**$127.00**	**$128.98**
4 "	125.25	127.50	130.14
5 "	125.50	128.00	131.30
6 "	125.75	128.50	132.46
Extra chain,			
No. 0559, per foot **2.25**		2.45	

With 26-inch copper art shade; with 6-inch holder; back-ground decorations, yellow, amber, green; border, purple grapes; yellow back-ground; green or autumn leaves.

Complete fixture includes

Hubbell pull sockets.............................each,	**$ 0.66**
No. 15124 26-inch copper art shade only................ "	**116.50**

WOOD FIXTURES

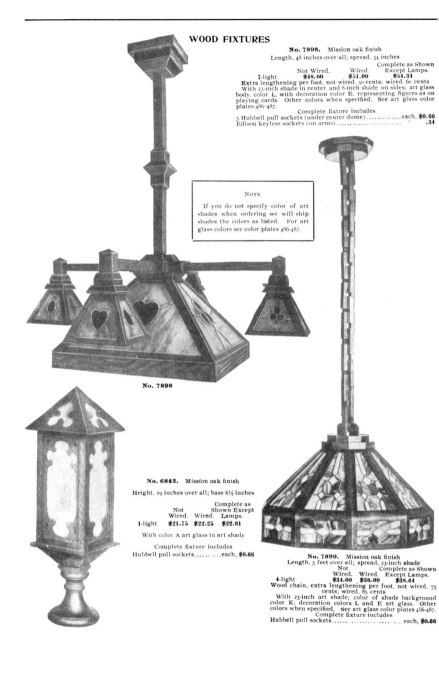

No. 7898. Mission oak finish

Length, 48 inches over all; spread, 31 inches

	Not Wired.	Wired.	Complete as Shown Except Lamps.
7-light	**$48.00**	**$51.00**	**$54.34**

Extra lengthening per foot, not wired, 50 cents; wired, 60 cents

With 23-inch shade in center and 8-inch shade on sides; art glass body, color L, with decoration color E, representing figures as on playing cards. Other colors when specified. See art glass color plates 486-487.

Complete fixture includes

3 Hubbell pull sockets (under center dome)..............each, **$0.66**
Edison keyless sockets (on arms)........................ " .34

NOTE

If you do not specify color of art shades when ordering we will ship shades the colors as listed. For art glass colors see color plates 486-487.

No. 7898

No. 6842. Mission oak finish

Height, 29 inches over all; base 6½ inches

	Not Wired.	Wired.	Complete as Shown Except Lamps.
1-light	**$21.75**	**$22.25**	**$22.91**

With color A art glass in art shade

Complete fixture includes
Hubbell pull sockets..........each, **$0.66**

No. 7899. Mission oak finish
Length, 5 feet over all; spread, 23-inch shade

	Not Wired.	Wired.	Complete as Shown Except Lamps.
4-light	**$34.00**	**$36.00**	**$38.64**

Wood chain, extra lengthening per foot, not wired, 75 cents; wired, 85 cents

With 23-inch art shade; color of shade background color K; decoration colors L and E art glass. Other colors when specified. See art glass color plates 486-487.
Complete fixture includes
Hubbell pull sockets........................each, **$0.66**

WOOD FIXTURES

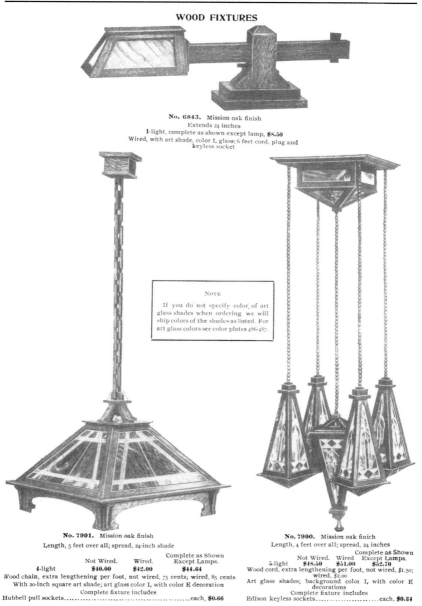

No. 6843. Mission oak finish
Extends 24 inches
1-light, complete as shown except lamp, **$8.50**
Wired, with art shade, color L glass; 6 feet cord, plug and
keyless socket

> NOTE
>
> If you do not specify color of art
> glass shades when ordering we will
> ship colors of the shades as listed. For
> art glass colors see color plates 486-487.

No. 7901. Mission oak finish
Length, 5 feet over all; spread, 24-inch shade

4-light	Not Wired.	Wired.	Complete as Shown Except Lamps.
	$40.00	**$42.00**	**$44.64**

Wood chain, extra lengthening per foot, not wired, 75 cents; wired, 85 cents
With 20-inch square art shade; art glass color L, with color E decoration
Complete fixture includes
Hubbell pull sockets...each, **$0.66**

No. 7900. Mission oak finish
Length, 4 feet over all; spread, 24 inches

5-light	Not Wired.	Wired	Complete as Shown Except Lamps.
	$48.50	**$51.00**	**$52.70**

Wood cord, extra lengthening per foot, not wired, $1.50;
wired, $2.00
Art glass shades; background color L, with color E
decorations
Complete fixture includes
Edison keyless sockets.....................each, **$0.34**

53

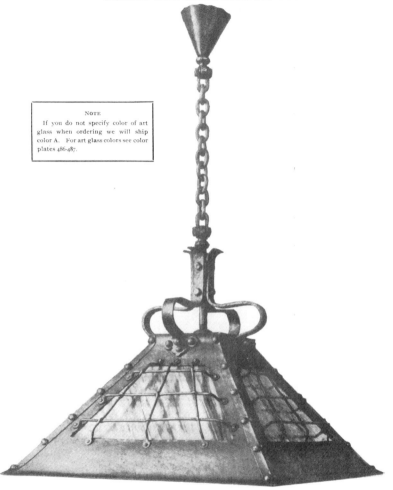

No. 7902. Hammered wrought iron
Length, 48 inches over all; spread, 20-inch shade

	Not Wired.	Wired.	Complete as Shown Except Lamps.
4-light	**$67.50**	**$70.00**	**$72.64**
Extra chain, per foot	**1.00**	**1.20**	

20-inch square shade, with art glass panels, color A glass
Complete fixture includes
Hubbell pull sockets...each. **$0.66**
Burnt brass, Swedish iron or verd antique
Add **20%** to list for special finishes

WROUGHT IRON DINING ROOM FIXTURE

NOTE

If you do not specify color of art glass when ordering we will ship color K. For art glass colors see plates 486-487.

No. 7903. Hammered wrought iron.
Length, 24 inches over all; spread, 18 inches

	Not Wired.	Wired.	Complete as Shown Except Lamps.
4-light	$60.00	$62.00	$64.64
Extra chain, per foot	1.00	1.20	

With four lanterns and art glass panels color K
Complete fixture includes
Hubbell pull sockets.............................each, $0.66
Burnt brass, Swedish iron or verd antique
Add 20% to list for special finishes

No. 7904. Old brass
Length, 42 inches over all; spread, 25 inches

	Not Wired.	Wired.	Complete as Shown Except Lamps.
5-light	**$57.50**	**$60.00**	**$64.42**

No. 7716 Teplitz shade and holder included in "not wired" and "wired" prices

Complete fixture includes

Edison keyless sockets (on bottom)............ ......each,			$ 0.34
Edison key sockets (on arms)..........................		"	.37
No. 24236 C. R. I. shades...........		"	.57
No. 7716 Teplitz "		"	10.00
2¼-inch electric holders.......		"	.08

1-inch casing on stem, extra lengthening per foot, not wired, 55 cents; wired, 65 cents

No. 7905. Brushed brass
Length, 36 inches over all; spread, 24 inches

Complete as Shown
Except Lamps.

					Not Wired.	Wired.	
6-light, 3 arms (3 inside bowl),					$50.00	$53.00	$55.04
7 "	4 "	3	"	"	54.00	57.50	59.88
8 "	5 "	3	"	"	58.00	62.00	64.72
9 "	6 "	3	"	"	62.00	66.50	69.56

10-inch C. R. I. bowl and No. 5817 3¼ x6-inch C. R. I. balls and 3¼-inch
spun holders included in "wired and "not wired" prices

Complete fixture includes

Edison keyless sockets	each,	$0.34
No. 2160 10-inch C. R. I. bowl	"	2.25
No. 5817 6-inch C. R. I. ball	"	.50

⅞-inch casing on stem, extra lengthening per foot, not wired, 45 cents; wired, 55 cents

TUNGSTEN FIXTURES

No. 7907. Brushed brass
Length, 36 inches over all; spread, 16 inches

	Not Wired.	Wired.	Complete as Shown Except Lamps.
2-light	$ 7.50	$ 8.50	$11.82
3 "	8.75	10.25	15.23
4 "	10.00	12.00	18.64
5 "	11.25	13.75	22.05
6 "	12.50	15.50	25.46

Complete fixture includes
Edison keyless sockets......................................each, $0.34
Form H holders... " .20
No. 6045 holophane shades............................ " 1.12

1-inch extra lengthening per foot, not wired, 45 cents, wired, 55 cents

No. 7906. Rich gilt
Length, 36 inches over all; spread, 14 inches

	Not Wired.	Wired.	Complete as Shown Except Lamps.
2-light	$3.50	$4.50	$ 7.82
3 "	4.00	5.50	10.48
4 "	4.50	6.50	13.14
5 "	5.00	7.50	15.80
6 "	5.50	8.50	18.46

Complete fixture includes
Edison keyless sockets................each, $0.34
Form H holders .... " .20
No. 6045 holophane shades.......... " 1.12

¾-inch extra lengthening per foot, not wired, 40 cents; wired, 50 cents

No. 7908. Brushed brass

Length, 36 inches over all; spread, 18 inches

	Not Wired.	Wired.	Complete as Shown Except Lamps.
2-light	$ 7.50	$ 8.50	$12.04
3 "	8.75	10.25	15.56
4 "	10.60	12.00	19.08

Complete fixture includes

Edison key sockets ....each, $0.37
Form H holders .... "   .20
No. 10613o holophane shades..... .... "   1.20

⅜-inch casing on stem, extra lengthening per foot, not wired, 45 cents; wired, 55 cents

59

TUNGSTEN FIXTURE

No. 7909. Rich gilt and satin
Length, 36 inches over all; spread, 16 inches

	Not Wired.	Wired.	Complete as Shown Except Lamps
2-light	$4.50	$5.50	$ 8.98
3 "	5.50	7.00	12.22
4 "	6.50	8.50	15.46

Complete fixture includes

Edison keyless sockets ....each, **$0.34**
Form H holders .... " **.20**
No. 106130 holophane shades .... " **1.20**

¾-inch extra lengthening per foot, not wired, 40 cents; wired, 50 cents

TUNGSTEN FIXTURE

No. 7910. Brushed brass
Length, 36 inches over all; spread, 20 inches

	Not Wired.	Wired.	Complete as Shown Except Lamps.
2-light	$ 6.50	$ 7.50	$11.82
3 "	7.75	9.25	15.73
4 "	9.00	11.00	19.64
5 "	10.25	12.75	23.55
6 "	11.50	14.50	27.46

Complete fixture includes

Edison keyless sockets ....each, $0.34
Form H holders ....   "   .20
No. 6060 holophane shades ....   "   1.62
1-inch casing on stem, extra lengthening per foot, not wired, 45 cents; wired, 55 cents

61

No. 7911. Brushed brass
Length, 36 inches over all; spread, 20 inches

	Not Wired.	Wired.	Complete as Shown Except Lamps.
2-light	$4.25	$ 5.25	$ 8.57
3 "	5.00	6.50	11.48
4 "	5.75	7.75	14.39
5 "	6.50	9.00	17.30
6 "	7.25	10.25	20.21

Complete fixture includes

Edison keyless sockets	each, $0.34
Form H holders	"	.20
No. 6045 holophane shades	"	1.12

¾-inch extra lengthening per foot, not wired, 40 cents; wired, 50 cents

TUNGSTEN FIXTURE

No. 7912. Brushed brass
Length, 36 inches over all; spread, 16 inches

	Not Wired.	Wired.	Complete as Shown Except Lamps.
2-light	$6.50	$ 7.50	$10.98
3 "	7.25	8.75	13.98
4 "	8.00	10.00	16.96
5 "	8.75	11.25	19.95
6 "	9.50	12.50	22.94

Complete fixture includes

Edison keyless sockets ....each, $0.34
Form H holders .... " .20
No. 106130 holophane shades.................................. " 1.20

⅜-inch casing on stem, extra lengthening per foot, not wired, 45 cents; wired, 55 cents

TUNGSTEN FIXTURE

No. 7913. Old brass
Length, 36 inches over all; spread, 24 inches

	Not Wired.	Wired.	Complete as Shown Except Lamps.
2-light	$20.50	$21.50	$25.82
3 "	22.75	24.25	30.73
4 "	25.00	27.00	35.64
5 "	27.25	29.75	40.55
6 "	29.50	32.50	45.46

Complete fixture includes

Edison keyless sockets...................................each, $0.34
Form H holders.. "   .20
No. 6061 holophane shades............................... "   1.62

1¼-inch extra lengthening per foot, not wired, 60 cents; wired 70 cents

TUNGSTEN FIXTURE

No. 7915. Brushed brass

Length, 36 inches over all; spread, 20 inches

	Not Wired.	Wired with Silk Cord.	Complete as Shown Except Lamps.
2-light	$16.50	$17.50	$20.98
4 "	21.50	23.50	30.46
Extra chain, No. 0556, per foot	2.50	2.70	

Complete fixture includes

Edison keyless sockets................................each, **$0.34**
Form H holders.. " **.20**
No. 106130 holophane shades................................ " **1.20**

TUNGSTEN FIXTURE

No. 7916. Brushed brass
Length, 36 inches over all; spread, 18 inches

	Not Wired.	Wired.	Complete as Shown Except Lamps.
2-light	**$16.00**	**$17.00**	**$20.48**
3 "	**19.00**	**20.50**	**25.72**
4 "	**22.00**	**24.00**	**30.96**

Complete fixture includes

Edison keyless sockets . . . . .each, $0.34
Form H holders. . . . . " .20
No. 106130 holophane shades. . . . . " 1.20

⅝-inch casing on stem, extra lengthening per foot, not wired, 45 cents; wired, 55 cents

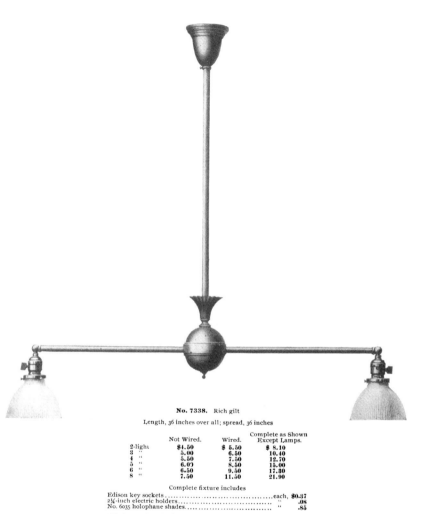

No. 7338. Rich gilt

Length, 36 inches over all; spread, 36 inches

	Not Wired.	Wired.	Complete as Shown Except Lamps.
2-light	$4.50	$ 5.50	$ 8.10
3 "	5.00	6.50	10.40
4 "	5.50	7.50	12.70
5 "	6.00	8.50	15.00
6 "	6.50	9.50	17.80
8 "	7.50	11.50	21.90

Complete fixture includes

Edison key sockets	each,	$0.37
2¼-inch electric holders	"	.08
No. 6035 holophane shades	"	.85

¾-inch extra lengthening per foot, not wired, 40 cents; wired 50 cents

No. 7340. Brushed brass

Length, 36 inches over all; spread, 34 inches

	Not Wired.	Wired.	Complete as Shown Except Lamps.
2-light	$ 6.75	$ 8.75	$ 9.41
3 "	8.00	9.50	11.99
4 "	9.25	11.25	14.57
5 "	10.50	13.00	17.15
6 "	11.75	14.75	19.73

Complete fixture includes

Edison key sockets . . . . each, **$0.37**
2½-inch electric holders . . . . " .08
No. 5671½ C. R. I. electric shades . . . . " **.38**
⅜-inch casing on stem, extra lengthening per foot, not wired, 45 cents; wired, 55 cents

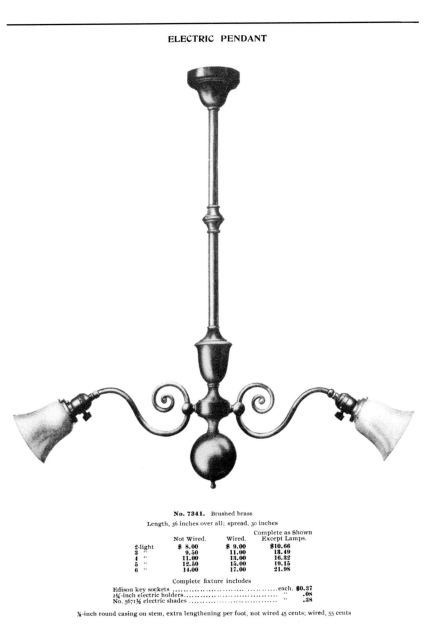

No. 7341. Brushed brass

Length, 36 inches over all; spread, 30 inches

	Not Wired.	Wired.	Complete as Shown Except Lamps.
2-light	$ 8.00	$ 9.00	$10.66
3 "	9.50	11.00	13.49
4 "	11.00	13.00	16.32
5 "	12.50	15.00	19.15
6 "	14.00	17.00	21.98

Complete fixture includes

Edison key sockets ....each,	$0.37
2¼-inch electric holders................................ "	.08
No. 5671½ electric shades .... "	.38

⅜-inch round casing on stem, extra lengthening per foot, not wired 45 cents; wired, 55 cents

ELECTRIC PENDANT

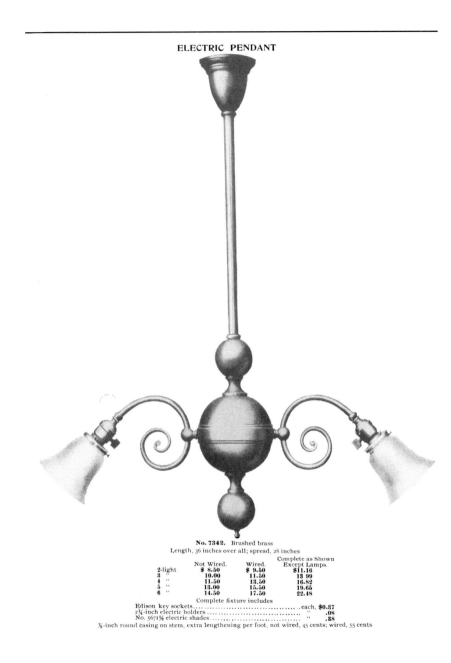

No. 7342. Brushed brass

Length, 36 inches over all; spread, 28 inches

	Not Wired.	Wired.	Complete as Shown Except Lamps.
2-light	$ 8.50	$ 9.50	$11.16
3 "	10.00	11.50	13.99
4 "	11.50	13.50	16.82
5 "	13.00	15.50	19.65
6 "	14.50	17.50	22.48

Complete fixture includes

Edison key sockets..................................each, $0.37
2¼-inch electric holders .... " .08
No. 5671½ electric shades.............................. " .38
⅝-inch round casing on stem, extra lengthening per foot, not wired, 45 cents; wired, 55 cents

No. 7343. Brushed brass

Length, 36 inches over all; spread, 28 inches

	Not Wired.	Wired.	Complete as Shown Except Lamps.
2-light	$ 6.50	$ 7.50	$ 9.16
3 "	8.00	8.50	10.99
4 "	9.50	11.50	14.82
5 "	11.00	13.50	17.65
6 "	12.50	15.50	20.48

Complete fixture includes

Edison key sockets . . . . each, $0.37
2¼-inch electric holders . . . . " .08
No. 5671½ electric shades . . . . " .38

⅜-inch round casing on stem, **extra lengthening per foot, not wired, 45 cents; wired, 55 cents**

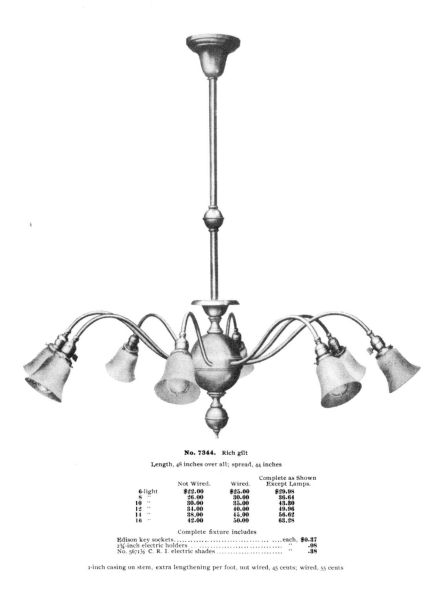

No. 7344. Rich gilt

Length, 48 inches over all; spread, 44 inches

	Not Wired.	Wired.	Complete as Shown Except Lamps.
6-light	$22.00	$25.00	$29.98
8 "	26.00	30.00	36.64
10 "	30.00	35.00	43.30
12 "	34.00	40.00	49.96
14 "	38.00	45.00	56.62
16 "	42.00	50.00	63.28

Complete fixture includes

Edison key sockets.............................each, **$0.37**
2¼-inch electric holders .... " .08
No. 5671½ C. R. I. electric shades .... " .38

1-inch casing on stem, extra lengthening per foot, not wired, 45 cents; wired, 55 cents

ELECTRIC FIXTURE

No. 7345. Old brass

Length, 42 inches over all ; spread, 30 inches

	Not Wired.	Wired.	Complete as Shown Except Lamps.
4-light	**$40.00**	**$42.00**	**$45.32**
5 "	48.00	50.50	54.65
6 "	56.00	59.00	63.98
8 "	72.00	76.00	82.64

Complete fixture includes

Edison key sockets ....each, **$0.37**
2¼-inch electric holders .... " .08
No. 5671½ C. R. I. electric shades...................... " .38
1-inch casing on stem, extra lengthening per foot, not wired 45 cents; wired, 55 cents

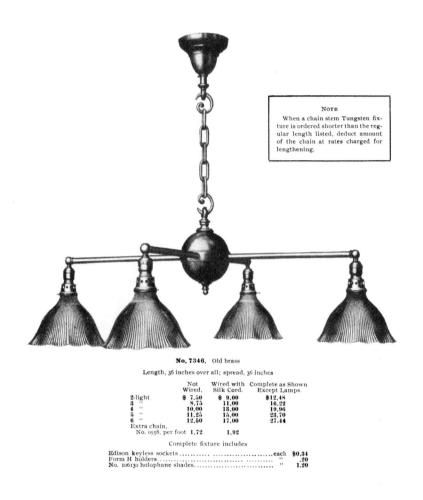

NOTE

When a chain stem Tungsten fixture is ordered shorter than the regular length listed, deduct amount of the chain at rates charged for lengthening.

No. 7346. Old brass

Length, 36 inches over all; spread, 36 inches

	Not Wired.	Wired with Silk Cord.	Complete as Shown Except Lamps.
2-light	$ 7.50	$ 9.00	$12.48
3 "	8.75	11.00	16.22
4 "	10.00	13.00	19.96
5 "	11.25	15.00	23.70
6 "	12.50	17.00	27.44
Extra chain, No. 0558, per foot	1.72	1.92	

Complete fixture includes

Edison keyless sockets	each	$0.34	
Form H holders	"	.20	
No. 106130 holophane shades	"	1.20	

TUNGSTEN FIXTURE

NOTE

When a chain stem Tungsten fixture is ordered shorter than the regular length listed, deduct amount of the chain at rates charged for lengthening.

No. 7347. Old brass

Length, 36 inches over all; spread, 36 inches

	Not Wired.	Wired with Silk Cord.	Complete as Shown Except Lamp.
2-light	$13.00	$14.50	$17.98
3 " (3 arms)	16.00	18.25	23.47
3 " (2 arms, 1 lt. on bottom)	13.50	15.75	20.97
4 " (4 arms)	19.00	22.00	28.97
4 " (3 arms, 1 lt. on bottom)	16.50	19.50	26.47
5 " (5 arms)	22.00	25.75	34.45
5 " (4 arms, 1 lt. on bottom)	19.50	23.25	31.95
6 " (5 arms, 1 lt. on bottom)	22.50	27.00	37.44
Extra chain, No. 0558 per foot	1.72	1.92	

Complete fixture includes

Edison keyless sockets..............................each, $0.34
Form H holders.................................... "   .20
No. 106130 holophane shades.... .... "   1.20

NOTE

When a chain stem Tungsten fixture is ordered shorter than the regular length listed, deduct at the rate charged for extra lengthening.

When fixture is ordered complete as shown we furnish No. 6045 shade except ordered otherwise.

No. 7348. Old brass

Length, 36 inches over all; spread, 18 inches

	Not Wired.	Wired.	Complete as Shown with No. 6060 60-watt shades, Except Lamps.	Complete as Shown with No. 6045 40-watt shades, Except Lamps.
2-light, (2 arms only)	$5.00	$ 6.00	$10.32	$ 9.32
3 " (2 arms, 1 lt. on bottom)	6.25	7.75	14.23	12.73
3 " (3 arms only)	5.75	7.25	13.73	12.23
4 " (4 arms only)	6.50	8.50	17.14	15.14
4 " (3 arms, 1 lt. on bottom)	7.00	9.00	17.64	15.64
5 " (4 arms, 1 lt. on bottom)	7.75	10.25	21.05	18.55
Extra chain, No. 0560, per foot	1.13	1.25		

Complete fixture includes

Edison keyless sockets	each,	$0.34
Form H holders	"	.20
No. 6045 holophane shades	"	1.12
No. 6060 holophane shades	"	1.62

TUNGSTEN FIXTURE

No. 7349. Brushed brass
Length, 36 inches over all; spread, 16 inches

	Not Wired.	Wired.	Complete as Shown with No. 6060 60-watt Shades, Except Lamps.	Complete as Shown with No. 6045 40-watt Shades, Except Lamps.
2-light (2 arms only)	$4.00	$5.00	$ 9.32	$ 8.32
3 " (3 arms only)	4.75	6.25	12.73	11.23
3 " (2 arms and 1-lt. on bottom)	4.25	5.75	12.23	10.73
4 " (3 arms and 1-lt. on bottom)	5.00	7.00	15.64	13.64
4 " (4 arms only)	5.50	7.50	16.14	14.14

Complete fixture includes

Edison keyless sockets..each,	$0.34
Form H holders .... "	.20
No. 6045 holophane shades... "	1.12
No. 6060 holophane shades... "	1.62

⅜-inch casing on stem, extra lengthening per foot, not wired, 45 cents; wired, 55 cents

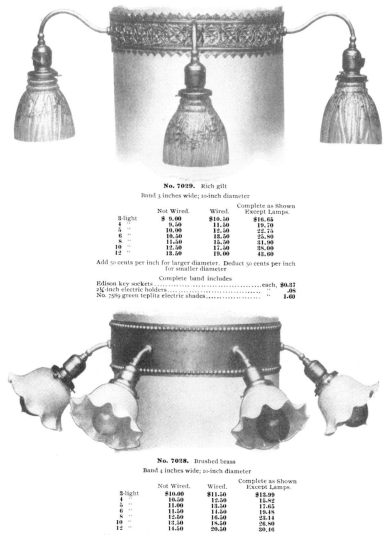

No. 7029. Rich gilt

Band 3 inches wide; 10-inch diameter

	Not Wired.	Wired.	Complete as Shown Except Lamps.
3-light	$ 9.00	$10.50	$16.65
4 "	9.50	11.50	19.70
5 "	10.00	12.50	22.75
6 "	10.50	13.50	25.80
8 "	11.50	15.50	31.90
10 "	12.50	17.50	38.00
12 "	13.50	19.00	43.60

Add 50 cents per inch for larger diameter. Deduct 50 cents per inch for smaller diameter

Complete band includes

Edison key sockets ....each, $0.37
2¼-inch electric holders.. "   .08
No. 7589 green teplitz electric shades.................... " 1.60

No. 7028. Brushed brass

Band 4 inches wide; 10-inch diameter

	Not Wired.	Wired.	Complete as Shown Except Lamps.
3-light	$10.00	$11.50	$13.99
4 "	10.50	12.50	15.82
5 "	11.00	13.50	17.65
6 "	11.50	14.50	19.48
8 "	12.50	16.50	23.14
10 "	13.50	18.50	26.80
12 "	14.50	20.50	30.46

Add 50 cents per inch for larger diameter. Deduct 50 cents per inch for smaller diameter

Complete band includes

Edison key sockets ....each, $0.37
2¼-inch electric holders...... .... " $0.08
No. 95½ electric plain opalescent shades................. "   .38

ELECTRIC COLUMN BANDS

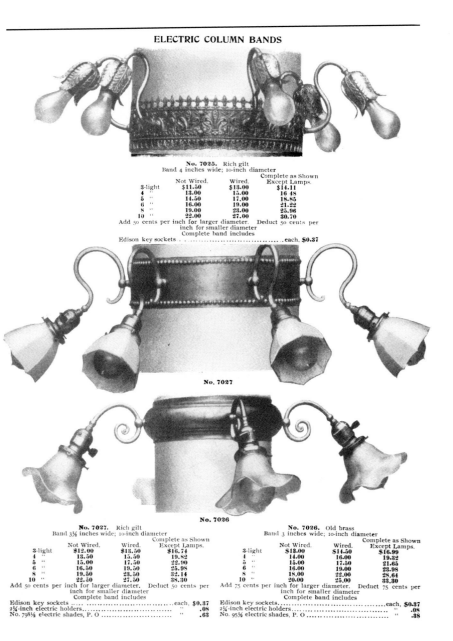

No. 7025. Rich gilt
Band 4 inches wide; 10-inch diameter

	Not Wired.	Wired.	Complete as Shown Except Lamps.
3-light	$11.50	$13.00	$14.11
4 "	13.00	15.00	16 48
5 "	14.50	17.00	18.85
6 "	16.00	19.00	21.22
8 "	19.00	23.00	25.96
10 "	22.00	27.00	30.70

Add 50 cents per inch for larger diameter. Deduct 50 cents per inch for smaller diameter
Complete band includes
Edison key sockets . . . . each, $0.37

No. 7027

No. 7026

No. 7027. Rich gilt
Band 3½ inches wide; 10-inch diameter

	Not Wired.	Wired.	Complete as Shown Except Lamps.
3-light	$12.00	$13.50	$16.74
4 "	13.50	15.50	19.82
5 "	15.00	17.50	22.90
6 "	16.50	19.50	25.98
8 "	19.50	23.50	32.14
10 "	22.50	27.50	38.30

Add 50 cents per inch for larger diameter. Deduct 50 cents per inch for smaller diameter
Complete band includes
Edison key sockets . . . . each, $0.37
2¼-inch electric holders. . . . . " .08
No. 798½ electric shades, P. O . . . . " .63

No. 7026. Old brass
Band 3 inches wide; 10-inch diameter

	Not Wired.	Wired.	Complete as Shown Except Lamps.
3-light	$13.00	$14.50	$16.99
4 "	14.00	16.00	19.32
5 "	15.00	17.50	21.65
6 "	16.00	19.00	23.98
8 "	18.00	22.00	28.64
10 "	20.00	25.00	33.30

Add 75 cents per inch for larger diameter. Deduct 75 cents per inch for smaller diameter
Complete band includes
Edison key sockets . . . . each, $0.37
2¼-inch electric holders. . . . . " .08
No. 95½ electric shades, P. O . . . . " .38

ELECTRIC PENDANTS

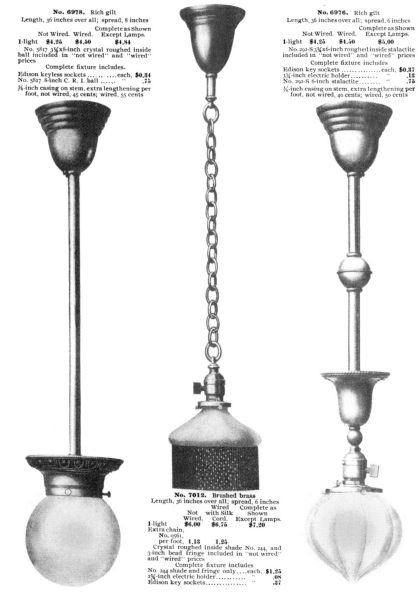

No. 6978. Rich gilt
Length, 36 inches over all; spread, 8 inches
Complete as Shown
Not Wired. Wired. Except Lamps.
1-light **$4.25** **$4.50** **$4.84**
No. 5817 3¼x8-inch crystal roughed inside
ball included in "not wired" and "wired"
prices

Complete fixture includes.

Edison keyless sockets .... each, **$0.34**
No. 5817 8-inch C. R. I. ball ...... " .75
⅜-inch casing on stem, extra lengthening per
foot, not wired, 45 cents; wired, 55 cents

No. 6976. Rich gilt
Length, 36 inches over all; spread, 6 inches
Complete as Shown
Not Wired. Wired. Except Lamps.
1-light **$4.25** **$4.50** **$5.00**
No. 292-S 3¼x6-inch roughed inside stalactite
included in "not wired" and "wired" prices
Complete fixture includes
Edison key sockets .... each, **$0.37**
3¼-inch electric holder.......... " .13
No. 292-S 6-inch stalactite........ " .75
¾-inch casing on stem, extra lengthening per
foot, not wired, 40 cents; wired, 50 cents

No. 7012. Brushed brass
Length, 36 inches over all; spread, 6 inches
Wired Complete as
Not with Silk Shown
Wired. Cord. Except Lamps.
1-light **$6.00** **$6.75** **$7.20**
Extra chain,
No. 0561,
per foot, 1.13 1.25
Crystal roughed inside shade No. 244, and
3-inch bead fringe included in "not wired"
and "wired" prices
Complete fixture includes
No. 244 shade and fringe only....each, **$1.25**
2¼-inch electric holder........... " .08
Edison key sockets............... " .37

ELECTRIC PENDANTS

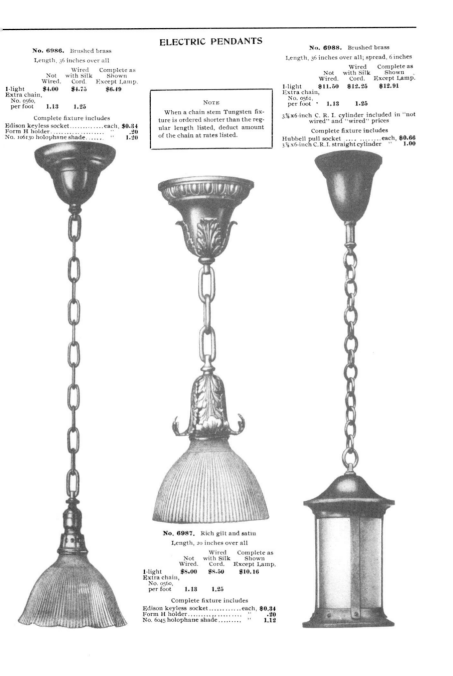

No. 6986. Brushed brass

Length, 36 inches over all

	Not Wired.	Wired with Silk Cord.	Complete as Shown Except Lamp.
1-light	$4.00	$4.75	$6.49
Extra chain, No. 0560, per foot	1.13	1.25	

Complete fixture includes

Edison keyless socket	each,	$0.34
Form H holder	"	.20
No. 106130 holophane shade	"	1.20

NOTE

When a chain stem Tungsten fixture is ordered shorter than the regular length listed, deduct amount of the chain at rates listed.

No. 6988. Brushed brass

Length, 36 inches over all; spread, 6 inches

	Not Wired.	Wired with Silk Cord.	Complete as Shown Except Lamp.
1-light	$11.50	$12.25	$12.91
Extra chain, No. 0561, per foot	1.13	1.25	

3⅜x6-inch C. R. I. cylinder included in "not wired" and "wired" prices

Complete fixture includes

Hubbell pull socket	each,	$0.66
3⅜x6-inch C.R.I. straight cylinder	"	1.00

No. 6987. Rich gilt and satin

Length, 20 inches over all

	Not Wired.	Wired with Silk Cord.	Complete as Shown Except Lamp.
1-light	$8.00	$8.50	$10.16
Extra chain, No. 0560, per foot	1.13	1.25	

Complete fixture includes

Edison keyless socket	each,	$0.34
Form H holder	"	.20
No. 6045 holophane shade	"	1.12

ELECTRIC PENDANTS

No. 7009. Brushed brass

Length, 43 inches over all; spread, 8 inches

	Not Wired.	Wired.	Complete as Shown Except Lamps.
1-light	**$4.25**	**$4.50**	**$5.00**

No. 4013 3¼x8-inch C. R. I. ball included in "not wired" and "wired" prices

Complete fixture includes

Edison key sockets .... each, **$0.37**
3¼-inch electric holders .... " .13
No. 4013 8-inch C. R. I. ball ...... " 1.68

¾-inch casing on stem; extra lengthening per foot, not wired, 50 cents, wired, 60 cents

No. 7011. Brushed brass

Length, 43 inches over all; spread, 6 inches

	Not Wired.	Wired.	Complete as Shown Except Lamps.
1-light	**$5.50**	**$5.75**	**$6.12**

No. 238 3¼x6-inch C. R. I. ball and 3¼-inch stamped socket cover holder included in "not wired" and "wired" prices

Complete fixture includes

Edison key sockets .... each, **$0.37**
No. 238 6-inch C. R. I. ball........ " .75
3¼-inch stamped socket cover holder .... " 1.25

¾-inch square casing on stem; extra lengthening per foot, not wired, 65 cents; wired, 75 cents

No. 7010. Brushed brass

Length, 43 inches over all; spread, 4½ inches

	Not Wired.	Wired.	Complete as Shown Except Lamps.
1-light	**$3.25**	**$3.50**	**$4.40**

Complete fixture includes

Edison key sockets .... each, **$0.37**
2¼-inch electric holders .... " .08
No 9321½ C. R. I. electric shade.. " .45

¾-inch square casing on stem; extra lengthening per foot, not wired, 65 cents; wired, 75 cents

82

ELECTRIC PENDANTS

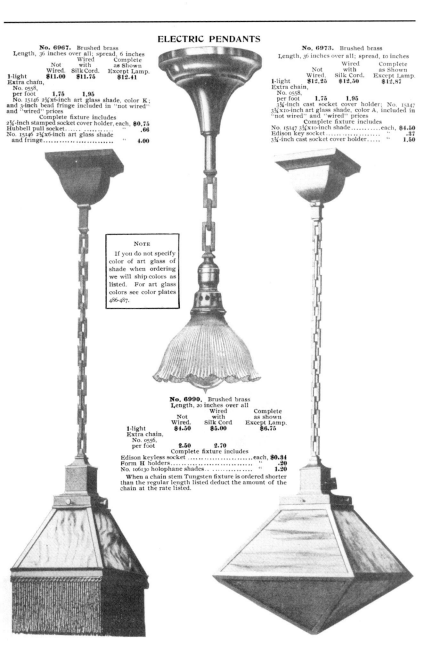

No. 6967. Brushed brass
Length, 36 inches over all; spread, 6 inches

	Wired	
	Not	with	Complete as Shown
	Wired.	Silk Cord.	Except Lamp.
1-light	**$11.00**	**$11.75**	**$12.41**
Extra chain, No. 0558, per foot	**1.75**	**1.95**	

No. 15146 2¼x6-inch art glass shade, color K; and 3-inch bead fringe included in "not wired" and "wired" prices

Complete fixture includes
2¼-inch stamped socket cover holder, each, **$0.75**
Hubbell pull socket...... .... " **.66**
No. 15146 2¼x6-inch art glass shade and fringe.......................... " **4.00**

NOTE

If you do not specify color of art glass of shade when ordering we will ship colors as listed. For art glass colors see color plates 486-487.

No. 6990. Brushed brass
Length, 20 inches over all

	Not	Wired with	Complete as shown
	Wired.	Silk Cord	Except Lamp.
1-light	**$4.50**	**$5.00**	**$6.75**
Extra chain, No. 0556, per foot	**2.50**	**2.70**	

Complete fixture includes
Edison keyless socket ....each, **$0.34**
Form H holders............................ " **.20**
No. 106130 holophane shades .. .. " **1.20**

When a chain stem Tungsten fixture is ordered shorter than the regular length listed deduct the amount of the chain at the rate listed.

No. 6973. Brushed brass
Length, 36 inches over all; spread, 10 inches

		Wired	
	Not	with	Complete as Shown
	Wired.	Silk Cord.	Except Lamp.
1-light	**$12.25**	**$12.50**	**$12.87**
Extra chain, No. 0558, per foot	**1.75**	**1.95**	

3¾-inch cast socket cover holder; No. 15147 3¾x10-inch art glass shade, color A, included in "not wired" and "wired" prices

Complete fixture includes
No. 15147 3¾x10-inch shade...........each, **$4.50**
Edison key socket .... " **.37**
3¾-inch cast socket cover holder..... " **1.50**

83

ELECTRIC PENDANTS

NOTE
If you do not specify color of
art glass when ordering we will
ship colors as listed.

No. 6991.

No. 6994.   No. 6992.

No. 6993.

No. 6994. Old brass
Length, 36 inches over all

	Not Wired.	Wired with Silk Cord.	Complete as Shown Except Lamp.
1-light	$11.00	$11.75	$12.41
Extra chain, No. 0561, per foot	1.13	1.25	

Complete fixture includes
Hubbell pull socket ....each, $0.66

No. 6992. Brushed brass
Length, 36 inches over all; spread, 6¼ inches

	Not Wired.	Wired with Silk Cord.	Complete as Shown Except Lamp.
1-light	$24.00	$24.75	$25.41
Extra chain, No. 0557, per foot	1.90	2.10	

Made of heavy cast brass frame; art glass panels; design in center,
color E; border, color C; body, K
Complete fixture includes
Hubbell pull socket ....each, $0.66

No. 6991. Old brass
Length, 36 inches over all

	Not Wired.	Wired with Silk Cord.	Complete as Shown Except Lamp.
1-light	$28.00	$28.75	$29.41
Extra chain, No. 0561, per foot	1.13	1.25	

Bent art glass panels; color F art glass
Complete fixture includes
Hubbell pull socket.................. ....each, $0.66

No. 6993. Old brass
Length, 18 inches over all

	Not Wired.	Wired.	Complete as Shown Except Lamp.
1-light	$2.50	$2.80	$4.46

¾-inch extra lengthening per foot, not wired, 45 cents; wired, 55 cents
Complete fixture includes
Edison keyless socket...................................each, $0.84
Form H holder........... .... ''   .20
No. 6045 holophane shade...... .... ''   1.12

84

ELECTRIC FIXTURES

No. 7810. Brushed brass

Length, 36 inches over all; spread, 9 inches

2-light	Not Wired.	Wired.	Complete as Shown Except Lamps.
2-light	$ 8.00	$ 9.00	$10.00
4 "	10.50	12.50	16.10

Complete fixture includes

Edison key sockets...................................each, $0.37
2¼-inch electric holders .... " .08
No. 9321½ C. R. I. electric shades........................ " .45
⅝-inch casing on stem, extra lengthening per foot, not wired, 75 cents; wired, 85 cents

No. 6998. Brushed brass

Length, 36 inches over all; spread, 12 inches

2-light	Not Wired.	Wired.	Complete as Shown Except Lamps.
2-light	$6.50	$ 7.25	$9.05

Complete fixture includes

Edison key sockets......................... ....each, $0.37
2½-inch electric holders .... " .08
No. 9321½ C. R. I. shades....................... " .45
⅝-inch casing on stem, extra lengthening per foot, not wired, 75 cents; wired, 85 cents

WOOD FIXTURE

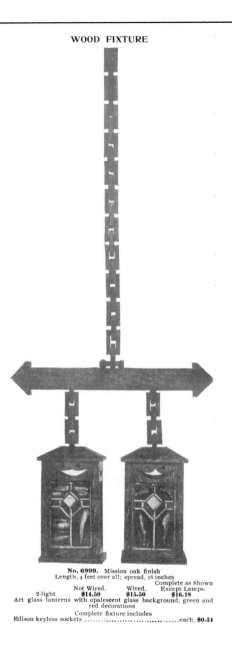

No. 6999. Mission oak finish
Length, 4 feet over all; spread, 18 inches

Complete as Shown
Except Lamps.

	Not Wired.	Wired.	
2-light	**$14.50**	**$15.50**	**$16.18**

Art glass lanterns with opalescent glass background; green and
red decorations

Complete fixture includes

Edison keyless sockets.................................each, **$0.34**

No. 6919. Iron, dull black
Length, 42 inches over all

		Complete as Shown
Not Wired.	Wired.	Except Lamps.
1-light **$12.20**	**$12.50**	**$12.84**

3¾x10-inch special opalescent stalactite included in "not wired" and "wired" prices.

Complete fixture includes
Edison keyless sockets .... each, **$0.34**
⅜-inch iron pipe stem, extra lengthening per foot, not wired, 15 cents; wired, 25 cents.

No. 7433. Iron, dull black
Length, 9 inches

		Complete as Shown
Not Wired.	Wired.	Except Lamps.
1-light **$7.25**	**$7.50**	**$7.84**

No. 132 3¾x8-inch twist opalescent ball included in "not wired" and "wired" prices.

Complete fixture includes
Edison keyless sockets ....each, **$0.34**
No. 132 8-inch T. O. ball .... " **.95**

No. 7438. Iron, dull black
Length, 11 inches; top, 9 inches

		Complete as Shown
Not Wired.	Wired.	Except Lamps.
1-light **$7.75**	**$8.00**	**$8.84**

No. 132 3¾x8-inch twist opalescent ball included in "not wired" and "wired" prices.

Complete fixture includes
Edison keyless sockets ....each, **$0.34**
No. 132 8-inch twist opalescent ball ....each, **.95**

No. 6920. Iron, dull black

Length, 36 inches over all

		Complete as Shown
Not Wired.	Wired.	Except Lamps.
1-light **$9.45**	**$9.75**	**$10.09**

3¾x10-inch special opalescent stalactite included in "not wired" and "wired" prices.

Complete fixture includes
Edison keyless sockets ...each, **$0.34**

⅜-inch iron pipe, extra lengthening per foot, not wired, 15 cents; wired, 25 cents.

No. 6922. Iron, dull black
Length, 36 inches over all

		Complete as Shown Except Lamps.
Not Wired.	Wired.	
1-light **$11.20**	**$11.50**	**$11.84**

No. 132 3¾x8-inch opalescent ball included in "not wired" and "wired" prices.

Complete fixture includes
Edison keyless sockets each, **$0.34**
No. 132 3¾x8-inch twist opalescent ball.......... each, **.95**

⅜-inch iron pipe, extra lengthening per foot, not wired, 15 cents; wired, 25 cents.

No. 7437. Iron, dull black
Length, 13 inches; top, 9 inches

		Complete as Shown
Not Wired.	Wired.	Except Lamps.
1-light **$8.25**	**$8.50**	**$8.84**

No. 132 4x10-inch opalescent ball included in "not wired" and "wired" prices.

Complete fixture includes
Edison keyless sockets ....each, **$0.34**
No. 132 4x10-inch opalescent twist ball................each, **1.25**

87

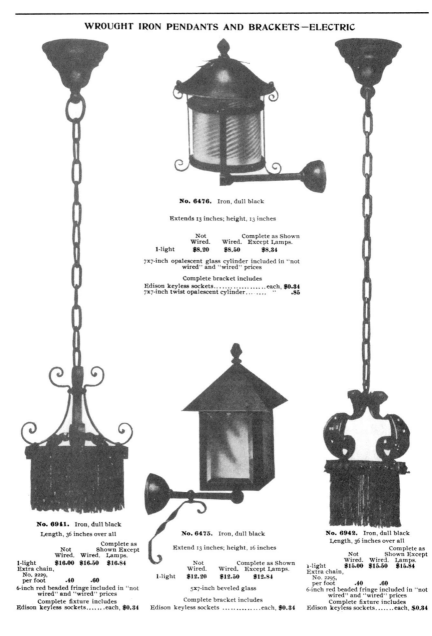

No. 6476. Iron, dull black

Extends 13 inches; height, 13 inches

	Not Wired.	Wired.	Complete as Shown Except Lamps.
1-light	$8.20	$8.50	$8.34

7x7-inch opalescent glass cylinder included in "not wired" and "wired" prices

Complete bracket includes

Edison keyless sockets....................each, $0.34
7x7-inch twist opalescent cylinder... .... "   .85

No. 6941. Iron, dull black
Length, 36 inches over all

	Not Wired.	Wired.	Complete as Shown Except Lamps.
1-light	$16.00	$16.50	$16.84
Extra chain, No. 2229, per foot	.40	.60	

6-inch red beaded fringe included in "not wired" and "wired" prices

Complete fixture includes
Edison keyless sockets......each, $0.34

No. 6475. Iron, dull black

Extend 13 inches; height, 16 inches

	Not Wired.	Wired.	Complete as Shown Except Lamps.
1-light	$12.20	$12.50	$12.84

5x7-inch beveled glass

Complete bracket includes
Edison keyless sockets ....each, $0.34

No. 6942. Iron, dull black
Length, 36 inches over all

	Not Wired.	Wired.	Complete as Shown Except Lamps.
1-light	$15.00	$15.50	$15.84
Extra chain, No. 2295, per foot	.40	.60	

6-inch red beaded fringe included in "not wired" and "wired" prices

Complete fixture includes
Edison keyless sockets.......each, $0.34

ELECTRIC CEILING LIGHTS

No. 7503. Old brass
Length, 10 inches over all

	Not Wired.	Complete as Shown Except Lamp.
1-light	$3.60	$3.94

With 5-inch red bead fringe No. F175; see
plate 485 for fringe
Complete fixture includes
Edison keyless socket............each, $0.34

NO. 7504. Brushed brass
Length, 11 inches over all

	Not Wired.	Complete as Shown Except Lamp.
1-light	$3.60	$3.94

With 5-inch green bead fringe No. F171; see
plate 485 for fringe

Complete fixture includes
Edison keyless socket..........each, $0.34

No. 7505. Old brass
Length, 10 inches over all

	Not Wired.	Complete as Shown Except Lamp.
1-light	$1.80	$2.14

With 5-inch gold bead fringe No. F181; see
plate 485 for fringe
Complete fixture includes
Edison keyless socket............each, $0.34

No. 7507. Brushed brass
Length, 12½ inches over all

	Not Wired.	Complete as Shown Except Lamp.
1-light	$3.00	$3.34

With 5-inch red bead fringe No. F175; see
plate 485 for fringe
Complete fixture includes
Edison keyless socket...........each, $0.34

No. 7506. Old brass
Length, 9¼ inches over all

	Not Wired.	Complete as Shown Except Lamp.
1-light	$1.60	$1.94

With 3¼-inch holder and 5-inch green bead
fringe No. F173; see plate 485 for fringe

Complete fixture includes
Edison keyless socket..........each, $0.34

No. 7508. Brushed brass
Length, 10 inches over all

	Not Wired.	Complete as Shown Except Lamp.
1-light	$2.25	$2.59

With 6-inch gold fringe No. F181; see plate
485 for fringe

Complete fixture includes
Edison keyless socket..........each, $0.34

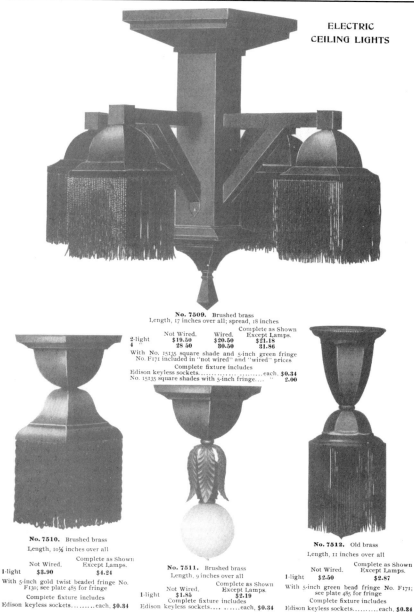

No. 7509. Brushed brass
Length, 17 inches over all; spread, 18 inches

	Not Wired.	Wired.	Complete as Shown Except Lamps.
2-light	$19.50	$20.50	$21.18
4 "	28.50	30.50	31.86

With No. 15135 square shade and 5-inch green fringe
No. F171 included in "not wired" and "wired" prices

Complete fixture includes
Edison keyless sockets............. ....each, $0.34
No. 15135 square shades with 5-inch fringe.... " **2.00**

No. 7510. Brushed brass
Length, 10½ inches over all

	Not Wired.	Complete as Shown Except Lamps.
1-light	$3.90	$4.24

With 5-inch gold twist beaded fringe No.
F130; see plate 485 for fringe
Complete fixture includes
Edison keyless sockets.........each, $0.34

No. 7511. Brushed brass
Length, 9 inches over all

	Not Wired.	Complete as Shown Except Lamps.
1-light	$1.85	$2.19

Complete fixture includes
Edison keyless sockets.... ......each, $0.34

No. 7512. Old brass
Length, 11 inches over all

	Not Wired.	Complete as Shown Except Lamps.
1-light	$2.50	$2.87

With 5-inch green bead fringe No. F171;
see plate 485 for fringe
Complete fixture includes
Edison keyless sockets.........each, $0.34

ELECTRIC CEILING LIGHTS

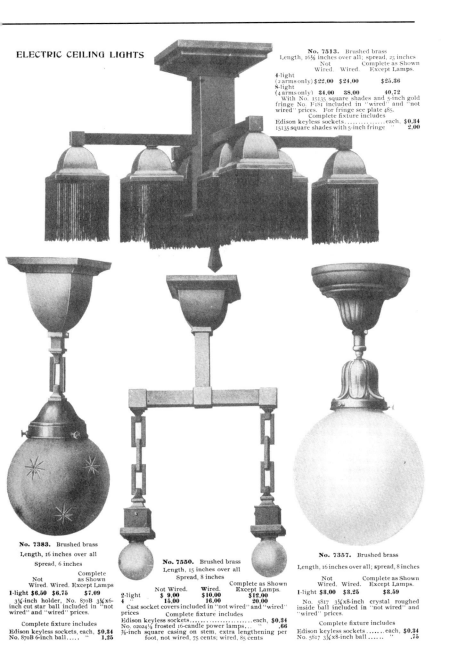

No. 7513. Brushed brass
Length, 16½ inches over all; spread, 23 inches

	Not Wired.	Wired.	Complete as Shown Except Lamps.
4-light (2 arms only)	$22.00	$24.00	$25.36
8-light (4 arms only)	34.00	38.00	40.72

With No. 15135 square shades and 5-inch gold fringe No. F181 included in "wired" and "not wired" prices. For fringe see plate 485.

Complete fixture includes
Edison keyless sockets...............each, $0.34
15135 square shades with 5-inch fringe " 2.00

No. 7383. Brushed brass
Length, 16 inches over all
Spread, 6 inches

	Not Wired.	Wired.	Complete as Shown Except Lamps.
1-light	$6.50	$6.75	$7.09

3¼-inch holder, No. 870B 3¼x6-inch cut star ball included in "not wired" and "wired" prices.

Complete fixture includes
Edison keyless sockets, each, $0.34
No. 870B 6-inch ball..... " 1.25

No. 7550. Brushed brass
Length, 15 inches over all
Spread, 8 inches

	Not Wired.	Wired.	Complete as Shown Except Lamps.
2-light	$ 9.00	$10.00	$12.00
4 "	15.00	16.00	20.00

Cast socket covers included in "not wired" and "wired" prices
Complete fixture includes
Edison keyless sockets.....................each, $0.34
No. 02024½ frosted 16-candle power lamps... " .66
⅞-inch square casing on stem, extra lengthening per foot, not wired, 75 cents; wired, 85 cents

No. 7357. Brushed brass
Length, 16 inches over all; spread, 8 inches

	Not Wired.	Wired.	Complete as Shown Except Lamps.
1-light	$3.00	$3.25	$3.59

No. 5817 3¼x8-inch crystal roughed inside ball included in "not wired" and "wired" prices.

Complete fixture includes
Edison keyless sockets ......each, $0.34
No. 5817 3¼x8-inch ball ...... " .75

91

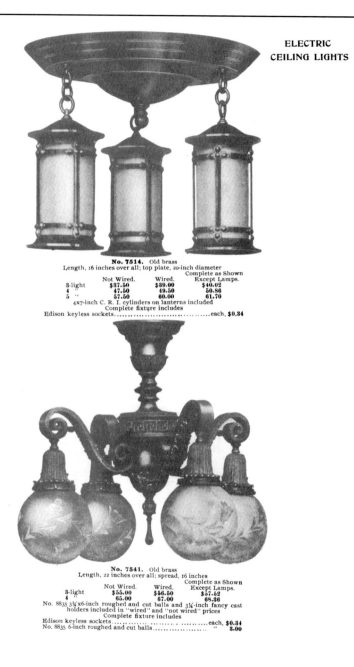

No. 7514. Old brass

Length, 16 inches over all; top plate, 20-inch diameter

	Not Wired.	Wired.	Complete as Shown Except Lamps.
3-light	$37.50	$39.00	$40.02
4 "	47.50	49.50	50.86
5 "	57.50	60.00	61.70

4x7-inch C. R. I. cylinders on lanterns included

Complete fixture includes

Edison keyless sockets...................................each, $0.34

No. 7541. Old brass

Length, 22 inches over all; spread, 16 inches

	Not Wired.	Wired.	Complete as Shown Except Lamps.
3-light	$55.00	$56.50	$57.52
4 "	65.00	67.00	68.36

No. 8835 3¼x6-inch roughed and cut balls and 3¼-inch fancy cast
holders included in "wired" and "not wired" prices

Complete fixture includes

Edison keyless sockets................................... each, $0.34

No. 8835 6-inch roughed and cut balls.................... " 3.00

ELECTRIC CEILING LIGHTS

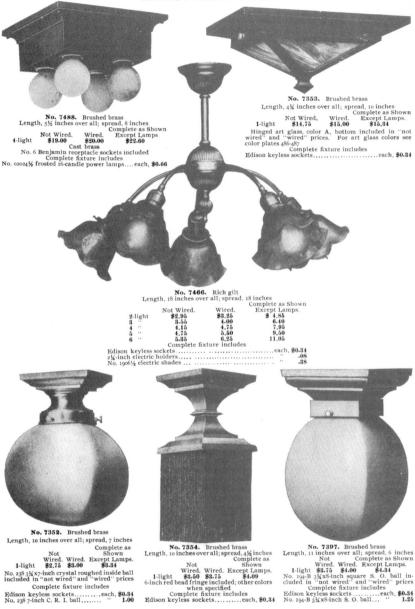

No. 7488. Brushed brass
Length, 5½ inches over all; spread, 8 inches
Complete as Shown

	Not Wired.	Wired.	Except Lamps.
4-light	**$19.00**	**$20.00**	**$22.60**

Cast brass
No. 6 Benjamin receptacle sockets included
Complete fixture includes
No. 0202¼ frosted 16-candle power lamps....each, **$0.66**

No. 7353. Brushed brass
Length, 4¾ inches over all; spread, 10 inches
Complete as Shown

	Not Wired.	Wired.	Except Lamps.
1-light	**$14.75**	**$15.00**	**$15.34**

Hinged art glass, color A, bottom included in "not
wired" and "wired" prices. For art glass colors see
color plates 486-487
Complete fixture includes
Edison keyless sockets......................each, **$0.34**

No. 7466. Rich gilt
Length, 18 inches over all; spread, 18 inches
Complete as Shown

	Not Wired.	Wired.	Except Lamps.
2-light	**$2.95**	**$3.25**	**$ 4.85**
3 "	**3.55**	**4.00**	6.40
4 "	4.15	4.75	7.95
5 "	4.75	5.50	9.50
6 "	5.35	6.25	11.05

Complete fixture includes
Edison keyless sockets ....each, **$0.34**
2¼-inch electric holders .... " .08
No. 1906½ electric shades ... . " .38

No. 7352. Brushed brass
Length, 10 inches over all; spread, 7 inches
Complete as Shown

	Not Wired.	Wired.	Except Lamps.
1-light	**$2.75**	**$3.00**	**$3.34**

No. 238 3¼x7-inch crystal roughed inside ball
included in "not wired" and "wired" prices
Complete fixture includes
Edison keyless sockets.........each, **$0.34**
No. 238 7-inch C. R. I. ball........ " **1.00**

No. 7354. Brushed brass
Length, 10 inches over all; spread, 4½ inches
Complete as Shown

	Not Wired.	Wired.	Except Lamps.
1-light	**$3.50**	**$3.75**	**$4.09**

6-inch red bead fringe included; other colors
when specified
Complete fixture includes
Edison keyless sockets.........each, **$0.34**

No. 7397. Brushed brass
Length, 11 inches over all; spread, 6 inches
Complete as Shown

	Not Wired.	Wired.	Except Lamps.
1-light	**$3.75**	**$4.00**	**$4.34**

No. 194-B 3¼x8-inch square S. O. ball in-
cluded in "not wired" and "wired" prices
Complete fixture includes
Edison keyless sockets.........each, **$0.34**
No. 194-B 3¼x8-inch S. O. ball... " **1.25**

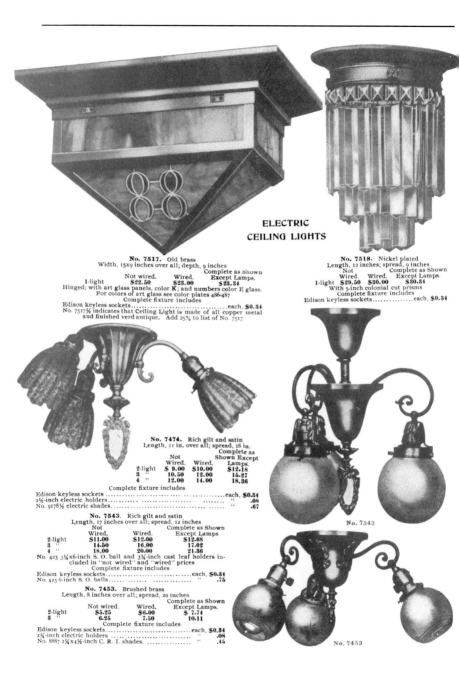

ELECTRIC
CEILING LIGHTS

No. 7517. Old brass
Width, 15x9 inches over all; depth, 9 inches
Complete as Shown

	Not wired.	Wired.	Except Lamps.
1-light	$22.50	$23.00	$23.34

Hinged; with art glass panels, color **K**; and numbers color E glass.
For colors of art glass see color plates 486-487
Complete fixture includes
Edison keyless sockets,......................each, **$0.34**
No. 7517½ indicates that Ceiling Light is made of all copper metal
and finished verd antique. Add 25% to list of No. 7517

No. 7518. Nickel plated
Length, 12 inches; spread, 9 inches
Complete as Shown
Except Lamps.

	Wired.	Wired.	
1-light	$29.50	$30.00	$30.34

With 5-inch colonial cut prisms
Complete fixture includes
Edison keyless sockets..............each. **$0.34**

No. 7474. Rich gilt and satin
Length, 11 in. over all; spread, 18 in.

	Not Wired.	Wired.	Complete as Shown Except Lamps.
2-light	$ 9.00	$10.00	$12.18
3 "	10.50	12.00	15.27
4 "	12.00	14.00	18.36

Complete fixture includes
Edison keyless sockets..........................each, **$0.34**
2¼-inch electric holders............................. " .08
No. 9178½ electric shades........................... " .67

No. 7543. Rich gilt and satin
Length, 17 inches over all; spread, 12 inches

	Not Wired.	Wired.	Complete as Shown Except Lamps
2-light	$11.00	$12.00	$12.68
3 "	14.50	16.00	17.02
4 "	18.00	20.00	21.36

No. 423 3¼x6-inch S. O. ball and 3¼-inch cast leaf holders in-
cluded in "not wired" and "wired" prices
Complete fixture includes
Edison keyless sockets..............................each, **$0.34**
No. 423 6-inch S. O. balls............. .... " .75

No. 7543

No. 7453. Brushed brass
Length, 8 inches over all; spread, 20 inches

	Not wired.	Wired.	Complete as Shown Except Lamps.
2-light	$5.25	$6.00	$ 7.74
3 "	6.25	7.50	10.11

Complete fixture includes
Edison keyless sockets..............................each, **$0.34**
2¼-inch electric holders .... " .08
No. 8887 2¼x4½-inch C. R. I. shades. .... " .45

No. 7453

94

No. 7522. Brushed brass
1-light, no glass..........each, $3.00
1 " with No. 106130
holophane.... .... "   4.20
Made with inner lamp receptacle. No lamp
included

No. 7519. Brushed brass
1-light, no glass, for 100-
watt lamp, 2¼-inch fitter
size......................each, $4.00
1-light, No. 7519½, no
glass, for 250-watt lamp,
3¼-inch fitter size....... "   6.00
Made with inner lamp receptacle. Can
furnish special holophane glass for this fixture. We recommend No. 106121 holophane,
at $2.45 each, net.

No. 7521. Brushed brass
1-light .... each, $1.20
1 "   complete as shown
with No. 7381 holophane
shade, less lamp . . . . "   2.00
No. 7381 holophane shade "   .80
Made with an inner lamp receptacle which
is part of the holder

No. 7544. Rich gilt and satin.
Made with hunge and lock

			Wired.	Complete as Shown Except Lamps.
3-light	10-inch bowl		$22.00	$23.02
4 "	12 "	"	30.00	31.36
5 "	14 "	"	38.00	39.70
6 "	14 "	"	39.00	41.04

Straw opalescent bowls included
Complete fixture includes
Edison keyless sockets ....each, $0.34
No. 427 10-inch straw opalescent bowl .... "   3.00
No. 427 12 "   "   "   " .... "   3.75
No. 427 14 "   "   "   " .... "   5.25

No. 7523. Brushed brass
1-light, no glass......... each, $2.50
1 "   with 8-inch C. R. I.
ball, 4-inch fitter....... "   3.25
Made with an inner lamp receptacle, forms
part of holder. No lamp included

No. 7520. Brushed brass
1-light......................each, $4.00
Includes No. 106130 holo-
phane shade .... "   1.20
Made with inner lamp receptacle. No
lamp included

No. 7467. Brushed brass
Length, 14 inches over all; top 6 inches wide

	Not Wired.	Wired.	Complete as Shown Except Lamp.
1-light	$12.70	$13.00	$13.34

No. 423 3¼x8-inch straw opalescent ball in-
cluded in "not wired" and "wired" prices
Complete fixture includes
Edison keyless socket............each, $0.34
No. 423 8-inch S. O. ball........... "   1.13

95

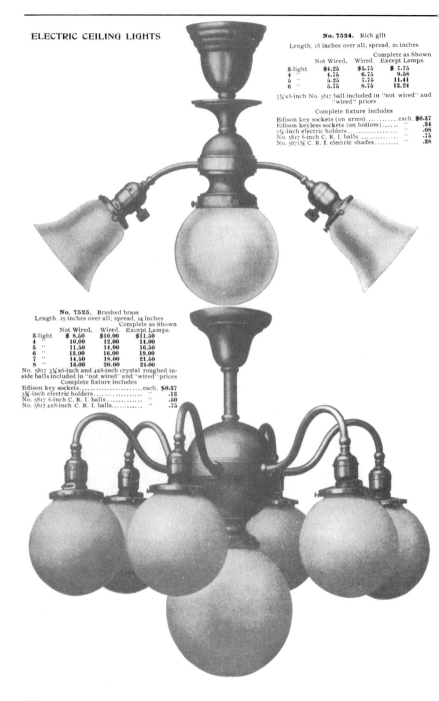

No. 7524. Rich gilt

Length, 18 inches over all; spread, 20 inches

	Not Wired.	Wired.	Complete as Shown Except Lamps.
3-light	$4.25	$5.75	$ 7.75
4 "	4.75	6.75	9.58
5 "	5.25	7.75	11.41
6 "	5.75	8.75	13.24

3¼x8-inch No. 5817 ball included in "not wired" and "wired" prices

Complete fixture includes

Edison key sockets (on arms)............each,	$0.37
Edison keyless sockets (on bottom)......	"	.34
2¼-inch electric holders..................	"	.08
No. 5817 8-inch C. R. I. balls	"	.75
No. 5671½ C. R. I. electric shades.........	"	.38

No. 7525. Brushed brass

Length, 25 inches over all; spread, 24 inches

	Not Wired.	Wired.	Complete as Shown Except Lamps.
3-light	$ 8.50	$10.00	$11.50
4 "	10.00	12.00	14.00
5 "	11.50	14.00	16.50
6 "	13.00	16.00	19.00
7 "	14.50	18.00	21.50
8 "	16.00	20.00	24.00

No. 5817 3¼x6-inch and 4x8-inch crystal roughed inside balls included in "not wired" and "wired" prices

Complete fixture includes

Edison key sockets.....................each,	$0.37
3¼-inch electric holders................	"	.13
No. 5817 6-inch C. R. I. balls............	"	.50
No. 5817 4x8-inch C. R. I. balls...........	"	.75

No. 7526. Brushed brass

Length, 15 inches over all; spread, 24 inches

	Not Wired.	Wired.	Complete as Shown Except Lamps.
2-light	$ 6.00	$ 7.00	$ 8.66
3 "	7.00	8.50	11.00
4 "	8.00	10.00	13.35
5 "	9.00	11.50	15.65
6 "	10.00	13.00	17.98
8 "	12.00	16.00	22.64

Complete fixture includes

Edison key sockets ....each, $0.37

2¼-inch electric holders.............. " .08

No. 5671½ C. R. I. electric shades.... " .38

⅜-inch casing on stem, extra lengthening per foot, not wired, 45 cents; wired, 55 cents

ELECTRIC CEILING LIGHTS

No. 7527, Brushed brass

Length, 27 inches over all; spread, 20 inches

	Not Wired.	Wired.	Complete as Shown Except Lamps.
2-light	$18.00	$19.00	$19.68
3 "	22.00	23.50	24.52
4 "	26.00	28.00	29.36
5 "	30.00	32.50	34.20

No. 5817 3¼x6-inch C. R. I. balls and 3¼-inch cast holder included in "wired" and "not wired" prices.

Complete fixture includes

Edison keyless sockets............... each, $0.34

No. 5817 6-inch crystal roughed inside balls............ " .... " .50

No. 0544½ 3¼-inch cast holders...... " .75

97

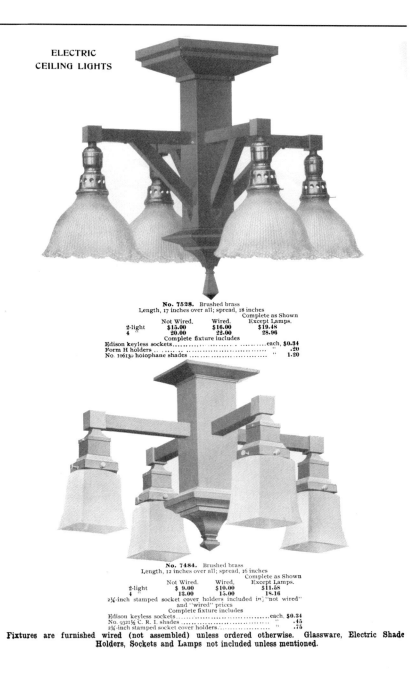

No. 7528. Brushed brass
Length, 17 inches over all; spread, 18 inches

	Not Wired.	Wired.	Complete as Shown Except Lamps.
2-light	$15.00	$16.00	$19.48
4 "	20.00	22.00	28.96

Complete fixture includes

Edison keyless sockets..............................	each,	$0.34
Form H holders	"	.20
No. 10613⁄ holophane shades	"	1.20

No. 7484. Brushed brass
Length, 12 inches over all; spread, 16 inches

	Not Wired.	Wired.	Complete as Shown Except Lamps.
2-light	$ 9.00	$10.00	$11.58
4 "	13.00	15.00	18.16

2¼-inch stamped socket cover holders included in "not wired"
and "wired" prices

Complete fixture includes

Edison keyless sockets...............................	each,	$0.34
No. 9321½ C. R. I. shades	"	.45
2¼-inch stamped socket cover holders..............	"	.75

Fixtures are furnished wired (not assembled) unless ordered otherwise. Glassware, Electric Shade Holders, Sockets and Lamps not included unless mentioned.

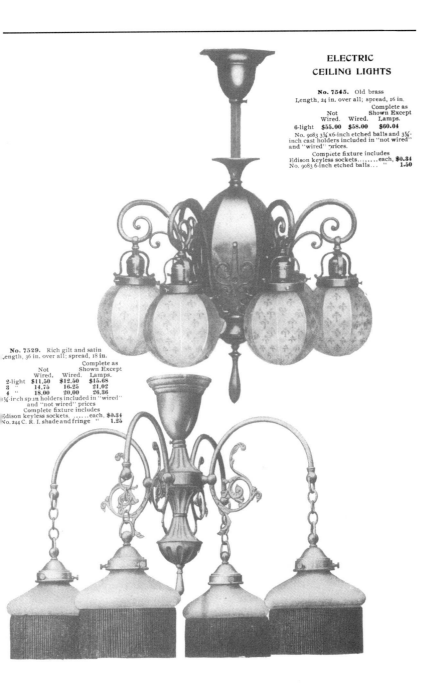

ELECTRIC
CEILING LIGHTS

No. 7545. Old brass

Length, 24 in. over all; spread, 16 in.

	Not Wired.	Wired.	Complete as Shown Except Lamps.
6-light	**$55.00**	**$58.00**	**$60.04**

No. 9083 3¼ x6-inch etched balls and 3¼-inch cast holders included in "not wired" and "wired" prices.

Complete fixture includes
Edison keyless sockets........each, **$0.34**
No. 9083 6-inch etched balls... " **1.50**

No. 7529. Rich gilt and satin

Length, 36 in. over all; spread, 18 in.

	Not Wired.	Wired.	Complete as Shown Except Lamps.
2-light	**$11.50**	**$12.50**	**$15.68**
3 "	14.75	16.25	21.02
4 "	18.00	20.00	26.36

3¼-inch span holders included in "wired" and "not wired" prices

Complete fixture includes
Edison keyless sockets. ......each, **$0.34**
No. 244 C. R. I. shade and fringe " **1.25**

No. 7530. Rich gilt and satin

Length, 16½ inches over all; spread, cast top plate, 20-inch diameter

	Not Wired.	Wired.	Complete as Shown Except Lamps.
4-light	**$45.00**	**$47.00**	**$53.96**

Cast husk covering both socket and Form H holder included in "not wired" and "wired" prices. Husk is our "Special Separable Make," so that assembling fixture is a very simple matter.

Complete fixture includes

Edison keyless sockets................................each,		**$0.34**
Form H holders	"	**.20**
No. 106130 holophane shades	"	**1.20**

No. 7531. Rich gilt and satin
Length, 26 inches over all; spread, 18 inches

	Not Wired.	Wired.	Complete as Shown Except Lamps.
2-light	$35.00	$36.00	$39.48
3 "	46.00	47.50	52.72
4 "	57.00	59.00	65.96

Cast husk covering both socket and Form H holder included in "not wired" and "wired" prices. Husk is our "Special Separable Make," so that assembling fixture is a very simple matter.

Complete fixture includes

Edison keyless sockets	each,	$0.34
Form H holders	"	.20
No. 106130 holophane shades	"	1.20

101

No. 7365. Brushed brass
Length, 39 inches over all; spread, 14 inches

	Not Wired.	Wired with Silk Cord.	Complete as Shown Except Lamps.
4-light (4 arms)	$31.00	$33.00	$34.36
5 " (4 arms and center)	37.50	40.00	41.70

No. 5817 3¼x6-inch crystal roughed inside balls and 3¼-inch spun holders included in "not wired" and "wired" prices

Complete fixture includes

Edison keyless sockets.......................................each, $0.34
No. 5817 6-inch C. R. I. balls............................. "   .50

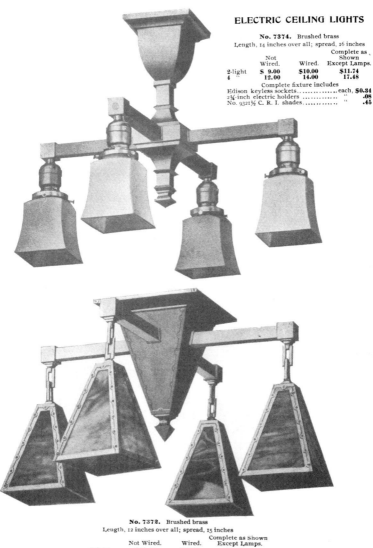

ELECTRIC CEILING LIGHTS

No. 7374. Brushed brass
Length, 14 inches over all; spread, 16 inches

	Not Wired.	Wired.	Complete as Shown Except Lamps.
2-light	$ 9.00	$10.00	$11.74
4 "	12.00	14.00	17.48

Complete fixture includes

Edison keyless sockets...............each,	$0.34
2¼-inch electric holders .... "	.08
No. 9321½ C. R. I. shades............. "	.45

No. 7372. Brushed brass
Length, 12 inches over all; spread, 15 inches

	Not Wired.	Wired.	Complete as Shown Except Lamps.
2-light	$16.00	$17.00	$17.68
4 "	27.00	29.00	30.36

No. 15140 5-inch art glass lanterns, color K, included in "not wired" and "wired" prices. For art glass colors see color plates 486 487

No. 15140 lanterns only ....each,	$3.00
Chain hangers .... "	1.00

Complete fixture includes

Edison keyless sockets ....each,	$0.34

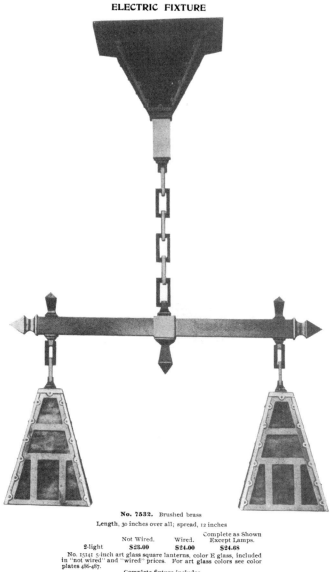

No. 7532. Brushed brass

Length, 30 inches over all; spread, 12 inches

	Not Wired.	Wired.	Complete as Shown Except Lamps.
2-light	$23.00	$24.00	$24.68

No. 15141 5-inch art glass square lanterns, color E glass, included in "not wired" and "wired" prices. For art glass colors see color plates 486-487.

Complete fixture includes

Edison keyless sockets.....................................each, $0.34

1-inch casing on stem, extra lengthening per foot, not wired, 75 cents; wired, 85 cents

ELECTRIC BRACKETS

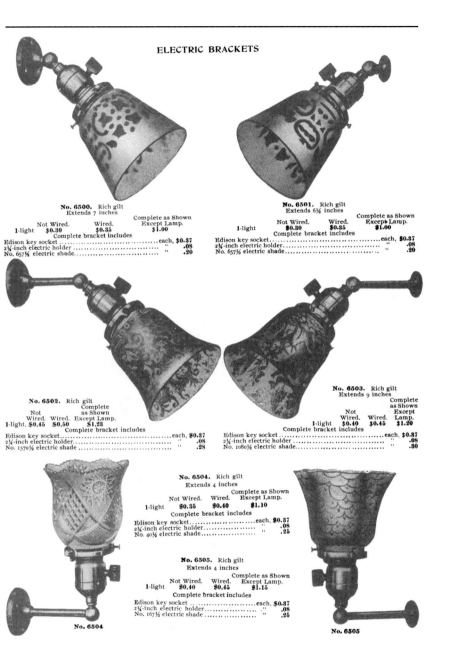

No. 6500. Rich gilt
Extends 7 inches

	Not Wired.	Wired.	Complete as Shown Except Lamp.
1-light	$0.30	$0.35	$1.00

Complete bracket includes

Edison key socket............................each, $0.37
2¼-inch electric holder............................ " .08
No. 657½ electric shade............................ " .20

No. 6501. Rich gilt
Extends 6½ inches

	Not Wired.	Wired.	Complete as Shown Except Lamp.
1-light	$0.30	$0.35	$1.00

Complete bracket includes

Edison key socket............................each, $0.37
2¼-inch electric holder............................ " .08
No. 657½ electric shade............................ " .20

No. 6502. Rich gilt

	Not Wired.	Wired.	Complete as Shown Except Lamp.
1-light,	$0.45	$0.50	$1.23

Complete bracket includes

Edison key socket............................each, $0.37
2¼-inch electric holder............................ " .08
No. 1570½ electric shade............................ " .28

No. 6503. Rich gilt
Extends 9 inches

	Not Wired.	Wired.	Complete as Shown Except Lamp.
1-light	$0.40	$0.45	$1.20

Complete bracket includes

Edison key socket............................each, $0.37
2¼-inch electric holder............................ " .08
No. 1080½ electric shade............................ " .30

No. 6504. Rich gilt
Extends 4 inches

	Not Wired.	Wired.	Complete as Shown Except Lamp.
1-light	$0.35	$0.40	$1.10

Complete bracket includes

Edison key socket............................each, $0.37
2¼-inch electric holder.................. " .08
No. 40½ electric shade.................. " .25

No. 6505. Rich gilt
Extends 4 inches

	Not Wired.	Wired.	Complete as Shown Except Lamp.
1-light	$0.40	$0.45	$1.15

Complete bracket includes

Edison key socket .. ..each, $0.37
2¼-inch electric holder.................. " .08
No. 167½ electric shade.................. " .25

No. 6504

No. 6505

ELECTRIC BRACKETS

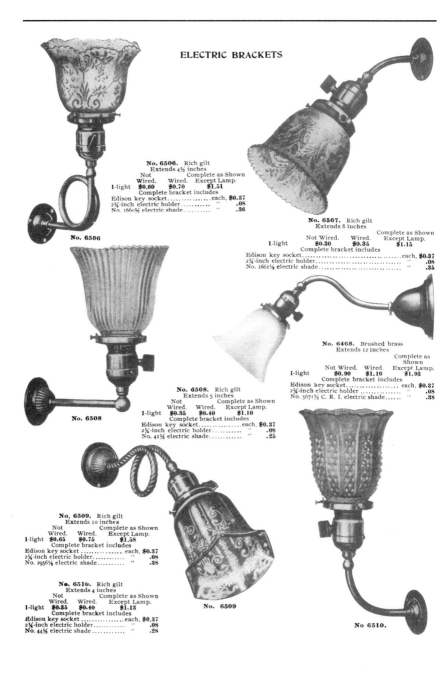

No. 6506. Rich gilt
Extends 4½ inches

	Not Wired.	Wired.	Complete as Shown Except Lamp.
1-light	**$0.60**	**$0.70**	**$1.51**

Complete bracket includes
Edison key socket..............each, $0.37
2¼-inch electric holder.......... " .08
No. 1660½ electric shade.......... " .36

No. 6506

No. 6507. Rich gilt
Extends 8 inches

	Not Wired.	Wired.	Complete as Shown Except Lamp.
1-light	**$0.30**	**$0.35**	**$1.15**

Complete bracket includes
Edison key socket...........................each, $0.37
2¼-inch electric holder............................ " .08
No. 1661½ electric shade............................ " .35

No. 6508. Rich gilt
Extends 5 inches

	Not Wired.	Wired.	Complete as Shown Except Lamp.
1-light	**$0.35**	**$0.40**	**$1.10**

Complete bracket includes
Edison key socket..............each, $0.37
2¼-inch electric holder.......... " .08
No. 41½ electric shade............ " .25

No. 6508

No. 6468. Brushed brass
Extends 12 inches

	Not Wired.	Wired.	Complete as Shown Except Lamp.
1-light	**$0.90**	**$1.10**	**$1.93**

Complete bracket includes
Edison key socket.............. each, $0.37
2¼-inch electric holder.............. " .08
No. 5671½ C. R. I. electric shade...... " .38

No. 6509. Rich gilt
Extends 10 inches

	Not Wired.	Wired.	Complete as Shown Except Lamp.
1-light	**$0.65**	**$0.75**	**$1.58**

Complete bracket includes
Edison key socket .... each, $0.37
2¼-inch electric holder............ " .08
No. 2956½ electric shade.......... " .38

No. 6510. Rich gilt
Extends 4 inches

	Not Wired.	Wired.	Complete as Shown Except Lamp.
1-light	**$0.35**	**$0.40**	**$1.13**

Complete bracket includes
Edison key socket .... each, $0.37
2¼-inch electric holder............ " .08
No. 44½ electric shade............ " .28

No. 6509

No 6510.

ELECTRIC BRACKETS

No. 6571. Rich gilt
Extends 10 inches

		Complete as Shown
	Not Wired.	Wired.	Except Lamp.
1-light	**$1.65**	**$1.75**	**$3.20**

Complete bracket includes
Edison key socket....................each, $0.37
2¼-inch electric holder................ " .08
No. 9115½ electric shade.............. " 1.00

No. 6467. Brushed brass
Extends 13 inches

			Complete as Shown
	Not Wired.	Wired.	Except Lamp.
1-light	**$1.50**	**$1.75**	**$2.58**

Complete bracket includes
Edison key socket.......................................each, $0.37
2¼-inch electric holder .... " .08
No. 396½ electric shade.................................. " .38

No. 6473. Brushed brass
Extends 6 inches

		Complete as Shown
	Not Wired.	Wired.	Except Lamp.
1-light	**$1.50**	**$1.75**	**$2.57**

Socket covers and 2¼-inch holder included in
"not wired" and "wired" prices
Complete bracket includes
Edison key socket....................each, $0.37
No. 8887 4½-inch C. R. I. shade .... " .45

No. 6511. Rich gilt
Extends 10 inches

	Not		Complete as Shown Except
	Wired.	Wired.	Lamp.
1-light	**$0.45**	**$0.50**	**$1.21**

Complete bracket includes
Edison key socket ....each, $0.37
2¼-inch electric holder....... " .08
No. 42½ electric shade........ " .26

No. 6465. Brushed brass
Extends 12 inches

			Complete as Shown
	Not Wired.	Wired.	Except Lamp.
1-light	**$0.75**	**$0.90**	**$1.73**

Canopy, 4½x4 inches deep
Complete bracket includes
Edison key socket.......................................each, $0.37
2¼-inch electric holder .... " .08
No. 1906½ electric shade .... " .38

No. 6568. Rich gilt
Extends 12 inches

		Complete as Shown
	Not Wired.	Wired.	Except Lamp.
1-light	**$0.90**	**$1.00**	**$1.73**

Complete bracket includes
Edison key socket.............................. ......each, $0.37
2¼-inch electric holder.................................... " .08
No. 1570½ electric shade .... " .28

No. 6559. Rich gilt
Extends 10 inches

	Not		Complete as Shown Except
	Wired.	Wired.	Lamp.
1-light	**$0.40**	**$0.45**	**$1.16**

Complete bracket includes
Edison key socket................each, $0.37
2¼-inch electric holder .... " .08
No. 42½ electric shade .... " .26

ELECTRIC BRACKETS

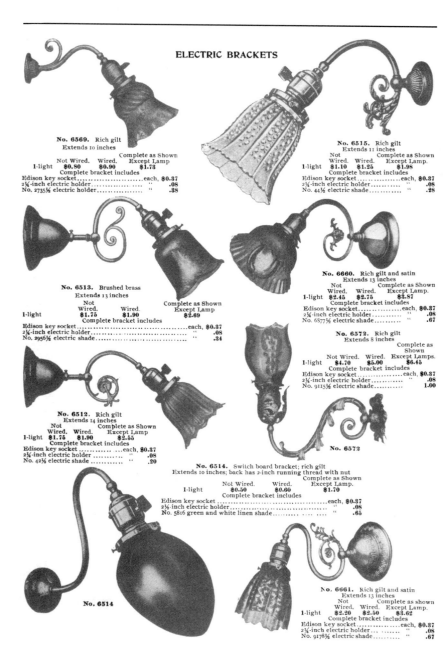

No. 6569. Rich gilt
Extends 10 inches
Complete as Shown

	Not Wired.	Wired.	Except Lamp
1-light	**$0.80**	**$0.90**	**$1.73**

Complete bracket includes
Edison key socket..........................each, **$0.37**
2¼-inch electric holder................ " .08
No. 2735½ electric holder................ " .38

No. 6515. Rich gilt
Extends 11 inches

	Not Wired.	Wired.	Complete as Shown Except Lamp.
1-light	**$1.10**	**$1.25**	**$1.98**

Complete bracket includes
Edison key socket.................each, **$0.37**
2¼-inch electric holder.......... " .08
No. 44½ electric shade........... " .28

No. 6513. Brushed brass
Extends 13 inches

	Not Wired.	Wired.	Complete as Shown Except Lamp
1-light	**$1.75**	**$1.90**	**$2.69**

Complete bracket includes
Edison key socket..............................each, **$0.37**
2¼-inch electric holder.................................. " .08
No. 2956½ electric shade................................. " .34

No. 6660. Rich gilt and satin
Extends 13 inches

	Not Wired.	Wired.	Complete as Shown Except Lamp.
1-light	**$2.45**	**$2.75**	**$3.87**

Complete bracket includes
Edison key socket.................each, **$0.37**
2¼-inch electric holder.......... " .08
No. 6877½ electric shade......... " .67

No. 6572. Rich gilt
Extends 8 inches
Complete as Shown

	Not Wired.	Wired.	Except Lamps.
1-light	**$4.70**	**$5.00**	**$6.45**

Complete bracket includes
Edison key socket.................each, **$0.37**
2¼-inch electric holder.......... " .08
No. 9115½ electric shade.......... 1.00

No. 6512. Rich gilt
Extends 14 inches

	Not Wired.	Wired.	Complete as Shown Except Lamp
1-light	**$1.75**	**$1.90**	**$2.55**

Complete bracket includes
Edison key socket............. each, **$0.37**
2¼-inch electric holder .... " .08
No. 42½ electric shade .... " .20

No. 6572

No. 6514. Switch board bracket; rich gilt
Extends 10 inches; back has 2-inch running thread with nut

	Not Wired.	Wired.	Complete as Shown Except Lamp.
1-light	**$0.50**	**$0.60**	**$1.70**

Complete bracket includes
Edison key socket ....each, **$0.37**
2½-inch electric holder.................................. " .08
No. 5816 green and white linen shade.......... .... " .65

No. 6514

No. 6661. Rich gilt and satin
Extends 13 inches

	Not Wired.	Wired.	Complete as shown Except Lamp.
1-light	**$2.20**	**$2.50**	**$3.62**

Complete bracket includes
Edison key socket.................each, **$0.37**
2¼-inch electric holder... .... " .08
No. 9178½ electric shade.......... " .67

ELECTRIC BRACKETS

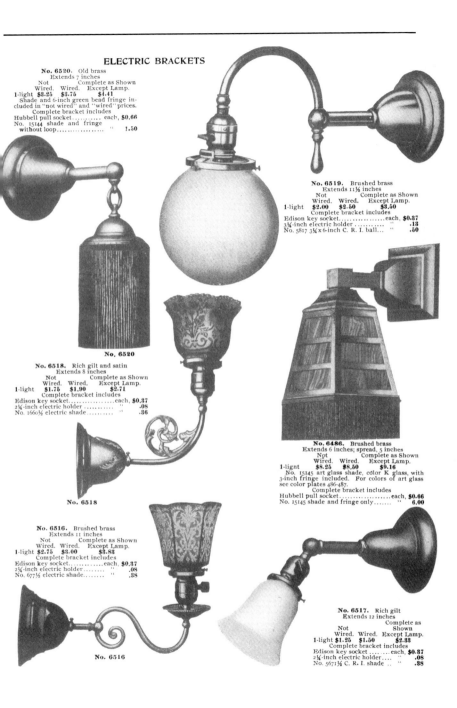

No. 6520. Old brass
Extends 7 inches
| | Not | Complete as Shown |
| | Wired. Wired. | Except Lamp. |

1-light **$3.25** **$3.75** **$4.41**
Shade and 6-inch green bead fringe included in "not wired" and "wired" prices.
Complete bracket includes
Hubbell pull socket.......... each, **$0.66**
No. 15144 shade and fringe
without loop................ " 1.50

No. 6519. Brushed brass
Extends 11½ inches
Not Complete as Shown
Wired. Wired. Except Lamp.
1-light **$2.00** **$2.50** **$3.50**
Complete bracket includes
Edison key socket...................each, **$0.37**
3¼-inch electric holder .... " .13
No. 5817 3¾ x 6-inch C. R. I. ball... " .50

No. 6520

No. 6518. Rich gilt and satin
Extends 8 inches
Not Complete as Shown
Wired. Wired. Except Lamp.
1-light **$1.75** **$1.90** **$2.71**
Complete bracket includes
Edison key socket................. each, **$0.37**
2¼-inch electric holder .... " .08
No. 1660½ electric shade.......... " .36

No. 6518

No. 6486. Brushed brass
Extends 6 inches; spread, 5 inches
Not Complete as Shown
Wired. Wired. Except Lamp.
1-light **$8.25** **$8.50** **$9.16**
No. 15145 art glass shade, color K glass, with
3-inch fringe included. For colors of art glass
see color plates 486-487.
Complete bracket includes
Hubbell pull socket...................each, **$0.66**
No. 15145 shade and fringe only....... " 6.00

No. 6516. Brushed brass
Extends 11 inches
Not Complete as Shown
Wired. Wired. Except Lamp.
1-light **$2.75** **$3.00** **$3.83**
Complete bracket includes
Edison key socket.............each, **$0.37**
2¼-inch electric holder........ " .08
No. 677½ electric shade........ " .38

No. 6516

No. 6517. Rich gilt
Extends 12 inches
Complete as
Not Shown
Wired. Wired. Except Lamp.
1-light **$1.25** **$1.50** **$2.33**
Complete bracket includes
Edison key socket ....each, **$0.37**
2¼-inch electric holder.... " .08
No. 5671½ C. R. I. shade .. " .38

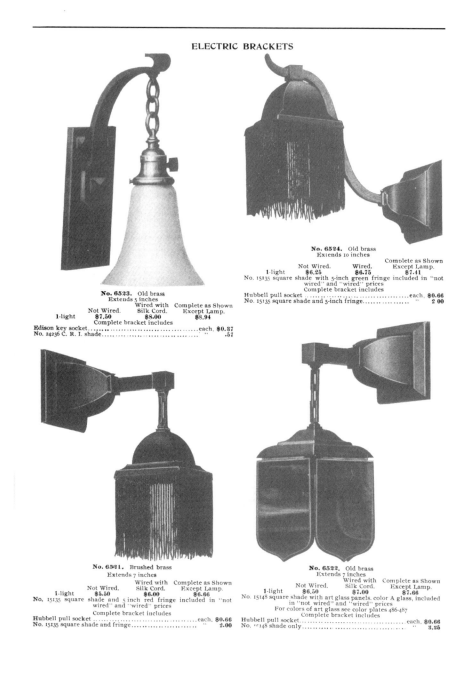

No. 6523. Old brass
Extends 5 inches

1-light	Not Wired.	Wired with Silk Cord.	Complete as Shown Except Lamp.
	$7.50	$8.00	$8.94

Complete bracket includes

Edison key socket...each, $0.37
No. 24236 C. R. I. shade...................................   "   .57

No. 6524. Old brass
Extends 10 inches

1-light	Not Wired.	Wired.	Complete as Shown Except Lamp.
	$6.25	$6.75	$7.41

No. 15135 square shade with 5-inch green fringe included in "not
wired" and "wired" prices
Complete bracket includes

Hubbell pull socket ....each, $0.66
No. 15135 square shade and 5-inch fringe................   "   2 00

No. 6521. Brushed brass
Extends 7 inches

1-light	Not Wired.	Wired with Silk Cord.	Complete as Shown Except Lamp.
	$5.50	$6.00	$6.66

No. 15135 square shade and 5 inch red fringe included in "not
wired" and "wired" prices
Complete bracket includes

Hubbell pull socket ....each, $0.66
No. 15135 square shade and fringe.......................   "   2.00

No. 6522. Old brass
Extends 7 inches

1-light	Not Wired.	Wired with Silk Cord.	Complete as Shown Except Lamp.
	$6.50	$7.00	$7.66

No. 15148 square shade with art glass panels, color A glass, included
in "not wired" and "wired" prices
For colors of art glass see color plates 486-487
Complete bracket includes

Hubbell pull socket...each, $0.66
No. 15148 shade only...   "   3.25

110

ELECTRIC BRACKETS

No. 6529. Brushed brass
Extends 9 inches

	Not Wired.	Wired.	Complete as Shown Except Lamp.
1-light	$7.00	$7.50	$8.16

No. 15160 square shade and art glass panels, color L glass, included in "not wired" and "wired" prices. For colors of art glass see color plates 486-487
Complete bracket includes

Hubbell pull socket . . . . each, $0.66
No. 15160 shade only . . . . " 3.25

No. 6526. Old brass
Extends 5½ inches

	Not Wired.	Wired.	Complete as Shown Except Lamp.
1-light	$2.50	$2.75	$4.45

Complete bracket includes

Edison key socket . . . . each, $0.37
2¼-inch electric holder . . . . " .08
No. 244 C. R. I. shade and 3-inch fringe . . . . " 1.25

No. 6525. Old brass
Extends 10 inches

	Not Wired.	Wired with Silk Cord.	Complete as Shown Except Lamp.
1-light	$7.75	$8.25	$8.91

No. 15148 square shade and art glass panels, color A glass, included in "not wired" and "wired" prices. For art glass colors see color plates 486-487
Complete bracket includes

Hubbell pull socket . . . . each, $0.66
No. 15148 shade only . . . . " 3.25

No. 6528. Old brass
Extends 7 inches

	Not Wired.	Wired with Silk Cord.	Complete as Shown Except Lamp.
1-light	$7.50	$8.00	$8.66

Complete bracket includes

Hubbell pull socket . . . . each, $0.66

111

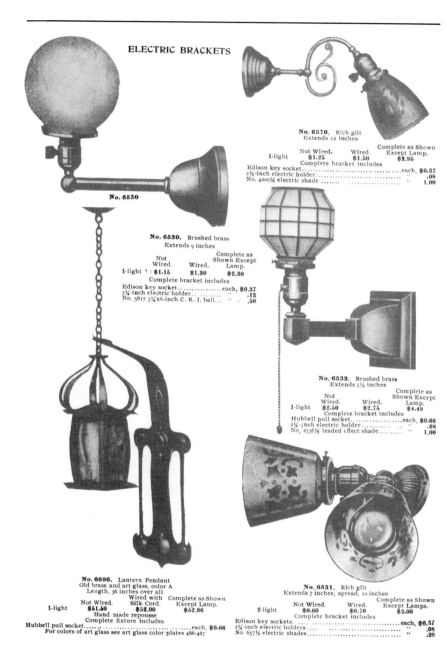

ELECTRIC BRACKETS

No. 6530

No. 6530. Brushed brass
Extends 9 inches

	Not Wired.	Wired.	Complete as Shown Except Lamp.
1-light	$1.15	$1.30	$2.30

Complete bracket includes

Edison key socket.....................each, $0.37
3¼-inch electric holder............... " .13
No. 5817 3¼x6-inch C. R. I. ball... " . .50

No. 6570. Rich gilt
Extends 12 inches

	Not Wired.	Wired.	Complete as Shown Except Lamp.
1-light	$1.25	$1.50	$2.95

Complete bracket includes

Edison key socket.....................each, $0.37
2½-inch electric holder................ " .08
No. 4200½ electric shade 1.00

No. 6532. Brushed brass
Extends 5½ inches

	Not Wired.	Wired.	Complete as Shown Except Lamp.
1-light	$2.50	$2.75	$4.49

Complete bracket includes

Hubbell pull socket...................each, $0.66
2¼-inch electric holder............. " .08
No. 2536½ leaded effect shade......... " 1.00

No. 6696. Lantern Pendant
Old brass and art glass, color A
Length, 36 inches over all

	Not Wired.	Wired with Silk Cord.	Complete as Shown Except Lamp.
1-light	$51.50	$52.00	$52.66

Hand made repousse
Complete fixture includes

Hubbell pull socket.....................................each, $0.66
For colors of art glass see art glass color plates 486-487

No. 6531. Rich gilt
Extends 7 inches; spread, 10 inches

	Not Wired.	Wired.	Complete as Shown Except Lamps.
2-light	$0.60	$0.70	$2.00

Complete bracket includes

Edison key sockets. ....each, $0.37
2¼-inch electric holders.... .... " .08
No. 657½ electric shades............................. " .20

ELECTRIC BRACKETS

No. 6453. Brushed brass
Extends 9½ inches

1-light	Not Wired.	Wired.	Complete as Show Except Lamp.
	$2.50	$3.00	$3.90

Complete bracket includes

Edison key socket		each,	$0.37
2¼-inch electric holder		"	.08
No. 9321½ C. R. I. shade		"	.45

No. 6455. Brushed brass
Extends 8 inches

1-light	Not Wired.	Wired.	Complete as Shown Except Lamp.
	$2.00	$2.50	$3.40

Complete bracket includes

Edison key socket		each,	$0.37
2¼-inch electric holder		"	.08
No. 9321½ C. R. I. shade		"	.45

No. 6456.
Old brass

Extends 5½ inches
Spread, 8½ inches

1-light	Not Wired.	Wired.	Complete as Shown Except Lamps.
	$4.75	$5.25	$5.99

Spun socket covers included in "wired" and "not wired" prices
Complete bracket includes

Edison key sockets		each,	$0.37

No. 6454. Brushed brass
Extends 14 inches

1-light	Not Wired.	Wired.	Complete as Shown Except Lamp.
	$2.25	$2.75	$3.65

Complete bracket includes

Edison key socket		each,	$0.37
2¼-inch electric holder		"	.08
No. 9321½ C. R. I. shade		"	.45

No. 6488. Brushed brass
Extends 6 inches

1-light	Not Wired.	Wired.	Complete as Shown Except Lamp.
	$2.75	$3.00	$4.50

Complete bracket includes

Edison key socket		each,	$0.37
2¼-inch electric holder		"	.08
No. 4501½ C. R. I. shade		"	1.05

No. 6470. Brushed brass
Extends 7 inches

1-light	Not Wired.	Wired.	Complete as Shown Except Lamp.
	$3.75	$4.00	$4.82

Cast 2¼-inch socket cover holder included in "not wired" and "wired" prices
Complete bracket includes

Edison key socket		each,	$0.37
No. 9321½ C. R. I. shade		"	.45
Cast 2¼-in. socket cover holder		"	1.25

No. 6488

No. 6470

ELECTRIC BRACKETS

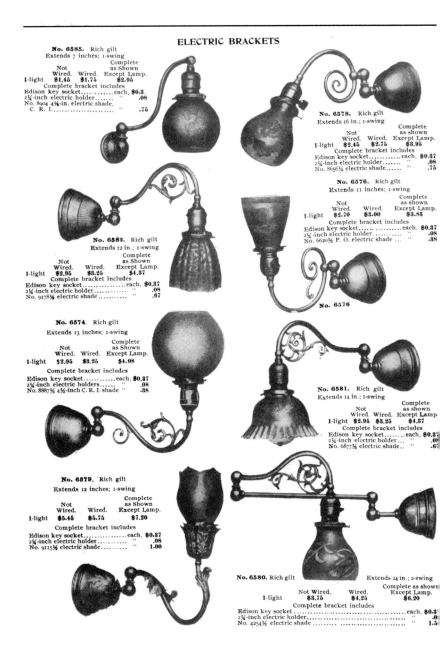

No. 6585. Rich gilt
Extends 7 inches; 1-swing

	Not Wired.	Wired.	Complete as Shown Except Lamp.
1-light	$1.45	$1.75	$2.95

Complete bracket includes
Edison key socket............each, $0.3.
2¼-inch electric holder...... " .08
No. 8904 4½-in. electric shade,
C. R. I................... " .75

No. 6578. Rich gilt
Extends 16 in.; 1-swing

	Not Wired.	Wired.	Complete as shown Except Lamp.
1-light	$2.45	$2.75	$3.95

Complete bracket includes
Edison key socket............each, $0.37
2¼-inch electric holder ...... " .08
No. 8656½ electric shade...... " .75

No. 6576. Rich gilt
Extends 11 inches; 1-swing

	Not Wired.	Wired.	Complete as Shown Except Lamp.
1-light	$2.70	$3.00	$3.83

Complete bracket includes
Edison key socket.............each, $0.37
2¼-inch electric holder .... " .08
No. 6620½ P. O. electric shade ... " .38

No. 6582. Rich gilt
Extends 12 in.; 1-swing

	Not Wired.	Wired.	Complete as Shown Except Lamp.
1-light	$2.95	$3.25	$4.37

Complete bracket includes
Edison key socket.............each, $0.37
2¼-inch electric holder............ " .08
No. 9178½ electric shade.......... " .67

No. 6574. Rich gilt
Extends 13 inches; 1-swing

	Not Wired.	Wired.	Complete as Shown Except Lamp.
1-light	$2.95	$3.25	$4.08

Complete bracket includes
Edison key socket.............each, $0.37
2¼-inch electric holders...... " .08
No. 8887½ 4½-inch C. R. I. shade " .38

No. 6581. Rich gilt
Extends 14 in.; 1-swing

	Not Wired.	Wired.	Complete as shown Except Lamp
1-light	$2.95	$3.25	$4.37

Complete bracket includes
Edison key socket........each, $0.3
2¼-inch electric holder... " .0
No. 6877½ electric shade.. " .6

No. 6579. Rich gilt
Extends 12 inches; 1-swing

	Not Wired.	Wired.	Complete as Shown Except Lamp.
1-light	$5.45	$5.75	$7.20

Complete bracket includes
Edison key socket..............each, $0.37
2¼-inch electric holder.......... " .08
No. 9115½ electric shade......... " 1.00

No. 6576

No. 6580. Rich gilt   Extends 24 in.; 2-swing

	Not Wired.	Wired.	Complete as shown Except Lamp.
1-light	$3.75	$4.25	$6.20

Complete bracket includes
Edison key socket..each, $0.3
2¼-inch electric holder................................... " .0
No. 4254½ electric shade .... " 1.5

114

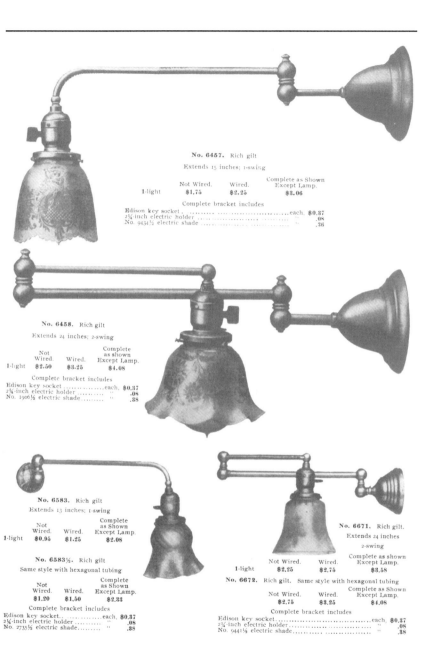

No. 6457. Rich gilt

Extends 15 inches; 1-swing

	Not Wired.	Wired.	Complete as Shown Except Lamp.
1-light	$1.75	$2.25	$3.06

Complete bracket includes

Edison key socket . ...each, $0.37
2¾-inch electric holder .. .. .08
No. 9434½ electric shade .... " .36

No. 6458. Rich gilt

Extends 24 inches; 2-swing

	Not Wired.	Wired.	Complete as shown Except Lamp.
1-light	$2.50	$3.25	$4.08

Complete bracket includes

Edison key socket ....each, $0.37
2¾-inch electric holder .... " .08
No. 1906½ electric shade......... " .38

No. 6583. Rich gilt

Extends 13 inches; 1-swing

	Not Wired.	Wired.	Complete as Shown Except Lamp.
1-light	$0.95	$1.25	$2.08

No. 6583½. Rich gilt

Same style with hexagonal tubing

Not Wired.	Wired.	Complete as Shown Except Lamp.
$1.20	$1.50	$2.33

Complete bracket includes

Edison key socket ....each, $0.37
2¾-inch electric holder .... " .08
No. 2735½ electric shade......... " .38

No. 6671. Rich gilt.

Extends 24 inches

2-swing

	Not Wired.	Wired.	Complete as shown Except Lamp.
1-light	$2.25	$2.75	$3.58

No. 6672. Rich gilt. Same style with hexagonal tubing

Not Wired.	Wired.	Complete as Shown Except Lamp.
$2.75	$3.25	$4.08

Complete bracket includes

Edison key socket.................................each, $0.37
2¾-inch electric holder................................ " .08
No. 9441½ electric shade................ .... " .38

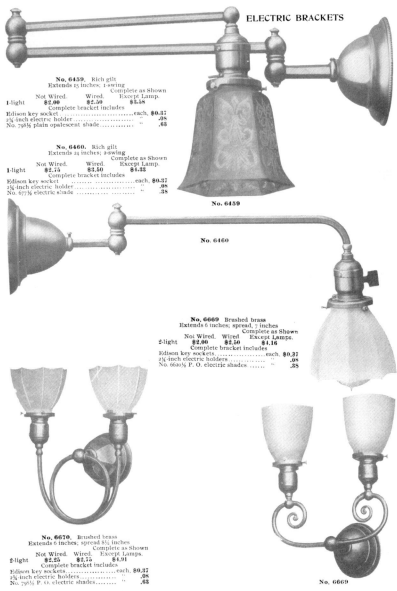

ELECTRIC BRACKETS

No. 6459. Rich gilt
Extends 15 inches; 1-swing

	Not Wired.	Wired.	Complete as Shown Except Lamp.
1-light	$2.00	$2.50	$3.58

Complete bracket includes

Edison key socket	each,	$0.37
2¼-inch electric holder	"	.08
No. 798½ plain opalescent shade	"	.63

No. 6460. Rich gilt
Extends 24 inches; 2-swing

	Not Wired.	Wired.	Complete as Shown Except Lamp.
1-light	$2.75	$3.50	$4.33

Complete bracket includes

Edison key socket	each,	$0.37
2¼-inch electric holder	"	.08
No. 677½ electric shade	"	.38

No. 6459

No. 6460

No. 6669 Brushed brass
Extends 6 inches; spread, 7 inches

	Not Wired.	Wired	Complete as Shown Except Lamps.
2-light	$2.00	$2.50	$4.16

Complete bracket includes

Edison key sockets	each,	$0.37
2¼-inch electric holders	"	.08
No. 6620½ P. O. electric shades	"	.38

No. 6670. Brushed brass
Extends 6 inches; spread 8½ inches

	Not Wired.	Wired.	Complete as Shown Except Lamps.
2-light	$2.25	$2.75	$4.91

Complete bracket includes

Edison key sockets	each,	$0.37
2¼-inch electric holders	"	.08
No. 798½ P. O. electric shades	"	.63

No. 6669

Fixtures are furnished wired (not assembled) unless ordered otherwise. Glassware, Electric Shade Holders, Sockets and Lamps not included unless mentioned.

ELECTRIC BRACKETS

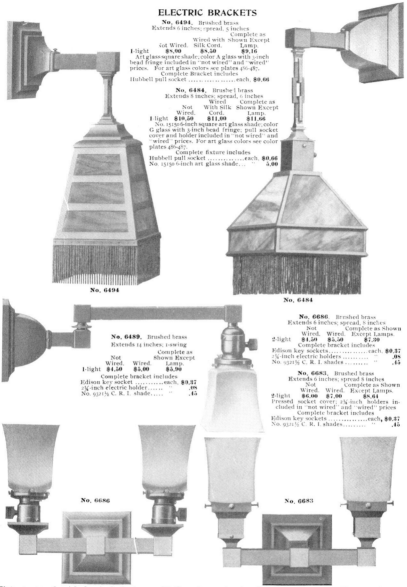

No. 6494. Brushed brass
Extends 6 inches; spread, 5 inches

		Complete as
	Wired with	Shown Except
Not Wired.	Silk Cord.	Lamp.
1-light	$8.00	$8.50	$9.16

Art glass square shade; color A glass with 3-inch
bead fringe included in "not wired" and "wired"
prices. For art glass colors see plates 486-487.
Complete Bracket includes
Hubbell pull socket ....each, $0.66

No. 6484. Brushed brass
Extends 8 inches; spread, 6 inches

	Wired	Complete as
Not	With Silk	Shown Except
Wired.	Cord.	Lamp.
1-light	$10.50	$11.00	$11.66

No. 15150 6-inch square art glass shade; color
G glass with 3-inch bead fringe; pull socket
cover and holder included in "not wired" and
"wired" prices. For art glass colors see color
plates 486-487.
Complete fixture includes
Hubbell pull socket ....each, $0.66
No. 15150 6-inch art glass shade... " 5.00

No. 6494

No. 6484

No. 6489. Brushed brass
Extends 14 inches; 1-swing

		Complete as
		Shown Except
Not		
Wired.	Wired.	Lamp.
1-light	$4.50	$5.00	$5.90

Complete bracket includes
Edison key socket ....each, $0.37
2¼-inch electric holder...... " .08
No. 9321½ C. R. I. shade..... " .45

No. 6686. Brushed brass
Extends 6 inches; spread, 8 inches

	Not	Complete as Shown
	Wired.	Wired.	Except Lamps.
2-light	$4.50	$5.50	$7.30

Complete bracket includes
Edison key sockets...............each, $0.37
2¼-inch electric holders .... " .08
No. 9321½ C. R. I. shades .... " .45

No. 6683. Brushed brass
Extends 6 inches; spread 8 inches

	Not	Complete as Shown
	Wired.	Wired.	Except Lamps.
2-light	$6.00	$7.00	$8.64

Pressed socket cover; 2¼-inch holders in-
cluded in "not wired" and "wired" prices
Complete bracket includes
Edison key sockets...............each, $0.37
No. 9321½ C. R. I. shades......... " .45

No. 6686

No. 6683

Fixtures are furnished wired (not assembled) unless ordered otherwise. Glassware, Electric Shade
Holders, Sockets and Lamps not included unless mentioned.

ELECTRIC BRACKETS

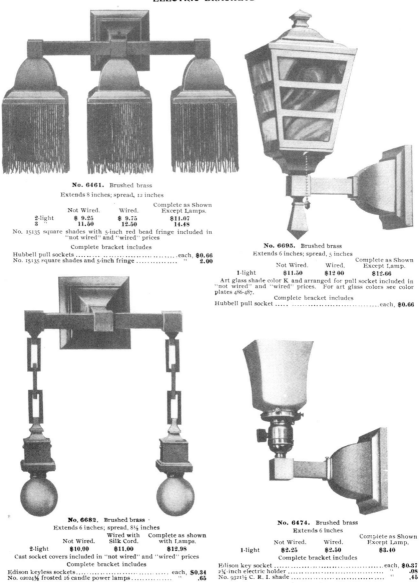

No. 6461. Brushed brass

Extends 8 inches; spread, 12 inches

	Not Wired.	Wired.	Complete as Shown Except Lamps.
2-light	$ 9.25	$ 9.75	$11.07
3 "	11.50	12.50	14.48

No. 15135 square shades with 5-inch red bead fringe included in
"not wired" and "wired" prices

Complete bracket includes

Hubbell pull sockets ....each, $0.66
No. 15135 square shades and 5-inch fringe .... " 2.00

No. 6695. Brushed brass

Extends 6 inches; spread, 5 inches

	Not Wired.	Wired.	Complete as Shown Except Lamp.
1-light	$11.50	$12 00	$12.66

Art glass shade color K and arranged for pull socket included in
"not wired" and "wired" prices. For art glass colors see color
plates 486-487.

Complete bracket includes

Hubbell pull socket ....each, $0.66

No. 6682. Brushed brass

Extends 6 inches; spread, 8¼ inches

	Not Wired.	Wired with Silk Cord.	Complete as shown with Lamps.
2-light	$10.00	$11.00	$12.98

Cast socket covers included in "not wired" and "wired" prices

Complete bracket includes

Edison keyless sockets............................... each, $0.34
No. 02024½ frosted 16 candle power lamps.............. " .65

No. 6474. Brushed brass

Extends 6 inches

	Not Wired.	Wired.	Complete as Shown Except Lamp.
1-light	$2.25	$2.50	$3.40

Complete bracket includes

Edison key socket .... each, $0.37
2¼-inch electric holder .... " .08
No. 9321½ C. R. I. shade .... " .45

118

ELECTRIC BRACKETS

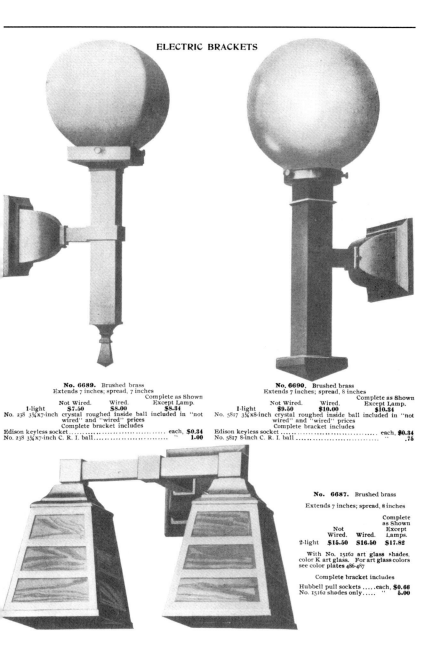

No. 6689. Brushed brass
Extends 7 inches; spread, 7 inches

	Not Wired.	Wired.	Complete as Shown Except Lamp.
1-light	**$7.50**	**$8.00**	**$8.34**

No. 238 3¼x7-inch crystal roughed inside ball included in "not wired" and "wired" prices

Complete bracket includes

Edison keyless socket................................... each, **$0.34**
No. 238 3¼x7-inch C. R. I. ball........................... " **1.00**

No. 6690. Brushed brass
Extends 7 inches; spread, 8 inches

	Not Wired.	Wired.	Complete as Shown Except Lamp.
1-light	**$9.50**	**$10.00**	**$10.34**

No. 5817 3¼x8-inch crystal roughed inside ball included in "not wired" and "wired" prices

Complete bracket includes

Edison keyless socket................................... each, **$0.34**
No. 5817 8-inch C. R. I. ball............................. " **.75**

No. 6687. Brushed brass

Extends 7 inches; spread, 8 inches

	Not Wired.	Wired.	Complete as Shown Except Lamps.
2-light	**$15.50**	**$16.50**	**$17.82**

With No. 15162 art glass shades, color K art glass. For art glass colors see color plates 486-487

Complete bracket includes

Hubbell pull sockets .....each, **$0.66**
No. 15162 shades only..... " **5.00**

119

ELECTRIC BRACKETS

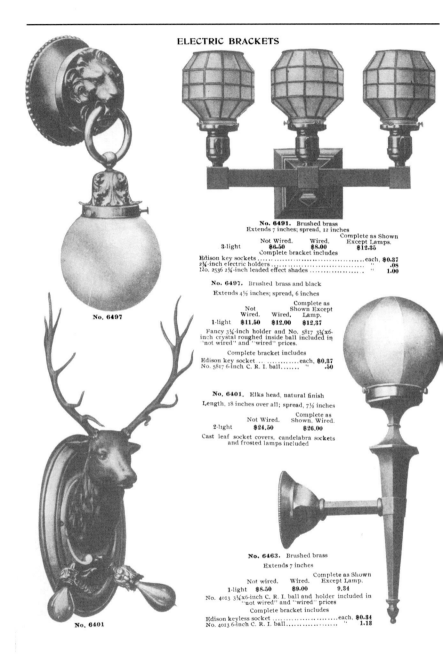

No. 6491. Brushed brass

Extends 7 inches; spread, 12 inches

	Not Wired.	Wired.	Complete as Shown Except Lamps.
3-light	$6.50	$8.00	$12.35

Complete bracket includes

Edison key sockets ....each, $0.37
2¼-inch electric holders .... " .08
No. 2536 2¼-inch leaded effect shades .... " 1.00

No. 6497. Brushed brass and black

Extends 4½ inches; spread, 6 inches

	Not Wired.	Wired.	Complete as Shown Except Lamp.
1-light	$11.50	$12.00	$12.37

Fancy 3¼-inch holder and No. 5817 3¼x6-inch crystal roughed inside ball included in "not wired" and "wired" prices.

Complete bracket includes

Edison key socket .. ..each, $0.37
No. 5817 6-inch C. R. I. ball....... " .50

No. 6401. Elks head, natural finish

Length, 18 inches over all; spread, 7½ inches

	Not Wired.	Complete as Shown, Wired.
2-light	$24.50	$26.00

Cast leaf socket covers, candelabra sockets and frosted lamps included

No. 6463. Brushed brass

Extends 7 inches

	Not wired.	Wired.	Complete as Shown Except Lamp.
1-light	$8.50	$9.00	9.34

No. 4013 3¼x6-inch C. R. I. ball and holder included in "not wired" and "wired" prices

Complete bracket includes

Edison keyless socket ....each, $0.34
No. 4013 6-inch C. R. I. ball.................. " 1.13

No. 6497

No. 6401

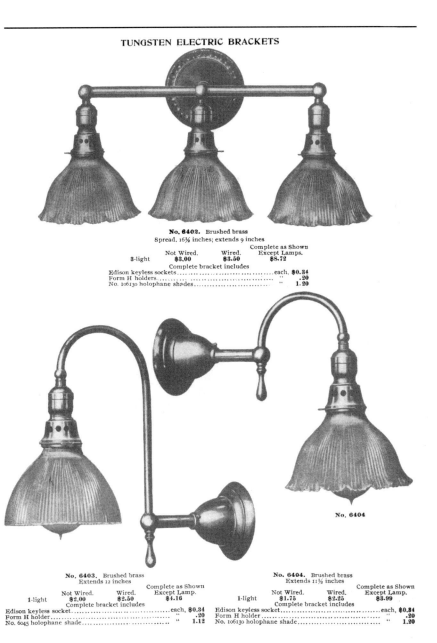

No. 6402. Brushed brass
Spread, 16¼ inches; extends 9 inches

	Not Wired.	Wired.	Complete as Shown Except Lamps.
3-light	$3.00	$3.50	$8.72

Complete bracket includes

Edison keyless sockets............................each, $0.34
Form H holders......................... " .20
No. 106130 holophane shades..................... " 1.20

No. 6404

No. 6403. Brushed brass
Extends 12 inches

	Not Wired.	Wired.	Complete as Shown Except Lamp.
1-light	$2.00	$2.50	$4.16

Complete bracket includes

Edison keyless socket............................each, $0.34
Form H holder......................... " .20
No. 6045 holophane shade................ " 1.12

No. 6404. Brushed brass
Extends 11½ inches

	Not Wired.	Wired.	Complete as Shown Except Lamp.
1-light	$1.75	$2.25	$3.99

Complete bracket includes

Edison keyless socket............................each, $0.34
Form H holder......................... " .20
No. 106130 holophane shade.................... " 1.20

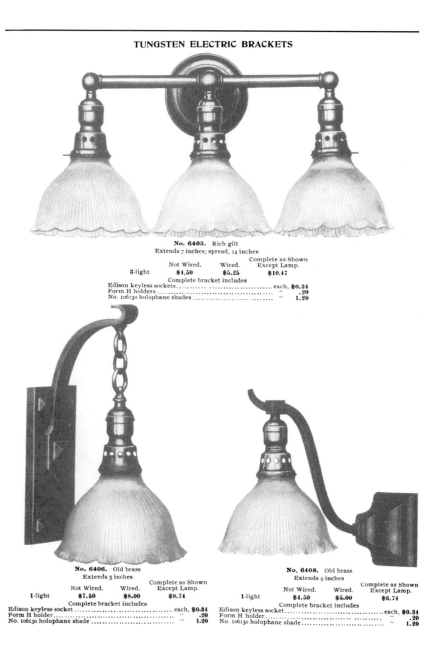

No. 6405. Rich gilt

Extends 7 inches; spread, 14 inches

	Not Wired.	Wired.	Complete as Shown Except Lamp.
3-light	**$4.50**	**$5.25**	**$10.47**

Complete bracket includes

Edison keyless sockets . . . . each, **$0.34**
Form H holders . . . . " **.20**
No. 106130 holophane shades . . . . " **1.20**

No. 6406. Old brass

Extends 5 inches

	Not Wired.	Wired.	Complete as Shown Except Lamp.
1-light	**$7.50**	**$8.00**	**$9.74**

Complete bracket includes

Edison keyless socket . . . . each, **$0.34**
Form H holder . . . . " **.20**
No. 106130 holophane shade . . . . " **1.20**

No. 6408. Old brass

Extends 9 inches

	Not Wired.	Wired.	Complete as Shown Except Lamp.
1-light	**$4.50**	**$5.00**	**$6.74**

Complete bracket includes

Edison keyless socket . . . . each, **$0.34**
Form H holder . . . . " **.20**
No. 106130 holophane shade . . . . " **1.20**

TUNGSTEN ELECTRIC BRACKETS

No. 6409. Old brass

Extends 12 inches; spread, 15 inches

	Not Wired.	Wired.	Complete as Shown Except Lamp.
2-light	**$7.50**	**$8.50**	**$11.82**

Complete bracket includes

Edison keyless sockets	each,	**$0.34**
Form H holders	"	**.20**
No. 6045 holophane shades	"	**1.12**

No. 6410. Brushed brass

Extends 7 inches

	Not Wired.	Wired.	Complete as Shown Except Lamp.
1-light	**$3.50**	**$4.00**	**$5.74**

Complete bracket includes

Edison keyless socket	each,	**$0.34**
Form H holder	"	**.20**
No. 106130 holophane shade	"	**1.20**

No. 6411. Old brass

Extends 7 inches

	Not Wired.	Wired.	Complete as Shown Except Lamp.
1-light	**$2.25**	**$2.75**	**$4.49**

Complete bracket includes

Edison keyless socket	each,	**$0.34**
Form H holder	"	**.20**
No. 106130 holophane shade	"	**1.20**

WOOD FIXTURES

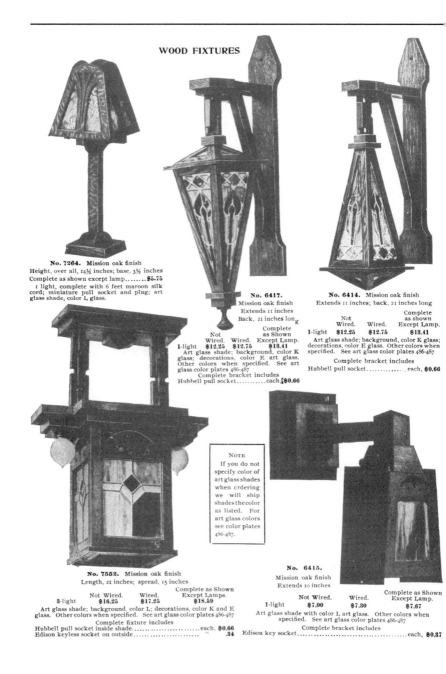

No. 7264. Mission oak finish
Height, over all, 14½ inches; base, 3½ inches
Complete as shown except lamp........**$5.75**
1 light, complete with 6 feet maroon silk cord; miniature pull socket and plug; art glass shade, color L glass.

No. 6417.
Mission oak finish
Extends 11 inches
Back, 21 inches long

	Not Wired.	Wired.	Complete as Shown Except Lamp.
1-light	**$12.25**	**$12.75**	**$13.41**

Art glass shade; background, color K glass; decorations, color E art glass. Other colors when specified. See art glass color plates 486-487
Complete bracket includes
Hubbell pull socket...........each,**$0.66**

No. 6414. Mission oak finish
Extends 11 inches; back, 21 inches long

	Not Wired.	Wired.	Complete as shown Except Lamp.
1-light	**$12.25**	**$12.75**	**$13.41**

Art glass shade; background, color K glass; decorations, color E glass. Other colors when specified. See art glass color plates 486-487

Complete bracket includes
Hubbell pull socket..............each, **$0.66**

NOTE
If you do not specify color of art glass shades when ordering we will ship shades the color as listed. For art glass colors see color plates 486-487.

No. 7552. Mission oak finish
Length, 21 inches; spread, 15 inches

	Not Wired.	Wired.	Complete as Shown Except Lamps.
3-light	**$16.25**	**$17.25**	**$18.59**

Art glass shade; background, color L; decorations, color K and E glass. Other colors when specified. See art glass color plates 486-487
Complete fixture includes
Hubbell pull socket inside shade.......................each, **$0.66**
Edison keyless socket on outside........................ " .34

No. 6415.
Mission oak finish
Extends 10 inches

	Not Wired.	Wired.	Complete as Shown Except Lamp.
1-light	**$7.00**	**$7.30**	**$7.67**

Art glass shade with color L, art glass. Other colors when specified. See art glass color plates 486-487
Complete bracket includes
Edison key socket.....................................each, **$0.37**

124

ADJUSTABLE BRACKETS

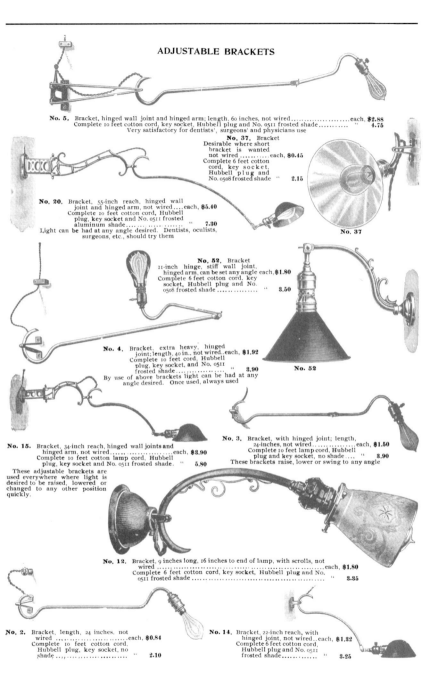

No. 5. Bracket, hinged wall joint and hinged arm; length, 60 inches, not wired ....each, **$2.88**
Complete 10 feet cotton cord, key socket, Hubbell plug and No. 0511 frosted shade .... " **4.75**
Very satisfactory for dentists', surgeons' and physicians use

No. 37. Bracket
Desirable where short
bracket is wanted
not wired .... each, **$0.45**
Complete 6 feet cotton
cord, key socket,
Hubbell plug and
No. 0508 frosted shade " **2.15**

No. 37

No. 20. Bracket, 55-inch reach, hinged wall
joint and hinged arm, not wired ... each, **$5.40**
Complete 10 feet cotton cord, Hubbell
plug, key socket and No. 0511 frosted
aluminum shade .... " **7.30**
Light can be had at any angle desired. Dentists, oculists,
surgeons, etc., should try them

No. 52. Bracket
11-inch hinge, stiff wall joint,
hinged arm, can be set any angle each, **$1.80**
Complete 6 feet cotton cord, key
socket, Hubbell plug and No.
0508 frosted shade .... " **3.50**

No. 52

No. 4. Bracket, extra heavy, hinged
joint; length; 40 in., not wired.. each, **$1.92**
Complete 10 feet cord, Hubbell
plug, key socket, and No. 0511
frosted shade................. " **3.90**
By use of above brackets light can be had at any
angle desired. Once used, always used

No. 15. Bracket, 34-inch reach, hinged wall joints and
hinged arm, not wired.... ....each, **$3.90**
Complete 10 feet cotton cord, Hubbell
plug, key socket and No. 0511 frosted shade. " **5.80**

These adjustable brackets are
used everywhere where light is
desired to be raised, lowered or
changed to any other position
quickly.

No. 3. Bracket, with hinged joint; length,
24-inches, not wired ....each, **$1.50**
Complete 10 feet lamp cord, Hubbell
plug and key socket, no shade ... " **3.90**
These brackets raise, lower or swing to any angle

No. 12. Bracket, 9 inches long, 16 inches to end of lamp, with scrolls, not
wired ....each, **$1.80**
Complete 6 feet cotton cord, key socket, Hubbell plug and No.
0511 frosted shade .... " **3.35**

No. 2. Bracket, length, 24 inches, not
wired ....each, **$0.84**
Complete 10 feet cotton cord,
Hubbell plug, key socket, no
shade ..,................ .... " **2.10**

No. 14. Bracket, 22-inch reach, with
hinged joint, not wired.. each, **$1.32**
Complete 10 feet cotton cord,
Hubbell plug and No. 0511
frosted shade............... " **3.25**

ELECTRIC CHURCH OR HALL FIXTURE

No. 7721. Rich gilt and satin
Length, 72 inches over all
Upper tier spreads 32 inches
Lower tier spreads 24 inches

	Not Wired.	Wired.	Complete as Shown Except Lamps.
11-light	$ 75.00	$ 80.50	$ 84.57
13 "	85.00	91.50	96.31
15 "	95.00	102.50	108.05
17 "	105.00	113.50	119.79
19 "	115.00	124.50	131.53

No. 423 3¼x6-inch straw opalescent balls included in "not wired" and "wired" prices

Complete fixture includes

Edison key sockets ....each.	**$0.37**
No. 423 6-inch S. O. balls	"	.75
3¼-inch fancy cast holder	"	1.25

1⅛-inch extra lengthening per foot, not wired 60 cents; wired, 70 cents

ELECTRIC CHURCH OR HALL FIXTURE

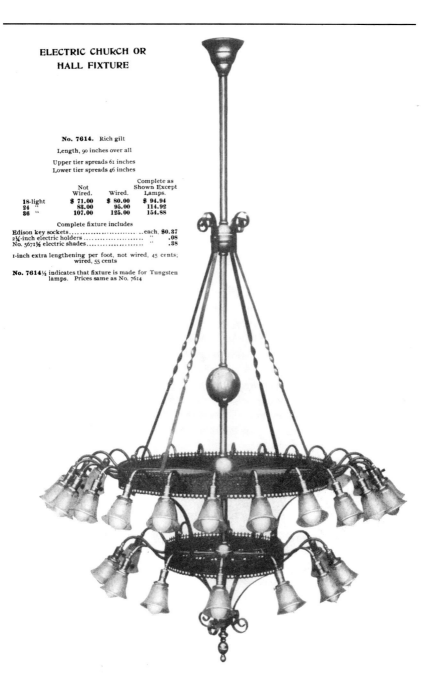

No. 7614. Rich gilt

Length, 90 inches over all

Upper tier spreads 61 inches
Lower tier spreads 46 inches

	Not Wired.	Wired.	Complete as Shown Except Lamps.
18-light	$ 71.00	$ 80.00	$ 94.94
24 "	88.00	95.00	114.92
36 "	107.00	125.00	154.88

Complete fixture includes

Edison key sockets.........................each,		$0.37
2¼-inch electric holders.....................	"	.08
No. 5671½ electric shades...................	"	.38

1-inch extra lengthening per foot, not wired, 45 cents;
wired, 55 cents

No. 7614½ indicates that fixture is made for Tungsten
lamps. Prices same as No. 7614

ELECTRIC CHURCH OR HALL FIXTURE

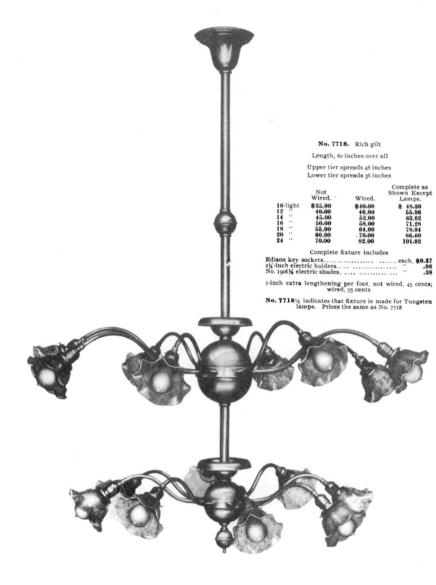

No. 7718. Rich gilt

Length, 60 inches over all

Upper tier spreads 48 inches
Lower tier spreads 36 inches

	Not Wired.	Wired.	Complete as Shown Except Lamps.
10-light	$35.00	$40.00	$ 48.30
12 "	40.00	46.00	55.96
14 "	45.00	52.00	63.62
16 "	50.00	58.00	71.28
18 "	55.00	64.00	78.94
20 "	60.00	.70.00	86.60
24 "	70.00	82.00	101.92

Complete fixture includes

Edison key sockets.................. ....each, **$0.37**
2½-inch electric holders.... .... " .08
No. 1906½ electric shades, ... " .38

1-inch extra lengthening per foot, not wired, 45 cents; wired, 55 cents

No. 7718½ indicates that fixture is made for Tungsten lamps. Prices the same as No. 7718

ELECTRIC DESK PORTABLES

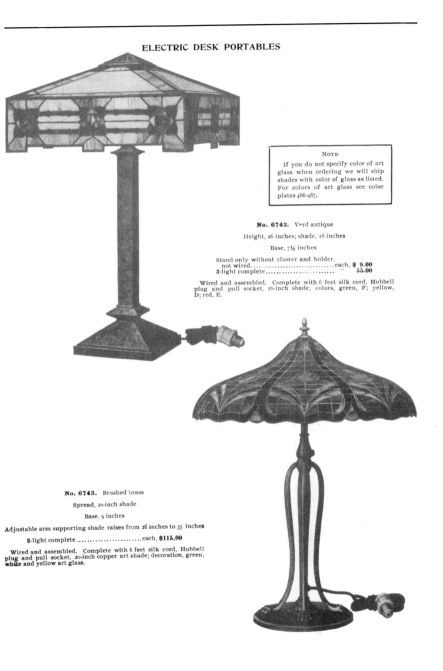

No. 6742. Verd antique

Height, 26 inches; shade, 16 inches

Base, 7½ inches

Stand only without cluster and holder,
not wired..............................each, $ 9.00
3-light complete......................   "   55.00

Wired and assembled. Complete with 6 feet silk cord, Hubbell
plug and pull socket, 16-inch shade; colors, green, F; yellow,
D; red, E.

No. 6743. Brushed brass

Spread, 20-inch shade

Base, 9 inches

Adjustable arm supporting shade raises from 26 inches to 35 inches

3-light complete.......................each, $115.00

Wired and assembled. Complete with 6 feet silk cord, Hubbell
plug and pull socket, 20-inch copper art shade; decoration, green,
white and yellow art glass.

129

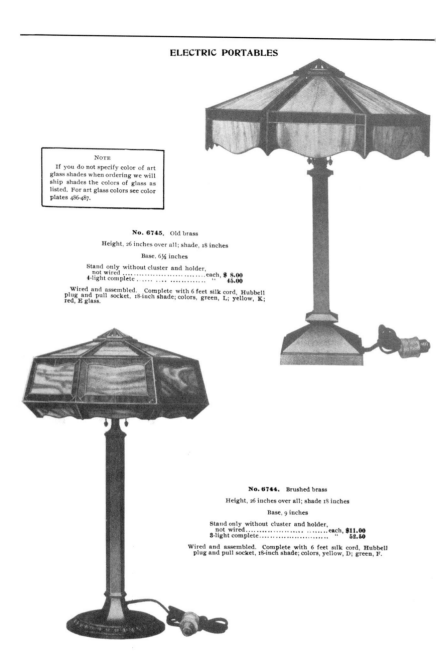

No. 6745. Old brass

Height, 26 inches over all; shade, 18 inches

Base. 6½ inches

Stand only without cluster and holder,
not wired ....each, $ 8.00
4-light complete .... " 45.00

Wired and assembled. Complete with 6 feet silk cord, Hubbell plug and pull socket, 18-inch shade; colors, green, L; yellow, K; red, E glass.

No. 6744. Brushed brass

Height, 26 inches over all; shade 18 inches

Base, 9 inches

Stand only without cluster and holder,
not wired...................... ....each, $11.00
3-light complete........................... " 52.50

Wired and assembled. Complete with 6 feet silk cord, Hubbell plug and pull socket, 18-inch shade; colors, yellow, D; green, F.

ELECTRIC PORTABLES

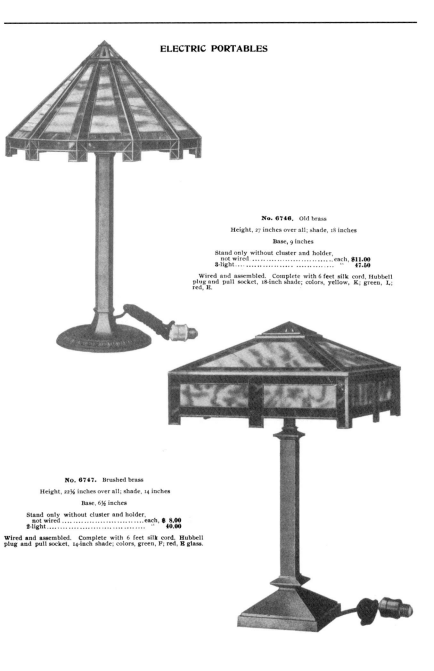

No. 6746. Old brass

Height, 27 inches over all; shade, 18 inches

Base, 9 inches

Stand only without cluster and holder,
not wired ....each, **$11.00**
3-light................................. " **47.50**

Wired and assembled. Complete with 6 feet silk cord, Hubbell plug and pull socket, 18-inch shade; colors, yellow, K; green, L; red, E.

No. 6747. Brushed brass

Height, 22½ inches over all; shade, 14 inches

Base, 6½ inches

Stand only without cluster and holder,
not wired ....each, **$ 8.00**
2-light................................. " **40.00**

Wired and assembled. Complete with 6 feet silk cord, Hubbell plug and pull socket, 14-inch shade; colors, green, F; red, E glass.

No. 6800. Old brass

Heigth, 34 inches over all; base, 5¼ inches

Stand only, not wired .... each, **$7.50**
Assembled. Complete .... " **9.85**

Wired with 6 feet silk cord, Hubbell plug and pull socket
and aluminum shade. Frosted inside

No. 6801. Old brass

Height, 20½ inches over all; base, 7 inches

1-light .... each, **$12.50**

Assembled. Complete with 6 feet silk cord,
Hubbell plug and key socket, stamped socket
cover holder, No. 114 shade and 2¾x10-inch green
cone shade.

No. 6898. Old brass

Height, 26 inches over all

Stand only, not wired .... each, **$7.75**
Assembled. Complete .... " **9.85**

Wired with 6 feet silk cord, Edison key socket, Hubbell
plug and 3¼-inch shade holder with 3¼x10-inch opal
shade.

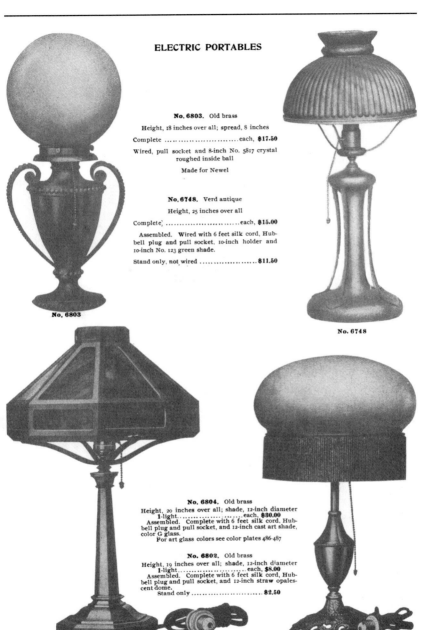

ELECTRIC PORTABLES

No. 6803. Old brass

Height, 18 inches over all; spread, 8 inches

Complete ....each, **$17.50**

Wired, pull socket and 8-inch No. 5817 crystal
roughed inside ball

Made for Newel

No. 6748. Verd antique

Height, 25 inches over all

Complete ....each, **$15.00**

Assembled. Wired with 6 feet silk cord, Hubbell plug and pull socket, 10-inch holder and
10-inch No. 123 green shade.

Stand only, not wired **$11.50**

No. 6803

No. 6748

No. 6804. Old brass

Height, 20 inches over all; shade, 12-inch diameter
1-light.....................each, **$30.00**

Assembled. Complete with 6 feet silk cord, Hubbell plug and pull socket, and 12-inch cast art shade,
color G glass.

For art glass colors see color plates 486-487

No. 6802. Old brass

Height, 19 inches over all; shade, 12-inch diameter
1-light.....................each, **$8.00**

Assembled. Complete with 6 feet silk cord, Hubbell plug and pull socket, and 12-inch straw opalescent dome.

Stand only **$2.50**

No. 6804

No. 6802

133

No. 6805. Old brass
Height, 23 inches over all; shade, 14-inch diameter
1-light.................................... each, **$20.00**
Assembled. Complete with 6 feet silk cord, Hubbell plug and pull socket, 14-inch art shade, color L, and bead fringe to match.
For art glass colors see color plates 486-487

No. 6749. Rich gilt and satin
Height, 28 inches over all
Complete ....each, **$18.00**
Assembled. Wired with 6 feet silk cord, Hubbell plug and pull socket and No. 1033 10-inch decorated globe and holder.
Stand only with 4-inch cast holder, not wired...................... **$10.50**

No. 6806. Brushed brass
Height, 15 inches over all
Shade, 6-inch diameter
1-light...............each, **$35.00**
Assembled. Complete with 6 feet silk cord, Hubbell plug and pull socket, 6-inch art shade, colors, yellow, K; green, I, and red, E. For art glass colors see color plates 486-487.

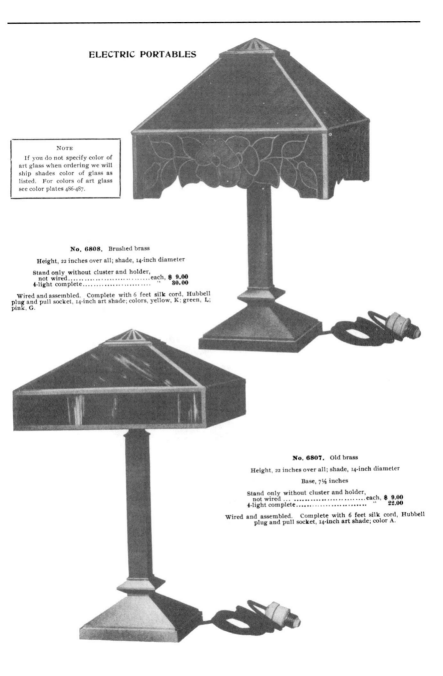

ELECTRIC PORTABLES

No. 6808. Brushed brass

Height, 22 inches over all; shade, 14-inch diameter

Stand only without cluster and holder,
    not wired.............................each, **$ 9.00**
4-light complete........................ " **30.00**

Wired and assembled. Complete with 6 feet silk cord, Hubbell plug and pull socket, 14-inch art shade; colors, yellow, K; green, L; pink, G.

No. 6807. Old brass

Height, 22 inches over all; shade, 14-inch diameter

Base, 7½ inches

Stand only without cluster and holder,
    not wired ... .each, **$ 9.00**
4-light complete........................ " **22.00**

Wired and assembled. Complete with 6 feet silk cord, Hubbell plug and pull socket, 14-inch art shade; color A.

No. 7260. Old brass

Height, 15½ inches over all; spread, 6½ inches
1-light stand only............................each, **$2.50**
Assembled. Complete with 6 feet silk cord, Hubbell
plug and pull socket, No. 430 7-inch green linen shade,
and clasp holder.............................each, **$4.75**
Linen shades can be had in colors of red, orange, pink
and light blue, when ordered; if not, we will furnish
green.

No. 6809. Brushed brass
Height, 21 inches over all
Shade, 16-inch diameter

2-light........................each, **$35.00**
Assembled. Complete with 6 feet silk
cord, Hubbell plug and pull socket, 16-
inch art shade; colors, yellow, R; green, F
and red, E. For art glass colors see
plates 486-487.

No. 6750. Old brass and black
Height, 27 inches over all

Complete....................................**$24.50**
Assembled. Wired with 6 feet silk cord, Hubbell plug
and pull socket, 4x10-inch, rose art glass shade and
4-inch cast holder.
Stand only, not wired.......................**$7.50**

No. 7261. Brushed brass
Height, 17 inches over all; spread, 6½ inches

Complete....................................**$4.25**
Assembled. Wired with 6 feet silk cord, Hubbell plug
and pull socket, No. 430 7-inch green linen shade and
clasp holder.
Stand only, not wired.......................**$2.00**

No. 6750

No. 7261

WOOD ELECTRIC PORTABLES

No. 6810. Mission oak finish

1-light complete.................each, **$22.50**

Wired and assembled. Complete with 6 feet silk cord, Hubbell plug and pull socket, art shade; color, G glass. For art glass colors see color plates 486-487.

No. 6811. Mission oak finish

1-light complete........ .... each, **$28.75**

Wired and assembled. Complete with 6 feet silk cord, Hubbell plug and pull socket, 6-inch shade and fringe. For art glass colors see color plates 486-487.

No. 6810

No. 6811

No. 7263. Wood Candelabra
Mission oak finish

1-light complete..................each, **$6.25**

Wired and assembled. Complete with 6 feet silk cord, Hubbell plug and miniature socket and frosted bulb.

No. 7262. Wood Candelabra
Mission oak finish

1-light complete .... each, **$5.88**

Wired and assembled. Complete with 6 feet silk cord, Hubbell plug, miniature socket and frosted bulb.

No. 6838. Wood Portable
Mission oak finish

Height, 21 inches over all; shade, 3½ inches

1-light complete as shown
except lamp .... each, **$14.00**

Wired and assembled. Complete with 6 feet cord, plug and keyless socket; color L glass in art shade. For art glass colors see color plates 486-487.

No. 6812. Mission oak finish

1-light complete........ each, **$12.88**

Wired and assembled. Complete with 6 feet silk cord, Hubbell plug and pull socket, art shade; color A glass. For color of art glass see color plates 486-487.

No. 6815. Mission oak finish

1-light complete........each, **$14.50**

Wired and assembled. Complete with 6 feet silk cord, Hubbell plug and pull socket, art glass; shade, color J. For art glass colors see color plates 486-487.

No. 6815

No. 6813. Mission oak finish

1-light complete .....each, **$31.88**

Wired and assembled. Complete with 6 feet silk cord, Hubbell plug and pull socket, art shade; color, L glass and bead fringe to match. For colors of art glass see color plates 486-487.

No. 6813

No. 7251

No. 6839. Wood Portable
Mission oak finish
Height, 22 inches over all; shade, 13½ inches diam.
2-light, complete as shown except
lamps.............................. each, **$18.50**
Assembled. Wired with 6 feet silk cord, Edison keyless sockets, plug and color L art glass in shade

No. 7251. Butler silver
Height, 23 inches over all; spread, 18 inches
Base, 6 inches diameter
5-light, complete as shown.......... ....each, **$47.50**
Assembled. Wired with 6 feet silk cord, Hubbell
plug and pull sockets, candles with silk candelabra
shades and holders.

No. 6814. Wood Portable
Mission oak finish
1-light **$21.25**
Assembled. Complete with 6 feet
silk cord, Hubbell plug and pull
socket, art shade, color H glass. For
art glass colors see color plates 486-487.

No. 6840. Wood Portable
Mission oak finish
Height, 24 inches over all
Shade, 15 inches diameter
1-light, complete as shown
except lamp.............each, **$6.00**
Assembled. Complete wired with
6 feet cotton cord, plug, socket and
art shade color E glass.

No. 6814

No. 6840

Fixtures are furnished wired (not assembled) unless ordered otherwise. Glassware, Electric Shade
Holders, Sockets and Lamps not included unless mentioned.

ELECTRIC DESK PORTABLES

No. 6818. Old brass
Height, 9 inches; extends 9½ inches; base, 6 inches
1-light..**$19.00**
Assembled. Complete with 6 feet silk cord, Hubbell plug and
pull socket, art shade, color K glass. For art glass colors see color
plates 486-487

No. 6751. Brushed brass
Wired complete with 6 feet silk cord, Hubbell plug and pull
socket, adjustable shade

Assembled. Complete as shown.........................**$6.25**
Portable only, not wired.............................. **5.00**

No. 6854. Brushed brass
Height, 21 inches over all
1-light...each, **$16.00**
Assembled. Wired with 6 feet silk cord, Edison key socket,
Hubbell plug, 8-inch square cast shade, art glass color A, socket
cover and adjustable sliding arm. For colors of art glass see color
plates 486-487.

No. 6817. Adjustable Desk Lamp
Heavy and strongly made. Has two swinging movements making
it adjustable
Nickel, old brass, oxidized copper, not wired...........each, **$5.00**
Assembled. Wired with 6 feet cotton cord, socket and
attaching plug............. . ... " **6.25**
The best thing for roll-top desks

ELECTRIC DESK PORTABLES

No. 6820. Rich gilt
Portable with adjustable hood
Stand and hood only, not wired.. each, **$6.50**
Assembled. Complete wired with
6 feet cotton lamp cord, Edison
key socket, Hubbell plug....... " **7.75**

No. 6821. Rich gilt
Portable
Stand only, with adjustable hood,
not wired................. ......each, **$6.00**
Assembled. Complete wired with
6 feet cotton lamp cord, Hubbell
plug and Edison key socket.... " **7.25**

No. 6819. Rich gilt
Portable
Height, 24 inches
Stand only, not wired............each, **$3.00**
Assembled. Complete wired with
6 feet cotton lamp cord, Edison
key socket, Hubbell plug, No.
114 2¾x7-inch green shade and
2¾-inch holder................,.... " **4.50**

No. 6860. Rich gilt
Height, 24 inches; raises and lowers
Stand only, not wired............ ....each, **$4.00**
Assembled. Complete with 6 feet cot-
ton lamp cord, Hubbell plug, Edison
key socket, No. 1133¾x10-inch green
shade and holder .... " **6.00**

No. 6891. Rich gilt
Height, 20 inches; adjustable
Stand only, not wired .... each, **$2.00**
Assembled. Complete with 6 feet cot-
ton lamp cord, Edison key socket,
Hubbell plug, No. 114 2¾x7-inch
green shade and holder............ " **3.50**

No. 6759. Rich gilt
Height, 24 inches; raises and lowers
Stand only, not wired ....each, **$2.50**
Assembled. Complete with
6 feet cotton lamp cord,
Hubbell plug, Edison
key socket, No. 114 2¾x7-
inch green shade and
holder.................. " **4.00**

No. 6891

140

No. 6753. Old brass
Height to shade, 16 inches
Stand only, not wired.....each, **$3.00**
Assembled. Complete with 6
feet silk cord, Hubbell plug,
Edison key socket, No. 0526
10-inch holder and No. 123 10-
inch green shade **5.50**

No. 6754. Rich gilt
Height to shade, 16 inches
Stand only, not wired. .. each, **$1.00**
Assembled. Complete with 6
feet cotton cord. Edison key
socket, Hubbell plug. No. 0526
10-inch holder and No. 113 10-
inch green shade........each, **3.00**

No. 6752. Rich gilt and satin
Height to shade, 14 inches
Stand only, not wired................. each, **$2.00**
Assembled. Complete with 6 feet cotton
lamp cord, Hubbell plug, Edison key
socket. No. 0526 10 inch holder and No.
113 10-inch green shade ....each, **4.00**

No. 6755. Rich gilt
Height, 23 inches; raises and lowers
Stand only, not wired .....each, **$6.00**
Assembled. Complete with 6
feet silk lamp cord, Hubbell
plug, Edison key socket, 3¼-
inch holder, No. 115 8-inch
green shade, ground bottom
globe ....each, **9.00**

No. 6757. Rich gilt
Height, 24 inches
Stand only, not wired....each, **$5.00**
Assembled. Complete with 6
feet silk cord, Hubbell plug,
Edison key socket, 3¼-inch
fancy holder and Kneeland
silvered glass reflector ..each, **8.50**

No. 6756. Rich gilt and satin
Height to shade, 16 inches
Stand only, not wired.....each, **$3.50**
Assembled. Complete with 6
feet silk cord, Hubbell plug,
Edison key socket, No. 0526
10-inch holder, No. 123 10-inch
green shade ....each, **6.00**

141

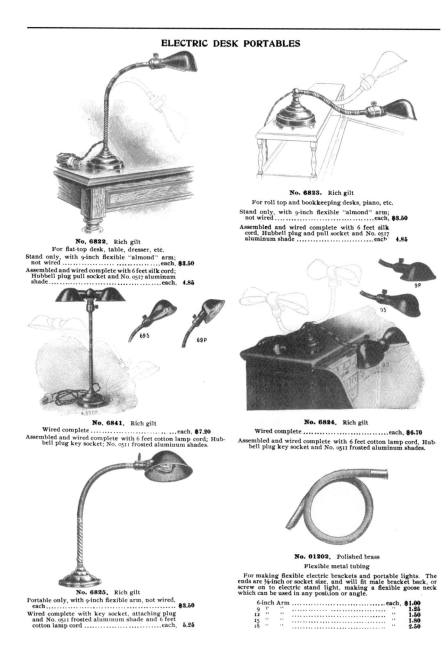

No. 6822. Rich gilt

For flat-top desk, table, dresser, etc.

Stand only, with 9-inch flexible "almond" arm; not wired ....each, **$3.50**

Assembled and wired complete with 6 feet silk cord; Hubbell plug pull socket and No. 0517 aluminum shade..each, **4.85**

No. 6823. Rich gilt

For roll top and bookkeeping desks, piano, etc.

Stand only, with 9-inch flexible "almond" arm; not wired..each, **$3.50**

Assembled and wired complete with 6 feet silk cord, Hubbell plug and pull socket and No. 0517 aluminum shade ....each **4.85**

No. 6841. Rich gilt

Wired complete .... each, **$7.20**

Assembled and wired complete with 6 feet cotton lamp cord; Hubbell plug key socket; No. 0511 frosted aluminum shades.

No. 6824. Rich gilt

Wired complete ....each, **$6.70**

Assembled and wired complete with 6 feet cotton lamp cord, Hubbell plug key socket and No. 0511 frosted aluminum shades.

No. 6825. Rich gilt

Portable only, with 9-inch flexible arm, not wired, each.. **$3.50**

Wired complete with key socket, attaching plug and No. 0511 frosted aluminum shade and 6 feet cotton lamp cord ....each, **5.25**

No. 01202. Polished brass

Flexible metal tubing

For making flexible electric brackets and portable lights. The ends are ½-inch or socket size, and will fit male bracket back, or screw on to electric stand light, making a flexible goose neck which can be used in any position or angle.

6-inch Arm ....each,		**$1.00**
9 " " .... "		**1.25**
12 " " .... "		**1.50**
15 " " .... "		**1.80**
18 " " .... "		**2.50**

142

ELECTRIC DESK PORTABLES

No. 6830. Rich gilt
Electric Portable
Stand only, not wired............................each, **$2.00**
Complete wired with 6 feet cotton lamp cord, socket,
plug, No. 114 7-inch green shade and No. 114 2¾-inch
holder .... " **3.75**

No. 6826. Rich gilt
Height, 24 inches; extends 18 inches
2-light Electric Portable. Arms are adjustable
Stand only...each, **$5.00**
Assembled. Complete with two 6-foot length cotton
lamp cords, plugs, sockets and 7-inch No. 0508 frosted
aluminum shades.. " **8.50**

No. 6830

No. 6826

No. 6829. Brushed brass
Height, 18 inches
Stand only, not wired...........each, **$2.75**
Assembled. Complete with 6 feet
cotton cord, key socket, Hubbell
plug, No. 0511..................... " **4.35**
For piano, office desk, library table, or any
place where an adjustable portable lamp is
needed.

No. 6828. Rich gilt
Electric Portable
Stand only, not wired............each, **$2.00**
Assembled. Complete wired with
6 feet cotton cord, Hubbell plug,
key socket, 3¾-inch holder and
3¾x10-inch green plated shade.. " **4.00**

No. 6831

No. 6832

No. 6831. Rich gilt
Adjustable Electric Portable
Stand only ....each, **$2.60**
Complete wired with 6 feet cotton
cord, key socket, Hubbell plug,
aluminum shade, 7-inch No. 0508 " **4.50**

No. 6832. Adjustable Desk Light
Raises from 16 to 22 inches........each, **$2.00**
Wired with 6 feet cotton cord,
socket and attaching plug, aluminum shade, No. 0500............ " **4.25**

No. 6827. Roll Top Desk Light
Frame and hood only, not wired ....each, **$4.50**
Assembled. Complete wired with 10 feet cotton lamp
cord, socket and Hubbell plug........................ " **5.75**

No. 6833. Metal Portable Hood
Hood only ....each, **$2.50**
Can be attached to any electric portable

ELECTRIC DESK PORTABLES

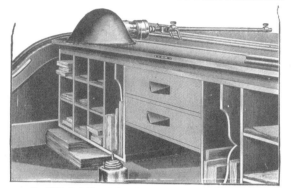

No. 6835. Desk Clamp (adjustable) on top of desks up to 15 inches wide
Clamp only, not wired..each, **$1.75**
Assembled. Complete, wired, 10 feet cotton lamp cord, socket and plug, 7-inch aluminum shade, No. 0511, frosted..each, **4.00**

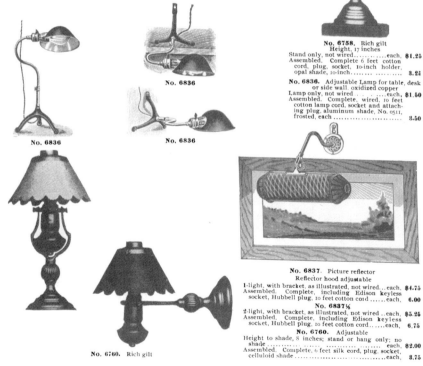

No. 6836

No. 6836

No. 6836

No. 6760. Rich gilt

No. 6758. Rich gilt
Height, 17 inches
Stand only, not wired.............each, **$1.25**
Assembled. Complete 6 feet cotton cord, plug, socket, 10-inch holder, opal shade, 10-inch...... .... **3.25**

No. 6836. Adjustable Lamp for table, desk or side wall. oxidized copper
Lamp only, not wired.. . .. .each, **$1.50**
Assembled. Complete, wired, 10 feet cotton lamp cord, socket and attaching plug. aluminum shade, No. 0511, frosted, each **3.50**

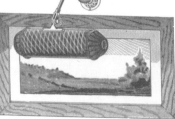

No. 6837. Picture reflector
Reflector hood adjustable
1-light, with bracket, as illustrated, not wired...each, **$4.75**
Assembled. Complete, including Edison keyless socket, Hubbell plug, 10 feet cotton cord ......each, **6.00**
No. 6837½.
2-light, with bracket, as illustrated, not wired ..each, **$5.25**
Assembled. Complete, including Edison keyless socket, Hubbell plug, 10 feet cotton cord......each, **6.75**
No. 6760. Adjustable
Height to shade, 8 inches; stand or hang only; no shade .... each, **$2.00**
Assembled. Complete, 6 feet silk cord, plug, socket, celluloid shade ....each, **3.75**

No. 6724. L'Art Noveau

Height, 29 inches over all; spread, 17 inches

Base, 6¾ inches

3-light, **$55.00**

Complete as shown with 16-candle power frosted Edison base lamps

No. 6722. L'Art Noveau

Height, 24½ inches over all; spread, 14 inches

Base, 6½ inches

3-light, **$50.00**

Complete as shown with round frosted 16-candle power Edison base lamps. 110 volt

No. 6722

145

No. 6717

No. 6717. L'Art Noveau
Height, 30 inches; spread, 16 inches
Base, 7 inches
4-light, **$55.00**
Complete as shown with 16-candle power round frosted lamps, Edison base

No. 6719. L'Art Noveau
Height, 26 inches; spread, 16 inches
Base, 7 inches
3-light, **$50.00**
Complete as shown with 16-candle power round frosted lamps, Edison base

No. 6719

ELECTRIC NEWELS AND STANDARDS

NOTE

Standard No. 6716 is also made to screw on newel posts when a stationary light is wanted. If made with a removable door on back to connect wiring add $6.50.

Standards will be shipped unless ordered for newel posts.

No. 6716. Antique bronze
Standard
Height, 25 inches over all; spread, 10 inches
Base, 6 inches
2-light **$28.00**
Complete with 16-candle power round frosted lamps, Edison base

No. 6728.   **No. 6732.**   **No. 6716.**   **No. 6731**

No. 6728. Brushed brass
Hexagonal
Height, 27 inches over all; base, 5 inches

	Not Wired.	Wired.	Complete as Shown Except Lamp.
1-light	**$11.00**	**$11.50**	**$11.84**

No. 4013 6-inch opalescent ball included in "not wired" and "wired" prices
Complete fixture includes
Edison keyless socket............each, **$0.34**
No. 4013 opalescent ball........... "   1.13

No. 6732. Rich gilt and satin
Height, 26 inches over all; base, 6¼ inches

	Not Wired.	Wired.	Complete as Shown Except Lamp.
1-light	**$16.00**	**$16.50**	**$16.84**

3¼x7-inch straw opalescent ball included in "not wired" and "wired" prices
Complete fixture includes
Edison keyless socket ....each, **$0.34**
No. 423 3¼x7-inch S. O. ball.... "   .92

No. 6731. Rich gilt and iridescent colors
Height, 34 inches over all; base, 7 inches

	Not Wired.	Wired.	Complete as Shown Except Lamp.
1-light	**$21.50**	**$22.00**	**$22.34**

No. 8768 3¼x6-inch etched ball included in "not wired" and "wired" prices
Complete bracket includes
Edison keyless socket.........each, **$0.34**
No. 8768 3¼x6-inch etched ball.. "   2.00

147

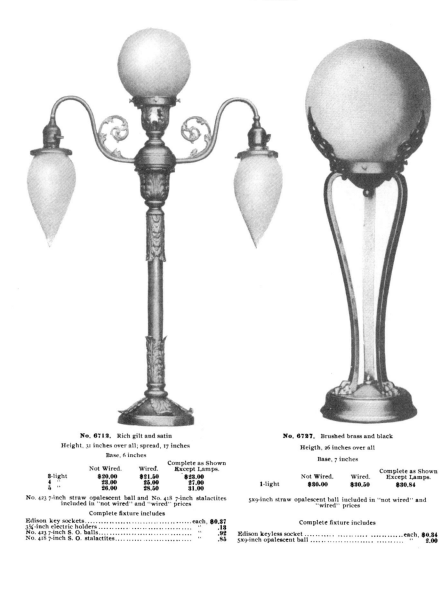

No. 6712. Rich gilt and satin

Height, 31 inches over all; spread, 17 inches

Base, 6 inches

	Not Wired.	Wired.	Complete as Shown Except Lamps.
3-light	$20.00	$21.50	$23.00
4 "	23.00	25.00	27.00
5 "	26.00	28.50	31.00

No. 423 7-inch straw opalescent ball and No. 418 7-inch stalactites included in "not wired" and "wired" prices

Complete fixture includes

Edison key sockets	each,	$0.37
3½-inch electric holders	"	.13
No. 423 7-inch S. O. balls	"	.92
No. 418 7-inch S. O. stalactites	"	.85

No. 6727. Brushed brass and black

Heigth, 26 inches over all

Base, 7 inches

	Not Wired.	Wired.	Complete as Shown Except Lamps.
1-light	$30.00	$30.50	$30.84

5x9-inch straw opalescent ball included in "not wired" and "wired" prices

Complete fixture includes

Edison keyless socket	each,	$0.84
5x9-inch opalescent ball	"	2.00

148

No. 6733. Rich gilt and satin

Height, 30 inches over all; base, 7 inches

1-light	Not Wired.	Wired.	Complete as Shown Except Lamp.
	$15.00	**$15.50**	**$15.84**

4x8-inch straw opalescent ball included in "not wired" and "wired" prices

Complete fixture includes

Edison keyless socket ....each,	**$0.34**
4x8-inch S. O. ball................................... "	**1.13**

No. 6736. Brushed brass

Height, 30 inches over all; spread, 22 inches

2-light	Not Wired.	Wired.	Complete as Shown Except Lamps.
	$4.00	**$5.00**	**$7.24**

Complete fixture includes

Edison key sockets ....each,	**$0.37**
2¼-inch electric holders................... .... "	.08
No. 6877½ electric shades............................. "	.67

COMBINATION FIXTURE

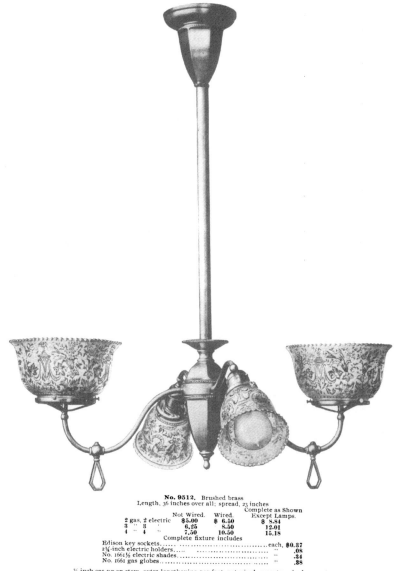

No. 9512. Brushed brass
Length, 36 inches over all; spread, 23 inches

	Not Wired.	Wired.	Complete as Shown Except Lamps.
2 gas, 2 electric	$5.00	$ 6.50	$ 8.84
3 " 3 "	6.25	8.50	12.01
4 " 4 "	7.50	10.50	15.18

Complete fixture includes

Edison key sockets............ ....each,		$0.37
2¼-inch electric holders.....	"	.08
No. 1661½ electric shades...............................	"	.34
No. 1651 gas globes................................	"	.38

⅜-inch cas ng on stem, extra lengthening per foot, not wired, 45 cents; wired, 55 cents

COMBINATION FIXTURE

No. 9517. Brushed brass
Length, 36 inches over all; spread, 23 inches

	Not Wired.	Wired.	Complete as Shown Except Lamps.
2 gas, 2 electric	$4.50	$ 6.00	$ 8.34
3 " 3 "	5.75	8.00	11.51
4 " 4 "	7.00	10.00	14.68

Complete fixture includes

Edison key sockets	each,	$0.37
2¼-inch electric holders	"	.08
No. 1661 gas globes	"	.38
No. 1661½ electric shades	"	.34

⅞-inch casing on stem, extra lengthening per foot, not wired, 45 cents; wired, 55 cents

COMBINATION FIXTURES

No. 9518. Rich gilt and satin

Length, 36 inches; spread, 20 inches

	Not Wired.	Wired.	Complete as Shown Except Lamps.
2 gas, 2 electric	$4.50	$6.00	$ 8.54
3 " 3 "	5.50	7.50	11.31
4 " 4 "	6.50	9.00	14.08

Complete fixture includes

Edison key sockets	each,	$0.37
2¼-inch electric holders	"	0.08
No. 2735½ electric shades	"	0.38
No. 2735 gas globes	"	0.44

⅞-inch casing on stem, extra lengthening per foot, not wired, 45 cents; wired, 55 cents

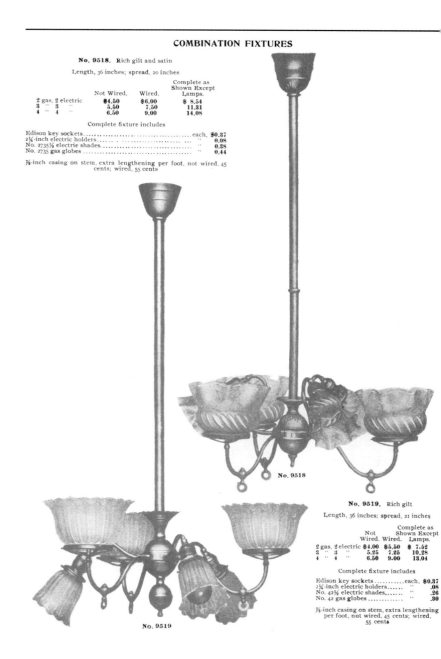

No. 9518

No. 9519. Rich gilt

Length, 36 inches; spread, 21 inches

	Not Wired.	Wired.	Complete as Shown Except Lamps.
2 gas, 2 electric	$4.00	$5.50	$ 7.52
3 " 3 "	5.25	7.25	10.28
4 " 4 "	6.50	9.00	13.04

Complete fixture includes

Edison key sockets	each,	$0.37
2¼-inch electric holders	"	.08
No. 42½ electric shades,	"	.26
No. 42 gas globes	"	.30

⅞-inch casing on stem, extra lengthening per foot, not wired, 45 cents; wired, 55 cents

No. 9519

COMBINATION FIXTURES

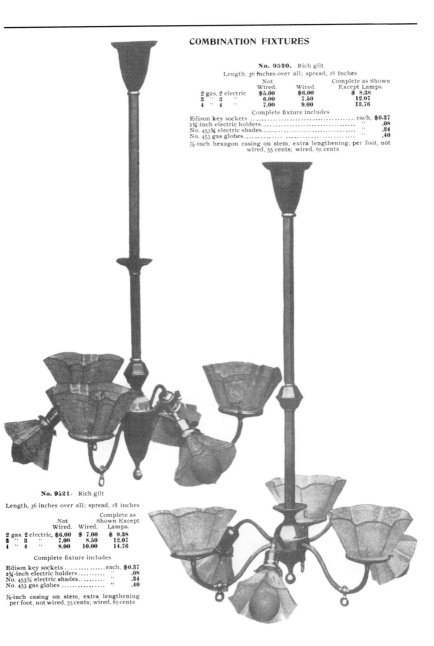

No. 9520. Rich gilt

Length, 36 inches over all; spread, 18 inches

	Not Wired.	Wired.	Complete as Shown Except Lamps.
2 gas, 2 electric	$5.00	$6.00	$ 8.38
3 " 3 "	6.00	7.50	12.07
4 " 4 "	7.00	9.00	13.76

Complete fixture includes

Edison key sockets.................................each,	$0.37
2¼-inch electric holders............................. "	.08
No. 453½ electric shades............................. "	.34
No. 453 gas globes............. .... "	.40

⅝-inch hexagon casing on stem, extra lengthening, per foot, not wired, 55 cents; wired, 65 cents

No. 9521. Rich gilt

Length, 36 inches over all; spread, 18 inches

	Not Wired.	Wired.	Complete as Shown Except Lamps.
2 gas, 2 electric,	$6.00	$ 7.00	$ 9.38
3 " 3 "	7.00	8.50	12.07
4 " 4 "	8.00	10.00	14.76

Complete fixture includes

Edison key sockets ....each,	$0.37
2¼-inch electric holders .... "	.08
No. 453½ electric shades......... "	.34
No. 453 gas globes .... "	.40

⅝-inch casing on stem, extra lengthening per foot, not wired, 55 cents; wired, 65 cents

No. 9522. Rich gilt
Length, 36 inches over all; spread, 18 inches

	Not Wired.	Wired.	Complete as Shown Except Lamps.
2 gas, 2 electric	$ 7.00	$ 8.50	$14.52
3 " 3 "	9.25	11.50	20.53
4 " 4 "	11.50	14.50	26.54

Complete fixture includes

Edison keyless sockets	each,	$0.34
Form H holders	"	.29
No. 6045 holophane shades	"	1.12
Welsbach Chic lights complete	"	1.35

⅞-inch casing on stem, extra lengthening per foot, not wired, 45 cents; wired, 55 cents
Arms made of Henoy ½-inch brass tube

154

No. 9523. Rich gilt and satin
Length, 36 inches over all; spread, 16½ inches

	Not Wired.	Wired.	Complete as Shown Except Lamps.
2 gas, 2 electric	$ 7.50	$ 9.00	$15.18
3 " 3 "	9.75	12.00	21.27
4 " 4 "	12.00	15.00	27.36

Complete fixture includes

Edison keyless sockets	each,	$0.34
Form H holders	"	.20
No. 106130 holophane shades	"	1.20
Welsbach chic lights complete	"	1.35

⅜-inch casing on stem, extra lengthening per foot, not wired, 45 cents; wired, 55 cents

Arms made of extra heavy ½-inch brass tube

No. 9524. Rich gilt and satin

Length 36 inches over all; spread, 22 inches

	Not Wired.	Wired.	Complete as Shown Except Lamps.
2 gas, 2 electric	$5.00	$ 6.50	$10.24
3 " 3 "	6.25	8.25	13.86
4 " 4 "	7.50	10.00	17.48

Complete fixture includes

Edison key sockets	each,	$0.37
2¼-inch electric holders	"	.08
No. 9178½ electric shades	"	.07
No. 9178 gas globes	"	.75

⅞-inch casing on stem, extra lengthening per foot, not-wired, 45 cents; wired, 55 cents

COMBINATION FIXTURE

No. 9554. Brushed brass
Length, 36 inches over all; spread, 18 inches

		Not Wired.	Wired.	Complete as Shown Except Lamps.
2 gas,	2 electric	$ 7.00	$ 8.50	$10.16
3 "	3 "	9.00	11.00	13.49
4 "	4 "	11.00	13.50	16.82
5 "	5 "	13.00	16.00	20.15
6 "	6 "	15.00	18.50	23.48

Complete candle trimmings included in "not wired" and "wired" prices

Complete fixture includes

Edison key sockets.	each,	$0.37
2¼-inch electric holders.................................	"	.08
No. 5671½ C. R. I. electric shades......................	"	.38
No. 451 opal candles......................................	"	.10
No. 37 opal flat bobache..................................	"	.11
No. 1 brass candle cup and stem..........................		.25

⅝-inch casing on stem, extra lengthening per foot, not wired, 45 cents; wired, 55 cents

No. 9525. Rich gilt and satin
Length, 36 inches over all; spread, 22 inches

	Not Wired.	Wired.	Complete as Shown Except Lamps.
2 gas, 2 electric	$ 7.00	$ 8.50	$10.24
3 " 3 "	9.00	11.00	13.61
4 " 4 "	11.00	13.50	16.98

Complete candle trimmings included in "not wired" and
"wired" prices
Complete fixture includes

Edison key sockets...each,		$0.37
2¼-inch electric holders.....	"	.08
No. 451 opal candles	"	.10
No. 452 crystal bobache................................	"	.10
No. 1 brass candle cup and stem.........................	"	.25
No. 6566½ electric shades...............................	"	.42

⅜-inch casing on stem, extra lengthening per foot, not wired, 45 cents; wired, 55 cents

COMBINATION FIXTURE

No. 9556. Brushed brass
Length, 36 inches over all; spread, 18 inches

	Not wired.	Wired.	Complete as Shown Except Lamps.
2 gas, 2 electric	$ 6.50	$ 8.00	$10.90
3 " 3 "	8.00	10.00	14.35
4 " 4 "	9.50	12.00	17.80
5 " 5 "	11.00	14.00	21.25
6 " 6 "	12.50	16.00	24.70

Complete fixture includes

Edison key sockets	...each,	**$0.37**
3¼-inch electric holders	"	.13
No. 5671 C. R. I. gas globes	"	.45
No. 5817 3¼x6-inch balls	"	.50

⅝-inch casing on stem, extra lengthening per foot, not wired, 45 cents; wired, 55 cents

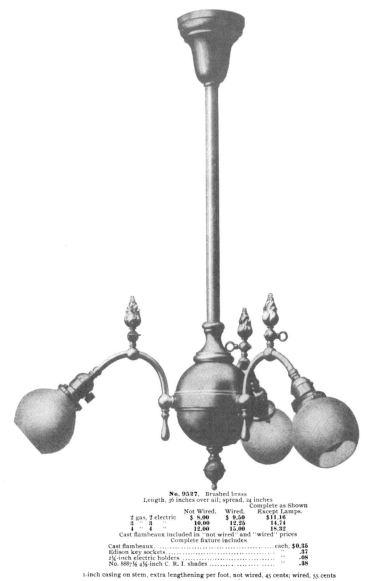

No. 9527. Brushed brass
Length, 36 inches over all; spread, 24 inches

	Not Wired.	Wired.	Complete as Shown Except Lamps.
2 gas, 2 electric	$ 8.00	$ 9.50	$11.16
3 " 3 "	10.00	12.25	14.74
4 " 4 "	12.00	15.00	18.32

Cast flambeaux included in "not wired" and "wired" prices
Complete fixture includes

Cast flambeaux.. each,	$0.35
Edison key sockets................................... "	.37
2¼-inch electric holders .... "	.08
No. 8887½ 4½-inch C. R. I. shades .... "	.38

1-inch casing on stem, extra lengthening per foot, not wired, 45 cents; wired, 55 cents

COMBINATION TUNGSTEN FIXTURE

No. 9528 Brushed brass
Length, 36 inches over all; spread, 20 inches

	Not Wired.	Wired.	Complete as Shown Except Lamps.
2 gas, 2 electric	$ 8.00	$ 9.50	$12.98
3 " 3 "	10.50	12.75	17.97
4 " 4 "	13.00	16.00	22.96
5 " 5 "	15.50	19.25	27.95
6 " 6 "	18.00	22.50	32.94

Cast flambeaux included in "not wired" and "wired" prices
Complete fixture includes

Cast flambeaux	each,	**$0.35**
Edison keyless sockets	"	.34
Form H holders	"	.20
No. 106130 holophane shades	"	1.20

⅜-inch extra lengthening per foot, not wired, 45 cents; wired, 55 cents

No. 9529. Holophane Reflector

Length, 42 inches over all; spread, 24 inches

	Not Wired.	Wired Complete as Shown Except Lamps.
2 gas, 6 electric	$18.00	$19.00
4 " 6 "	21.00	22.00

Emergency gas tips, holophane glassware and 6-light Benjamin cluster included in "not wired" and "wired" prices

Complete fixture includes

No. 2683 holophane electric shades........................each, $0.60
No. 2522 4x16-inch holophane reflector.................... " 4.00

COMBINATION FIXTURE

No. 9557. Brushed brass
Length, 36 inches over all; spread, 22 inches

	Not Wired.	Wired.	Complete as Shown Except Lamps.
2 gas, 2 electric	$10.00	$12.00	$13.80
4 " 4 "	14.00	16.00	19.60

Complete candle trimmings included in "not wired" and "wired" prices

Complete fixture includes

Edison key sockets	each,	$0.37
2¼-inch electric holders	"	.08
No. 94 C. R. I. electric shades	"	.45
No. 40 opal square candles	"	.13
No. 5 brass candle cup and stem	"	.25

1-inch casing on stem, extra lengthening per foot, not wired, 75 cents; wired, 85 cents

No. 8723. Brushed brass

Length, 36 inches over all; spread, 36 inches

	Not Wired.	Wired.	Complete as Shown Except Lamps.
2 gas, 2 electric	$13.50	$14.50	$16.30
4 " 4 "	17.50	19.50	23.10

Complete candle trimmings included in "not wired" and "wired" prices

Complete fixture includes

Edison key sockets	each,	$0.37
2¼-inch electric holders	"	.08
No. 9321½ C. R. I. electric shades	"	.45
No. 40 opal square candles	"	.13
No. 41 opal square bobache	"	.13
No. 5 brass candle cup and stem	"	.25

1-inch casing on stem, extra lengthening per foot, not wired, 75 cents; wired, 85 cents

COMBINATION FIXTURE

NOTE

If you do not specify color of art glass when ordering we will ship shades color **K** art glass. For colors of art glass see color plates 486-487.

No. 9531. Brushed brass

Length, 36 inches over all; spread, 20 inches

	Not Wired.	Wired.	Complete as Shown Except Lamps.
2 gas, 2 electric	**$22.00**	**$23.50**	**$24.82**
4 " 4 "	**38.00**	**41.00**	**43.64**

Complete candle trimmings and art glass shades, color **K** glass, included in "not wired" and "wired" prices

For colors of art glass see color plates 486-487

Complete fixture includes

No. 40 opal square candles		each,	**$0.13**
No. 41 opal square bobache		"	**.13**
No. 5 brass candle cup and stem		"	**.25**
No. 15152 square shade with art glass panels, color K glass		"	**3.50**
Hubbell pull sockets		"	**.66**

COMBINATION FIXTURE

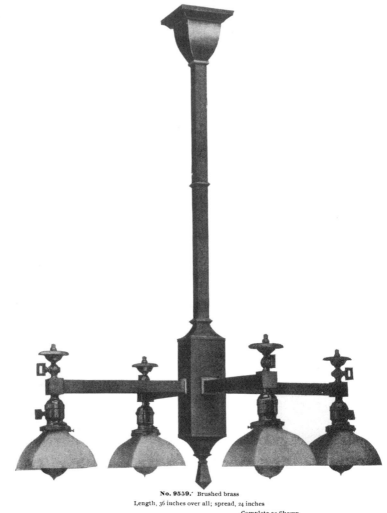

No. 9559. Brushed brass

Length, 36 inches over all; spread, 24 inches

	Not Wired.	Wired.	Complete as Shown Except Lamps.
2 gas, 2 electric	$15.50	$17.00	$19.04
4 " 4 "	19.00	22.00	26.08

Emergency cups and burners included in "not wired" and "wired" prices

Complete fixture includes

Edison key sockets	each,	$0.37
2¼-inch electric holders	"	.08
No. 258 C. R. I. electric shades	"	.57

1-inch casing on stem, extra lengthening per foot, not wired, 75 cents; wired, 85 cents

COMBINATION FIXTURE

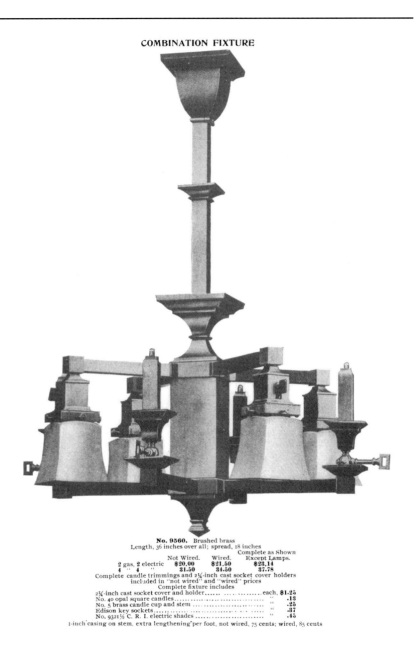

No. 9560. Brushed brass
Length, 36 inches over all; spread, 18 inches

	Not Wired.	Wired.	Complete as Shown Except Lamps.
2 gas, 2 electric	$20.00	$21.50	$23.14
4 " 4 "	31.50	34.50	37.78

Complete candle trimmings and 2¼-inch cast socket cover holders
included in "not wired" and "wired" prices
Complete fixture includes

2¼-inch cast socket cover and holder...... ....each,		$1.25
No. 40 opal square candles..............................	"	.13
No. 5 brass candle cup and stem	"	.25
Edison key sockets......................	"	.37
No. 9321½ C. R. I. electric shades	"	.45

1-inch casing on stem, extra lengthening per foot, not wired, 75 cents; wired, 85 cents

COMBINATION FIXTURES

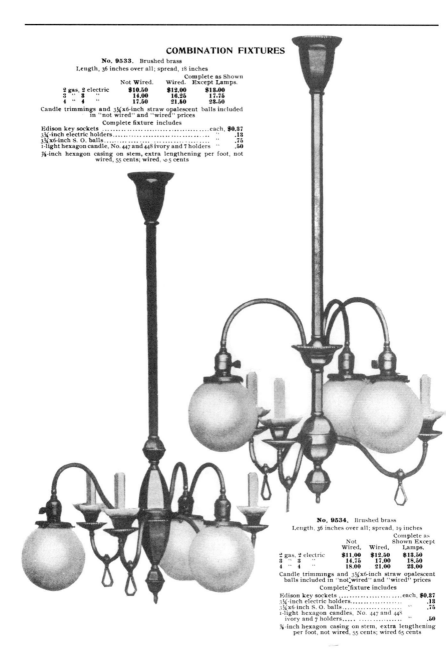

No. 9533. Brushed brass

Length, 36 inches over all; spread, 18 inches

	Not Wired.	Wired.	Complete as Shown Except Lamps.
2 gas, 2 electric	**$10.50**	**$12.00**	**$13.00**
3 " 3 "	14.00	16.25	17.75
4 " 4 "	17.50	21.50	23.50

Candle trimmings and 3¼x6-inch straw opalescent balls included in "not wired" and "wired" prices

Complete fixture includes

Edison key sockets ....each,	**$0.37**
3¼-inch electric holders............................... "	.13
3¼x6-inch S. O. balls................................. "	.75
1-light hexagon candle, No. 447 and 448 ivory and 7 holders "	.50

⅞-inch hexagon casing on stem, extra lengthening per foot, not wired, 55 cents; wired, 65 cents

No. 9534. Brushed brass

Length, 36 inches over all; spread, 19 inches

	Not Wired.	Wired.	Complete as Shown Except Lamps.
2 gas, 2 electric	**$11.00**	**$12.50**	**$13.50**
3 " 3 "	14.75	17.00	18.50
4 " 4 "	18.00	21.00	23.00

Candle trimmings and 3¼x6-inch straw opalescent balls included in "not wired" and "wired" prices

Complete fixture includes

Edison key sockets ....each,	**$0.37**
3¼-inch electric holders.................. "	.13
3¼x6-inch S. O. balls.................... "	.75
1-light hexagon candles, No. 447 and 448 ivory and 7 holders, "	.50

⅞-inch hexagon casing on stem, extra lengthening per foot, not wired, 55 cents; wired 65 cents

COMBINATION FIXTURE

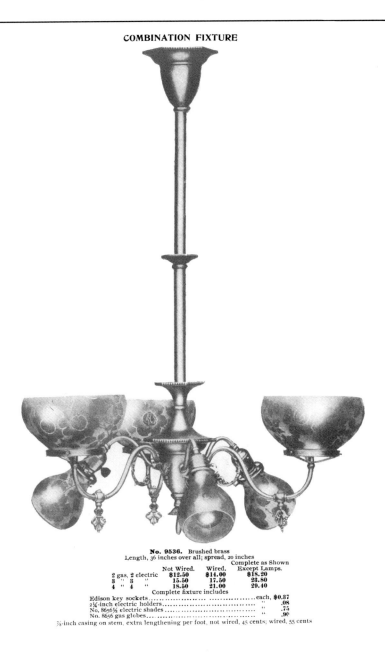

No. 9536. Brushed brass
Length, 36 inches over all; spread, 20 inches

	Not Wired.	Wired.	Complete as Shown Except Lamps.
2 gas, 2 electric	$12.50	$14.00	$18.20
3 " 3 "	15.50	17.50	23.80
4 " 4 "	18.50	21.00	29.40

Complete fixture includes

Edison key sockets	each, $0.37
2¼-inch electric holders	" .08
No. 8656½ electric shades	" .75
No. 8656 gas globes	" .90

⅞-inch casing on stem, extra lengthening per foot, not wired, 45 cents; wired, 55 cents

COMBINATION FIXTURES

No. 9538. Brushed brass

Length, 36 inches over all; spread, 18 inches

	Not Wired.	Wired.	Complete as Shown Except Lamps.
2 gas, 2 electric	**$30.00**	**$31.50**	**$32.50**
3 " 3 "	**36.00**	**38.00**	**39.50**

Candle trimmings and No. 657 S, 7-inch stalactites included in "not wired" and "wired" prices

Complete fixture includes

Edison key sockets	each,	**$0.37**
3¼-inch electric holders	"	.12
No. 657 S, 7-inch silver etched and cut stalactite	"	1.65
No. 451 opal candles	"	.10
No. 37 opal flat bobaches	"	.11

⅝-inch casing on stem, extra lengthening per foot, not wired, 45 cents; wired, 55 cents

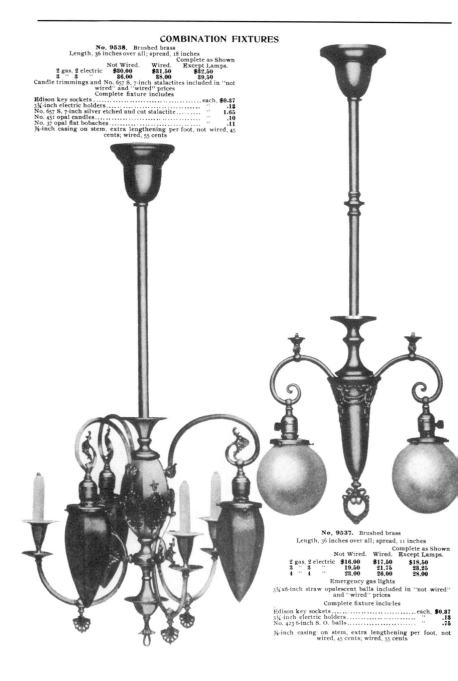

No. 9537. Brushed brass

Length, 36 inches over all; spread, 11 inches

	Not Wired.	Wired.	Complete as Shown Except Lamps.
2 gas, 2 electric	**$16.00**	**$17.50**	**$18.50**
3 " 3 "	**19.50**	**21.75**	**23.25**
4 " 4 "	**23.00**	**26.00**	**28.00**

Emergency gas lights

3¼ x6-inch straw opalescent balls included in "not wired" and "wired" prices

Complete fixture includes

Edison key sockets	each,	**$0.37**
3¼-inch electric holders	"	.12
No. 423 6-inch S. O. balls	"	.75

⅝-inch casing on stem, extra lengthening per foot, not wired, 45 cents; wired, 55 cents

COMBINATION FIXTURE

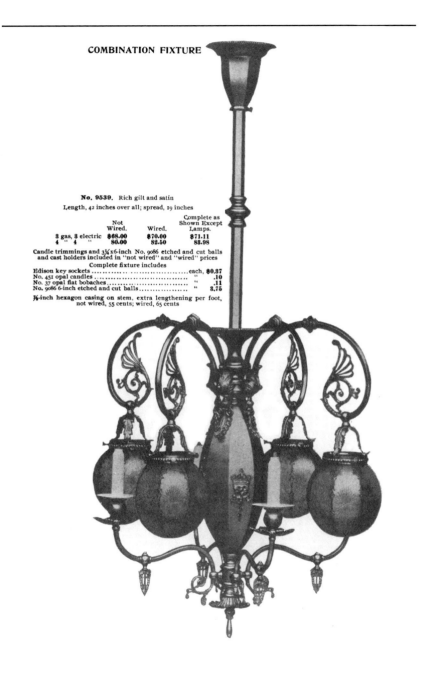

No. 9539. Rich gilt and satin

Length, 42 inches over all; spread, 19 inches

	Not Wired.	Wired.	Complete as Shown Except Lamps.
3 gas, 3 electric	$68.00	$70.00	$71.11
4 " 4 "	80.00	82.50	83.98

Candle trimmings and 3¼x6-inch No. 9086 etched and cut balls and cast holders included in "not wired" and "wired" prices

Complete fixture includes

Edison key sockets	each,	$0.37
No. 451 opal candles	"	.10
No. 37 opal flat bobaches	"	.11
No. 9086 6-inch etched and cut balls	"	3.75

⅞-inch hexagon casing on stem, extra lengthening per foot, not wired, 55 cents; wired, 65 cents

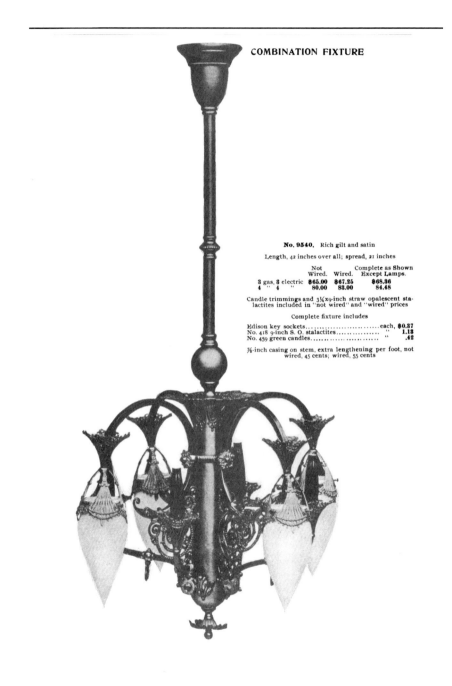

No. 9540. Rich gilt and satin

Length, 42 inches over all; spread, 21 inches

	Not Wired.	Wired.	Complete as Shown Except Lamps.
3 gas, 3 electric	$65.00	$67.25	$68.36
4 " 4 "	80.00	83.00	84.48

Candle trimmings and 3½x9-inch straw opalescent stalactites included in "not wired" and "wired" prices

Complete fixture includes

Edison key sockets.........................each, $0.37
No. 418 9-inch S. O. stalactites............... " 1.13
No. 459 green candles....................... " .42

¾-inch casing on stem, extra lengthening per foot, not
wired, 45 cents; wired, 55 cents

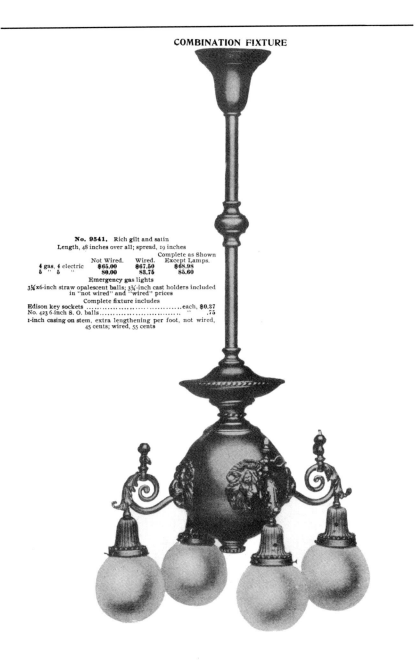

No. 9541. Rich gilt and satin

Length, 48 inches over all; spread, 19 inches

	Not Wired.	Wired.	Complete as Shown Except Lamps.
4 gas, 4 electric	$65.00	$67.50	$65.98
5 " 5 "	80.00	83.75	85.60

Emergency gas lights

3¼x6-inch straw opalescent balls; 3¼-inch cast holders included in "not wired" and "wired" prices

Complete fixture includes

Edison key sockets ....each, $0.37

No. 423 6-inch S. O. balls.............................   "   .75

1-inch casing on stem, extra lengthening per foot, not wired, 45 cents; wired, 55 cents

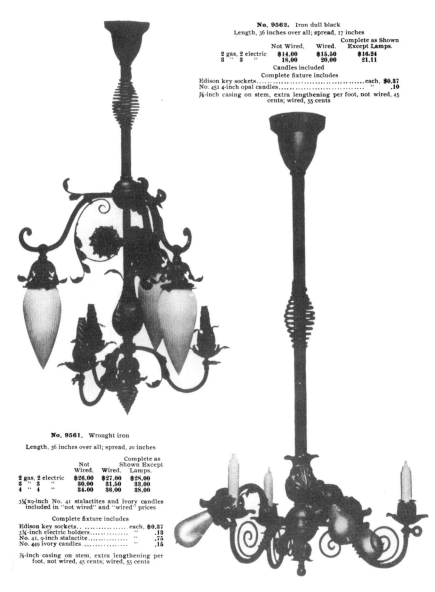

No. 9562. Iron dull black

Length, 36 inches over all; spread, 17 inches

	Not Wired.	Wired.	Complete as Shown Except Lamps.
2 gas, 2 electric	$14.00	$15.50	$16.24
3 " 3 "	18.00	20.00	21.11

Candles included

Complete fixture includes

Edison key sockets......................................each, $0.37
No. 451 4-inch opal candles................................ " .10

⅞-inch casing on stem, extra lengthening per foot, not wired, 45 cents; wired, 55 cents

No. 9561. Wrought iron

Length, 36 inches over all; spread, 20 inches

	Not Wired.	Wired.	Complete as Shown Except Lamps.
2 gas, 2 electric	$26.00	$27.00	$28.00
3 " 3 "	30.00	31.50	33.00
4 " 4 "	34.00	36.00	38.00

3¼x9-inch No. 41 stalactites and ivory candles included in "not wired" and "wired" prices

Complete fixture includes

Edison key sockets.. ....each, $0.37
3¾-inch electric holders.............. " .13
No. 41, 9-inch stalactite............... " .75
No. 449 ivory candles .... " .15

⅞-inch casing on stem, extra lengthening per foot, not wired, 45 cents; wired, 55 cents

WROUGHT IRON COMBINATON FIXTURES

No. 9563. Iron, dull black

Length, 36 inches over all; spread, 15 inches

	Not Wired.	Wired.	Complete as Shown Except Lamps.
3 gas, 3 electric	**$35.00**	**$37.00**	**$38.11**

Complete candle trimmings and 3¼x6-inch No. 5817 crystal roughed inside balls included in "not wired" and "wired" prices

Complete fixture includes

Edison key sockets	each,	$0.37
No. 5817 6-inch C. R. I. balls	"	.50
No. 451 opal candles	"	.10

¾-inch casing on stem, extra lengthening per foot, not wired. 45 cents; wired, 55 cents

No. 9564. Iron, dull black

Length, 42 inches over all; spread, 16½ inches

	Not Wired.	Wired.	Complete as Shown Except Lamps.
2 gas, 3 electric	**$18.00**	**$20.00**	**$21.08**
3 " 4 "	**22.50**	**25.00**	**26.45**

One electric inside bottom ball, complete candle trimmings and 3¼x8-inch No. 5817 crystal roughed inside ball included in "not wired" and "wired" prices.

Complete fixture includes

Edison key sockets (on arms)	each,	$0.37
Edison keyless sockets (in balls)	"	.84
No. 5817 3½x8-inch C. R. I. ball	"	.75
No. 451 opal candle	"	.10

¾-inch casing on stem, extra lengthening per foot, not wired, 45 cents; wired, 55 cents

No. 9564

No. 9563

WROUGHT IRON COMBINATION FIXTURES

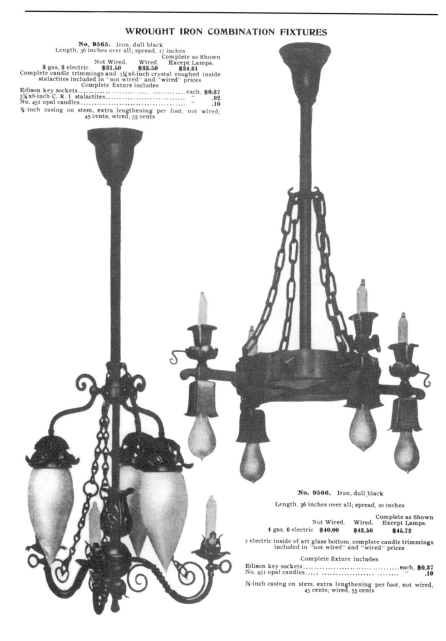

No. 9565. Iron, dull black
Length, 36 inches over all; spread, 17 inches

	Not Wired.	Wired.	Complete as Shown Except Lamps.
3 gas, 3 electric	$31.50	$33.50	$34.61

Complete candle trimmings and 3¼x8-inch crystal roughed inside
stalactites included in "not wired" and "wired" prices

Complete fixture includes

Edison key sockets......................... ....each,	$0.37
3¼x8-inch C. R. I. stalactites............................ "	.92
No. 451 opal candles...................................... "	.10

⅝-inch casing on stem, extra lengthening per foot, not wired,
45 cents; wired, 55 cents

No. 9566. Iron, dull black

Length, 36 inches over all; spread, 20 inches

	Not Wired.	Wired.	Complete as Shown Except Lamps.
4 gas, 6 electric	$40.00	$43.50	$45.72

2 electric inside of art glass bottom, complete candle trimmings
included in "not wired" and "wired" prices

Complete fixture includes

Edison key sockets...................................each,	$0.37
No. 451 opal candles..... .... "	.10

⅞-inch casing on stem, extra lengthening per foot, not wired,
45 cents; wired, 55 cents

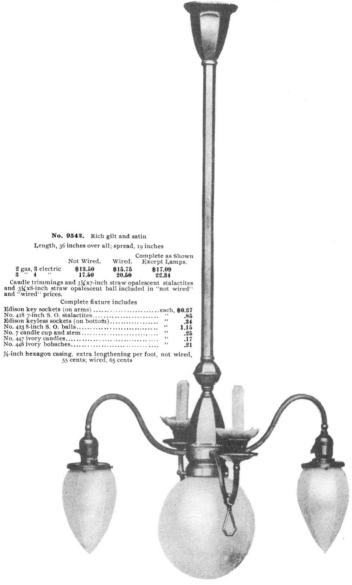

No. 9542. Rich gilt and satin

Length, 36 inches over all; spread, 19 inches

	Not Wired.	Wired.	Complete as Shown Except Lamps.
2 gas, 3 electric	$13.50	$15.75	$17.09
3 " 4 "	17.50	20.50	22.34

Candle trimmings and 3¼x7-inch straw opalescent stalactites and 3¼x8-inch straw opalescent ball included in "not wired" and "wired" prices.

Complete fixture includes

Edison key sockets (on arms)	each,	$0.37
No. 418 7-inch S. O. stalactites	"	.85
Edison keyless sockets (on bottom)	"	.34
No. 423 8-inch S. O. balls	"	1.15
No. 7 candle cup and stem	"	.25
No. 447 ivory candles	"	.17
No. 448 ivory bobaches	"	.21

⅞-inch hexagon casing, extra lengthening per foot, not wired, 55 cents; wired, 65 cents

COMBINATION DOME FIXTURE

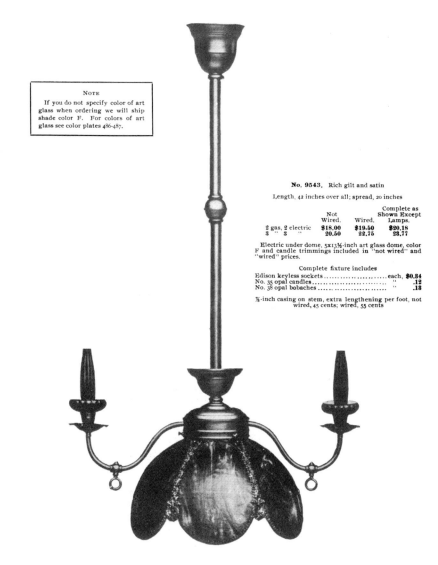

No. 9543. Rich gilt and satin

Length, 42 inches over all; spread, 20 inches

	Not Wired.	Wired.	Complete as Shown Except Lamps.
2 gas, 2 electric	$18.00	$19.50	$20.18
3 " 3 "	20.50	22.75	23.77

Electric under dome, 5x13½-inch art glass dome, color F and candle trimmings included in "not wired" and "wired" prices.

Complete fixture includes

Edison keyless sockets.........................each,	$0.34
No. 35 opal candles........................... "	.12
No. 38 opal bobaches......................... "	.13

⅝-inch casing on stem, extra lengthening per foot, not wired, 45 cents; wired, 55 cents

178

COMBINATION DOME FIXTURE

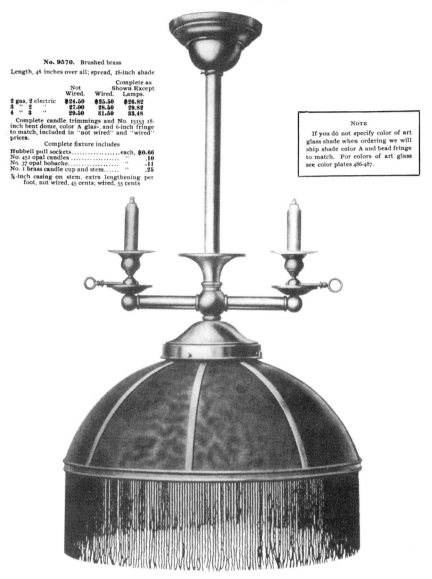

No. 9570. Brushed brass

Length, 48 inches over all; spread, 18-inch shade

	Not Wired.	Wired.	Complete as Shown Except Lamps.
2 gas, 2 electric	$24.50	$25.50	$26.82
3 " 2 "	27.00	28.50	29.82
4 " 3 "	29.50	31.50	33.48

Complete candle trimmings and No. 15153 18-inch bent dome, color A glass, and 6-inch fringe to match, included in "not wired" and "wired" prices.

Complete fixture includes

Hubbell pull sockets..................each,	$0.66
No. 451 opal candles .... "	.10
No. 37 opal bobache................. "	.11
No. 1 brass candle cup and stem...... "	.25

⅝-inch casing on stem, extra lengthening per foot, not wired, 45 cents; wired, 55 cents

NOTE

If you do not specify color of art glass shade when ordering we will ship shade color A and bead fringe to match. For colors of art glass see color plates 486-487.

179

COMBINATION DOME FIXTURE

NOTE

If you do not specify color of art glass when ordering we will ship shade, color A, and bead fringe to match. For colors of art glass see color plates 486-487.

No. 9567. Brushed brass
Length, 42 inches over all; spread, 18-inch shade

	Not Wired.	Wired.	Complete as Shown Except Lamps.
2 gas. 2 electric	**$23.50**	**$25.00**	**$25.74**

Complete candle trimmings and No. 15154 4x18-inch art glass shade, color A glass, and 4-inch bead fringe included in "not wired" and "wired" prices.

Complete fixture includes

Edison key sockets	each,	**$0.37**
No. 40 opal square candles	"	.13
No. 41 opal square bobache	"	.13
No. 5 candle, stem and holders	"	.25
No. 15154 shade and fringe only	"	14.00
No. 15154 16-inch shade	"	12.00
No. 15154 14-inch shade	"	10.00

1-inch casing on stem, extra lengthening per foot, not wired, 75 cents; wired, 85 cents

180

COMBINATION DOME FIXTURE

No. 9545. Brushed brass
Length, 48 inches over all; gas spread, 10 inches

	Not Wired.	Wired.	Complete as Shown Except Lamps.
2 gas, 2 electric	**$36.50**	**$38.00**	**$39.32**

Complete candle trimmings and No. 15156 20-inch square art shade with grape border design included in "not wired" and "wired" prices.

Complete fixture includes

Hubbell pull sockets	each,	$0.66
No. 40 opal candles	"	.13
No. 41 opal bobache	"	.13
No. 5 brass cup and stem	"	.25
No. 15156 art shade only	"	27.00

1-inch casing on stem, extra lengthening per foot, not wired, 75 cents; wired 85 cents

181

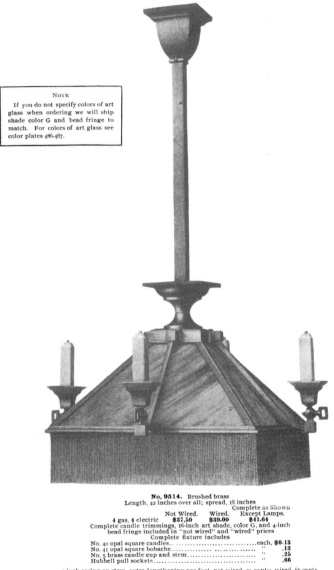

NOTE

If you do not specify colors of art glass when ordering we will ship shade color G and bead fringe to match. For colors of art glass see color plates 486-487.

No. 9514. Brushed brass
Length, 42 inches over all; spread, 18 inches

Complete as Shown

	Not Wired.	Wired.	Except Lamps.
4 gas, 4 electric	**$37.50**	**$39.00**	**$41.64**

Complete candle trimmings, 16-inch art shade, color G, and 4-inch bead fringe included in "not wired" and "wired" prices

Complete fixture includes

No. 40 opal square candles..	each,	**$0.13**
No. 41 opal square bobache	"	**.13**
No. 5 brass candle cup and stem	"	**.25**
Hubbell pull sockets	"	**.66**

1-inch casing on stem, extra lengthening per foot, not wired, 75 cents; wired, 85 cents

182

COMBINATION DOME FIXTURE
(Patented Combination Chain)

NOTE

If you do not specify color of art glass when ordering we will ship body of shade color K; leaves, color A, and bunches of grapes color B. For colors of art glass see color plates 486-487.

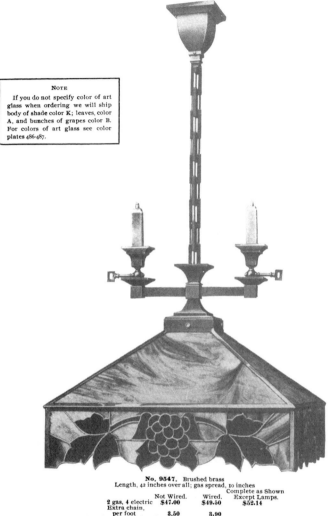

No. 9547. Brushed brass
Length, 42 inches over all; gas spread, 10 inches

	Not Wired.	Wired.	Complete as Shown Except Lamps.
2 gas, 4 electric	**$47.00**	**$49.50**	**$52.14**
Extra chain, per foot	**3.50**	**3.90**	

Complete candle trimmings and No. 15156 art glass shade with grape border included in "not wired" and "wired" prices

Complete fixture includes

Hubbell pull sockets	each, $	0.66
No. 40 opal candles	"	.13
No. 41 opal bobache	"	.13
No. 5 brass candle cup and stem	"	.25
No. 15156 20-inch art glass shade only	"	27.00

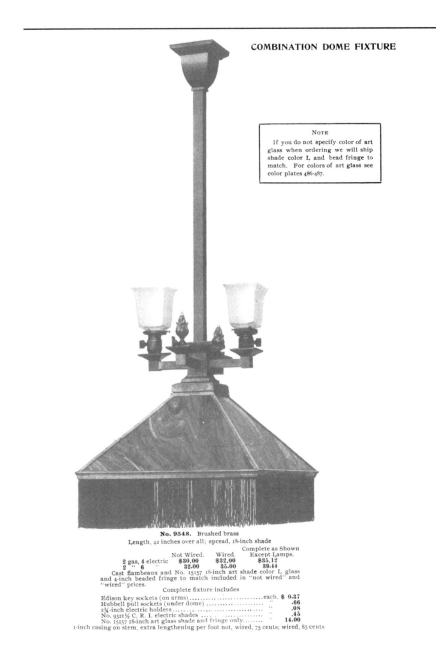

NOTE

If you do not specify color of art glass when ordering we will ship shade color L and bead fringe to match. For colors of art glass see color plates 486-487.

No. 9548. Brushed brass

Length, 42 inches over all; spread, 18-inch shade

	Not Wired.	Wired.	Complete as Shown Except Lamps.
2 gas, 4 electric	$30.00	$32.00	$35.12
2 " 6 "	32.00	35.00	39.44

Cast flambeaux and No. 15157 18-inch art shade color L glass and 4-inch beaded fringe to match included in "not wired" and "wired" prices.

Complete fixture includes

Edison key sockets (on arms) ....each,	$	0.37
Hubbell pull sockets (under dome)	"	.66
2¼-inch electric holders	"	.08
No. 9321½ C, R. I. electric shades	"	.45
No. 15157 18-inch art glass shade and fringe only........	"	14.00

1-inch casing on stem, extra lengthening per foot not, wired, 75 cents; wired, 85 cents

COMBINATION DOME FIXTURE

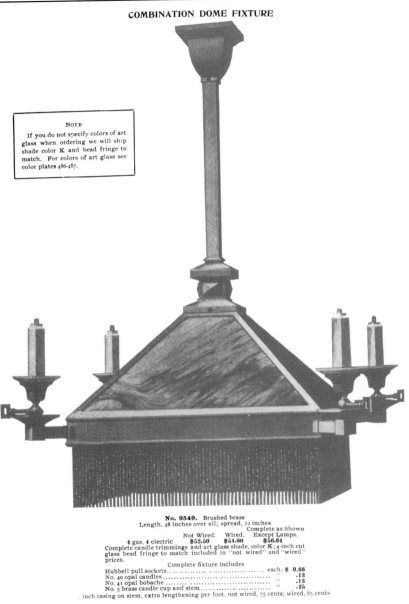

NOTE

If you do not specify colors of art glass when ordering we will ship shade color K and bead fringe to match. For colors of art glass see color plates 486-487.

No. 9549. Brushed brass
Length, 48 inches over all; spread, 22 inches

	Not Wired.	Wired.	Complete as Shown Except Lamps.
4 gas, 4 electric	**$52.50**	**$54.00**	**$56.64**

Complete candle trimmings and art glass shade, color K; 4-inch cut glass bead fringe to match included in "not wired" and "wired" prices.

Complete fixture includes

Hubbell pull sockets............	each.	$ 0.66
No. 40 opal candles............	"	.13
No. 41 opal bobache	"	.13
No. 5 brass candle cup and stem............	"	.25

. inch casing on stem, extra lengthening per foot, not wired, 75 cents; wired, 85 cents

185

COMBINATION DOME FIXTURE

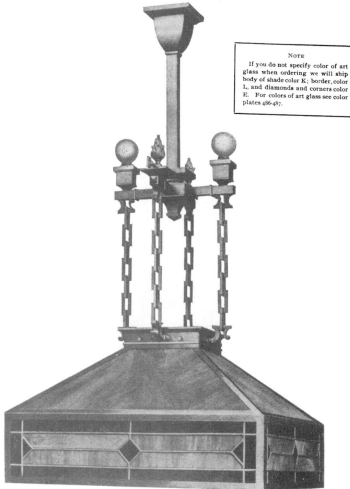

No. 9568. Brushed brass
Length, 42 inches over all; shade, 22 inches wide

	Not Wired.	Wired.	Complete as Shown Except Lamps.
2 gas, 6 electric	$61.50	$65.00	$68.32

Cast flambeaux, socket covers and 22-inch square art shade included
Color K body, color L, border and color E diamonds
Complete fixture includes

Hubbell pull sockets (under dome).............. ....each,	$0.66
Edison keyless sockets (on arms)...................... "	.84
Cast flambeaux.. "	.85

COMBINATION DOME FIXTURE

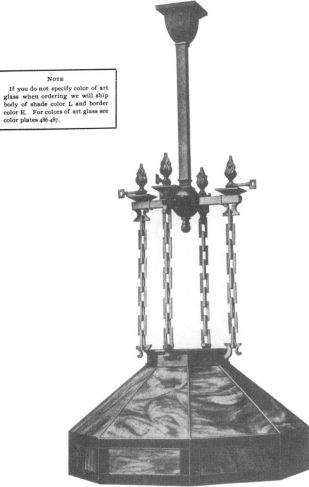

NOTE

If you do not specify color of art glass when ordering we will ship body of shade color L and border color E. For colors of art glass see color plates 486-487.

No. 9550. Brushed brass

Length, 48 inches over all; spread, 24 inches

	Not Wired.	Wired.	Complete as Shown Except Lamps.
4 gas, 4 electric	$67.50	$70.00	$72.64

Cast flambeaux and 22-inch art dome shade included in "not wired" and "wired" prices

Complete fixture includes

Hubbell pull sockets.....................................each, $0.66
Cast flambeaux .... " .35

1-inch casing on stem, extra lengthening per foot, not wired, 75 cents; wired, 85 cents

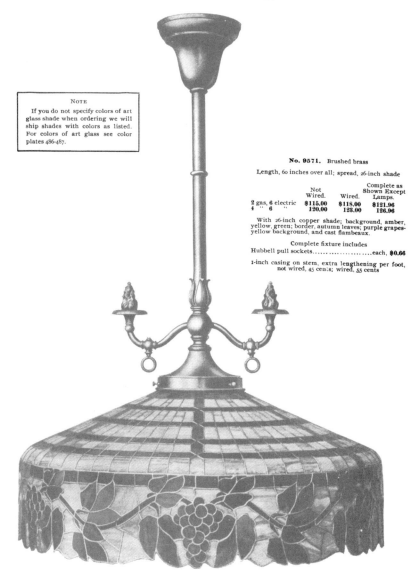

No. 9571. Brushed brass

Length, 60 inches over all; spread, 26-inch shade

	Not Wired.	Wired.	Complete as Shown Except Lamps.
2 gas, 6 electric	$115.00	$118.00	$121.96
4 " 6 "	120.00	123.00	126.96

With 26-inch copper shade; background, amber, yellow, green; border, autumn leaves; purple grapes-yellow background, and cast flambeaux.

Complete fixture includes

Hubbell pull sockets.....................each, **$0.66**

1-inch casing on stem, extra lengthening per foot, not wired, 45 cents; wired, 55 cents

COMBINATION DOME FIXTURE

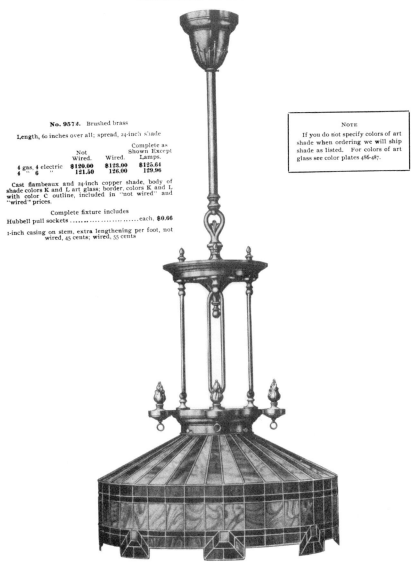

No. 9572. Brushed brass

Length, 60 inches over all; spread, 24-inch shade

	Not Wired.	Wired.	Complete as Shown Except Lamps.
4 gas, 4 electric	**$120.00**	**$123.00**	**$125.64**
4 " 6 "	121.50	126.00	129.96

Cast flambeaux and 24-inch copper shade, body of shade colors K and L art glass; border, colors K and L with color C outline, included in "not wired" and "wired" prices.

Complete fixture includes

Hubbell pull sockets ....each, $0.66

1-inch casing on stem, extra lengthening per foot, not wired, 45 cents; wired, 55 cents

STORE PENDANTS

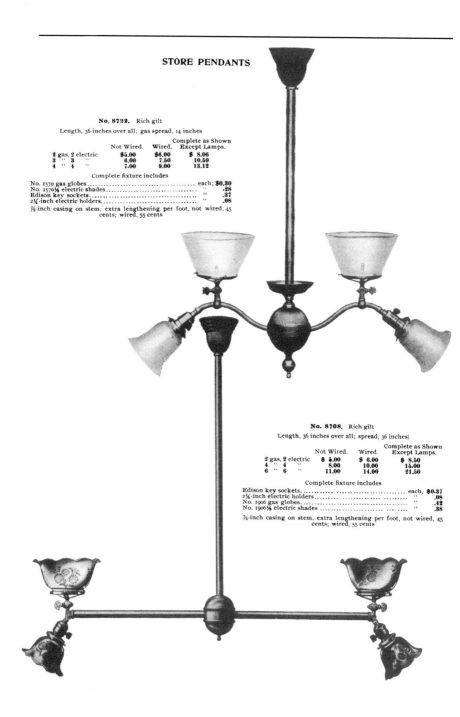

No. 8722. Rich gilt

Length, 36 inches over all; gas spread, 14 inches

	Not Wired.	Wired.	Complete as Shown Except Lamps.
2 gas, 2 electric	$5.00	$6.00	$ 8.06
3 " 3 "	6.00	7.50	10.59
4 " 4 "	7.00	9.00	13.12

Complete fixture includes

No. 1570 gas globes...................................	each;	$0.30
No. 1570½ electric shades.........................	"	.28
Edison key sockets.................................	"	.37
2¼-inch electric holders...........................	"	.08

⅞-inch casing on stem, extra lengthening per foot, not wired, 45 cents; wired, 55 cents

No. 8708. Rich gilt

Length, 36 inches over all; spread, 36 inches|

	Not Wired.	Wired.	Complete as Shown Except Lamps.
2 gas, 2 electric	$ 5.00	$ 6.00	$ 8.50
4 " 4 "	8.00	10.00	15.00
6 " 6 "	11.00	14.00	21.50

Complete fixture includes

Edison key sockets............................	each,	$0.37
2¼-inch electric holders.......................	"	.08
No. 1906 gas globes...........................	"	.42
No. 1906½ electric shades.....................	"	.38

⅞-inch casing on stem, extra lengthening per foot, not wired, 45 cents; wired, 55 cents

TUNGSTEN COMBINATION FIXTURE

No. 8717. Rich gilt

Length, 36 inches over all; spread, 25 inches

	Not Wired.	Wired.	Complete as Shown Except Lamps.
2 gas, 2 electric	$6.50	$ 8.00	$12.82
3 " 3 "	8.00	10.25	16.78
4 " 4 "	9.50	12.50	21.14

Complete fixture includes

Edison keyless sockets.................................each,	$0.34
Form H holders.................................... "	.20
No. 6060 holophane shades....................... "	1.62

¾-inch casing on stem, extra lengthening per foot, not wired, 45 cents; wired, 55 cents

No. 8718. Brushed brass
Length, 36 inches over all; spread, 24 inches

	Not Wired.	Wired.	Complete as Shown Except Lamps.
2 gas, 2 electric	$10.00	$11.50	$14.98
3 " 3 "	12.50	14.75	19.97
4 " 4 "	15.00	18.00	24.96
5 " 5 "	17.50	21.25	29.95

Cast flambeaux and plates included in "not wired" and "wired" prices

Complete fixture includes

Edison keyless sockets ....each, $0.34
Form H holders .... " .20
No. 106130 holophane shades .... " 1.20

1-inch casing on stem, extra lengthening per foot, not wired, 45 cents; wired, 55 cents

No. 8721. Brushed brass
Length, 42 inches over all; spread, 24 inches

	Not Wired.	Wired.	Complete as Shown Except Lamps.
2 gas, 3 electric	$20.00	$22.25	$28.36
4 " 5 "	28.50	32.25	34.10

Complete candle trimmings, 3¾x6-inch C. R. I. balls and cast socket cover holders included in "not wired" and "wired" prices

Complete fixture includes

Edison key sockets	each,	$0.37
No. 5817 6-inch C. R. I. balls	"	.50
No. 40 opal square candles	"	.13
No. 41 opal square bobache	"	.13
No. 5 brass candle cup and stem	"	.25
3¾-inch cast socket cover holders	"	1.50

1-inch casing on stem, extra lengthening per foot, not wired, 75 cents; wired, 85 cents

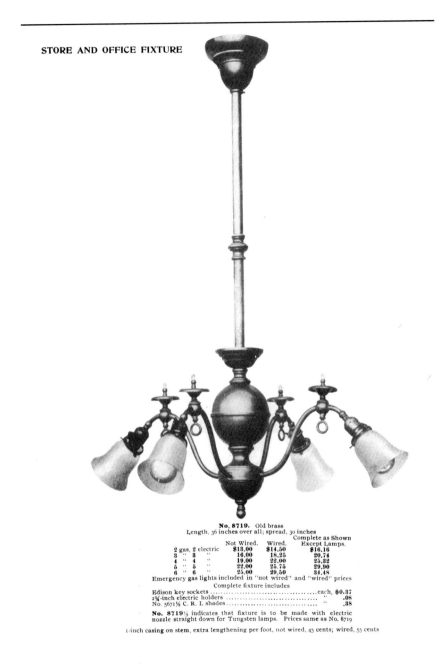

No. 8719. Old brass
Length, 36 inches over all; spread, 30 inches

		Not Wired.	Wired.	Complete as Shown Except Lamps.
2 gas,	2 electric	$13.00	$14.50	$16.16
3 "	3 "	16.00	18.25	20.74
4 "	4 "	19.00	22.00	25.32
5 "	5 "	22.00	25.75	29.90
6 "	6 "	25.00	29.50	34.48

Emergency gas lights included in "not wired" and "wired" prices

Complete fixture includes

Edison key sockets	each,	$0.37
2¼-inch electric holders	"	.08
No. 5671½ C. R. I. shades	"	.38

No. 8719½ indicates that fixture is to be made with electric nozzle straight down for Tungsten lamps. Prices same as No. 8719

1-inch casing on stem, extra lengthening per foot, not wired, 45 cents; wired, 55 cents

No. 8720. Old brass

Length, 42 inches over all; spread, 36 inches

	Not Wired.	Wired.	Complete as Shown Except Lamps.
2 gas, 2 electric	$14.00	$15.50	$17.16
3 " 3 "	16.50	18.75	21.24
4 " 4 "	19.00	22.00	25.32
5 " 5 "	21.50	25.25	29.40
6 " 6 "	24.00	28.50	33.48

Emergency gas lights included in "not wired" and "wired" prices

Complete fixture includes

Edison key sockets...each, **$0.37**

2¼-inch electric holders.................................. " .08

No. 5671½ C. R. I. shades................................ " .38

No. 8720½ indicates that fixture is to be made with electric nozzle straight down for Tungsten lamps. Prices same as No. 8720

1-inch casing on stem, extra lengthening per foot, not wired, 45 cents; wired, 55 cents

195

COMBINATION GAS AND ELECTRIC 1-LIGHT PENDANTS

No. 8879. Rich gilt
Length, 36 inches over all; spread, 14 inches

	Not Wired.	Wired.	Complete as Shown Except Lamp.
1 gas, 1 electric	$3.25	$4.00	$4.79

Complete candle trimmings included in "not wired" and "wired" prices

Complete fixture includes

Edison key sockets	each,	$0.37
2¼-inch electric holders	"	.08
No. 2956½ electric shades	"	.34
No. 451 opal candle	"	.10
No. 452 crystal bobache	"	.10
No. 1 brass candle cup and stem	"	.25

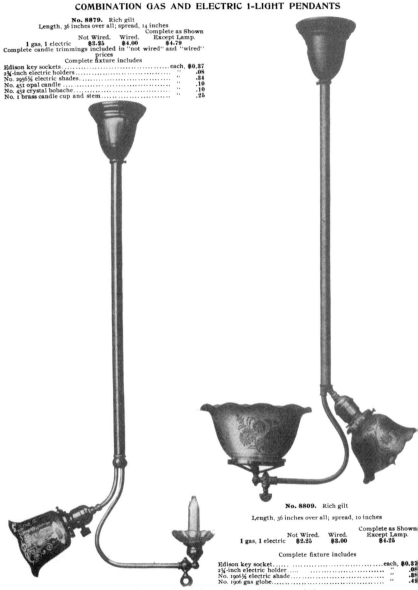

No. 8809. Rich gilt

Length, 36 inches over all; spread, 10 inches

	Not Wired.	Wired.	Complete as Shown Except Lamp.
1 gas, 1 electric	$2.25	$3.00	$4.25

Complete fixture includes

Edison key socket	each,	$0.37
2¼-inch electric holder	"	.08
No. 1906½ electric shade	"	.85
No. 1906 gas globe	"	.45

¼-inch casing on stem, extra lengthening per foot, not wired, 40 cents; wired, 50 cents

196

COMBINATION GAS AND ELECTRIC 1-LIGHT PENDANTS

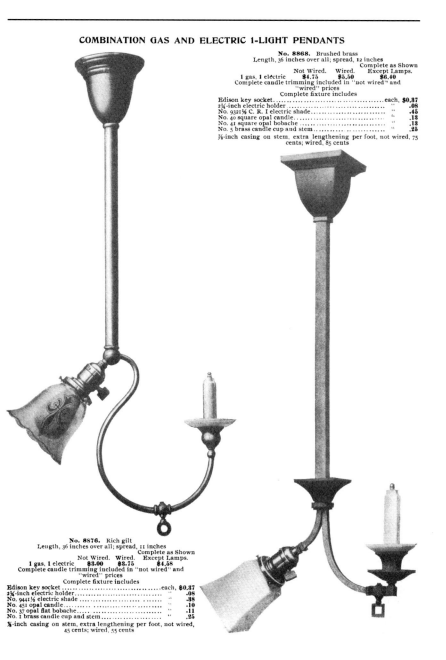

No. 8868. Brushed brass
Length, 36 inches over all; spread, 12 inches

	Not Wired.	Wired.	Complete as Shown Except Lamps.
1 gas, 1 electric	$4.75	$5.50	$6.40

Complete candle trimming included in "not wired" and
"wired" prices
Complete fixture includes

Edison key socket......................................each,	$0.37
2¼-inch electric holder .... "	.08
No. 9321½ C. R. I electric shade........................ "	.45
No. 40 square opal candle................................ "	.13
No. 41 square opal bobache.............................. "	.13
No. 5 brass candle cup and stem........................ "	.25

¾-inch casing on stem, extra lengthening per foot, not wired, 75
cents; wired, 85 cents

No. 8876. Rich gilt
Length, 36 inches over all; spread, 11 inches

	Not Wired.	Wired.	Complete as Shown Except Lamps.
1 gas, 1 electric	$3.00	$3.75	$4.58

Complete candle trimming included in "not wired" and
"wired" prices
Complete fixture includes

Edison key socket......................................each,	$0.37
2¼-inch electric holder............................... "	.08
No. 9441½ electric shade.............................. "	.38
No. 451 opal candle................................... "	.10
No. 37 opal flat bobache............................. "	.11
No. 1 brass candle cup and stem..................... "	.25

¾-inch casing on stem, extra lengthening per foot, not wired,
45 cents; wired, 55 cents

No. 8881. Brushed brass
Length, 36 inches over all; spread, 10 inches

		Complete as Shown
Not Wired.	Wired.	Except Lamps.
2 gas, 1 electric $8.00	$9.00	$9.34

Emergency gas lights
No. 5909 5x9-inch opalescent stalactite included in "not wired" and "wired" prices
Complete bracket includes
Edison keyless sockets.................................each, $0.34
No. 5909 opalescent stalactites .... " 1.25
⅜-inch casing on stem, extra lengthening per foot, not wired, 45 cents; wired, 55 cents

No. 8880. Rich gilt and satin
Length, 36 inches over all; spread, 10 inches

		Complete as Shown
Not Wired.	Wired.	Except Lamp.
1 gas, 1 electric $5.25	$6.00	$6.88

Candle trimmings included in "not wired" and "wired" prices
Complete fixture includes
No. 8887 4½-inch pearl opalescent shade.. ....each, $0.38
No. 451 opal candle................................... " .10
No. 37 flat bobache .... " .11
No. 1 candle holder.................................. " .25
Edison key socket.................................... " .37
2¼-inch electric holder............................... " .08
⅜-inch casing on stem, extra lengthening per foot, not wired, 45 cents; wired, 55 cents

VESTIBULE AND HALL FIXTURES

No. 8883. Rich gilt and satin

Length, 36 inches over all; spread, 9 inches

	Not Wired.	Wired.	Complete as Shown Except Lamps.
2 gas, 2 electric	$18.00	$19.50	$19.84

Holophane ball included in "not wired" and "wired" prices

Complete fixture includes

Edison keyless sockets ....each, **$0.34**
No. 3556 holophane ball, 6x8 inches............ " **3.20**
1-inch casing on stem, extra lengthening per foot, not wired, 45 cents; wired, 55 cents

No. 8882. Brushed brass

Length, 36 inches over all; spread, 12 inches

	Not Wired.	Wired.	Complete as Shown Except Lamps.
1 gas, 1 electric	$3.50	$4.25	$5.15

Complete candle trimming included in "not wired" and "wired" prices

Complete fixture includes

Edison key socket ....each, **$0.37**
2¼-inch electric holder.................................. " **.08**
No. 8887½ C .R. I. electric shade........................ " **.45**
No. 45. opal candle.................................... " **.10**
No. 37 flat bobache................................... " **.11**
No. 1 brass candle cup and stem...................... " **.25**
⅝-inch casing on stem, extra lengthening per foot, not wired, 45 cents; wired, 55 cents

199

COMBINATION GAS AND ELECTRIC 1-LIGHT PENDANTS

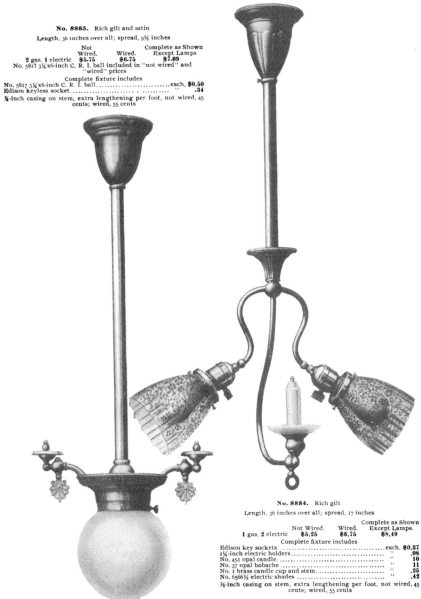

No. 8885. Rich gilt and satin

Length, 36 inches over all; spread, 9½ inches

	Not Wired.	Wired.	Complete as Shown Except Lamps
2 gas, 1 electric	$5.75	$6.75	$7.09

No. 5817 3¼x6-inch C. R. I. ball included in "not wired" and "wired" prices

Complete fixture includes

No. 5817 3¼x6-inch C. R. I. ball.........................each, $0.50
Edison keyless socket.............................. " .34

⅜-inch casing on stem, extra lengthening per foot, not wired, 45 cents; wired, 55 cents

No. 8884. Rich gilt

Length, 36 inches over all; spread, 17 inches

	Not Wired.	Wired.	Complete as Shown Except Lamps.
1 gas, 2 electric	$5.25	$6.75	$8.49

Complete fixture includes

Edison key sockets...each, $0.37
2¼-inch electric holders............................... " .08
No. 451 opal candle................................... " .10
No. 37 opal bobache .... " .11
No. 1 brass candle cup and stem....................... " .25
No. 6566½ electric shades .... " .42

⅜-inch casing on stem, extra lengthening per foot, not wired, 45 cents; wired, 55 cents

200

No. 8887. Brushed brass

Length, 36 inches over all; spread, 8 inches

	Not Wired.	Wired.	Complete as Shown Except Lamps.
2 gas, 1 electric	**$11.00**	**$12.00**	**$12.23**

With flambeaux and No. 4013 8-inch opalescent ball included in "not wired" and "wired" prices

Complete fixture includes

Edison keyless socket .... each, **$0.34**
No. 4013 8-inch opalescent ball........... " **1.50**

⅞-inch casing on stem, extra lengthening per foot, not wired, 45 cents; wired, 55 cents

No. 8886. Rich gilt and satin

Length, 36 inches over all; spread, 10 inches

	Not Wired.	Wired.	Complete as Shown Except Lamp.
1 gas, 1 electric	**$6.00**	**$6.75**	**$7.25**

Complete candle trimming and No. 5817 8-inch ball included in "not wired" and "wired" prices

Complete fixture includes

No. 5817 8-inch C. R. I. ball .... each, $0.75
No. 449 ivory candle .... " .15
No. 450 ivory bobache .... " .36
No. 2 brass candle cup and stem .... " .25
Edison key socket .... " .37
3¼-inch electric holder .... " .13

⅞-inch casing on stem, extra lengthening per foot, not wired, 45 cents; wired, 55 cents

201

VESTIBULE AND HALL FIXTURE

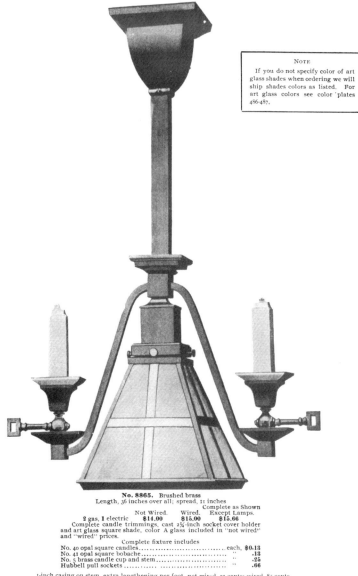

No. 8865. Brushed brass
Length, 36 inches over all; spread, 11 inches

	Not Wired.	Wired.	Complete as Shown Except Lamps.
2 gas, 1 electric	**$14.00**	**$15.00**	**$15.66**

Complete candle trimmings, cast 2¼-inch socket cover holder and art glass square shade, color A glass included in "not wired" and "wired" prices.

Complete fixture includes

No. 40 opal square candles	each,	$0.13
No. 41 opal square bobache	"	.13
No. 5 brass candle cup and stem	"	.25
Hubbell pull sockets	"	.66

1-inch casing on stem, extra lengthening per foot, not wired, 75 cents; wired, 85 cents

WROUGHT IRON VESTIBULE AND HALL FIXTURES

No. 8890. Iron, dull black

Length, 42 inches over all; spread, 9 inches

	Not Wired.	Wired.	Complete as Shown Except Lamp.
1 gas, 1 electric	$13.50	$14.50	$14.87

Candle included in "not wired" and "wired" prices

Complete fixture includes

Edison key socket.......,.............. each, $0.37
No. 451 opal candle...................... " .10

⅞-inch casing on stem, extra lengthening per foot, not wired, 45 cents; wired, 55 cents

No. 8889. Wrought iron

Length, 36 inches over all; spread, 8 inches

	Not Wired.	Wired.	Complete as Shown Except Lamp.
1 gas, 1 electric	$16.00	$16.50	$17.00

Special 3¼x9-inch stalactite and No. 445½ opal candle included in "not wired" and "wired" prices

Complete fixture includes

Edison key socket.........................each, $0.37
3¼-inch electric holder.................. " .13
No. 445½ opal candle.................... " .15
3¼x9-inch special stalactite............. " .65

⅞-inch casing on stem, extra lengthening per foot, not wired, 45 cents; wired, 55 cents

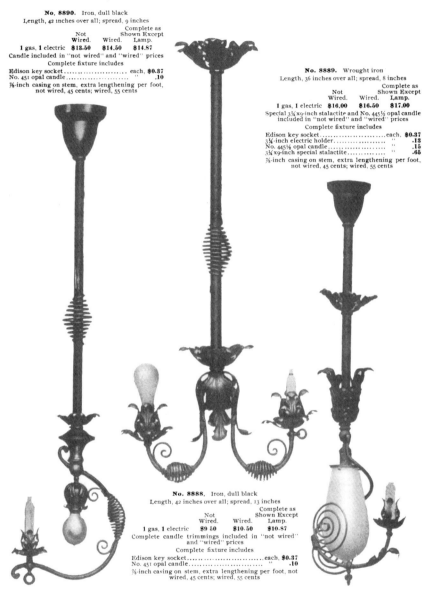

No. 8888. Iron, dull black

Length, 42 inches over all; spread, 13 inches

	Not Wired.	Wired.	Complete as Shown Except Lamp.
1 gas, 1 electric	$9.50	$10.50	$10.87

Complete candle trimmings included in "not wired" and "wired" prices

Complete fixture includes

Edison key socket............................each, $0.37
No. 451 opal candle........................... " .10

⅞-inch casing on stem, extra lengthening per foot, not wired, 45 cents; wired, 55 cents

203

WROUGHT IRON VESTIBULE AND HALL FIXTURES

No. 8892. Iron, dull black

Length, 42 inches over all; spread, 9½ inches

	Not Wired.	Wired.	Complete as Shown Except Lamp.
1 gas, 1 electric	**$16.00**	**$17.00**	**$17.37**

Complete candle trimmings included in "not wired" and "wired" prices

Complete fixture includes

Edison key socket...........................each, **$0.37**
No. 451 opal candle..................................... " .10

⅝-inch casing on stem, extra lengthening per foot, not wired, 45 cents; wired, 55 cents

No. 8891. Wrought iron

Length, 36 inches over all; spread, 12 inches

	Not Wired.	Wired.	Complete as Shown Except Lamp.
1 gas, 1 electric,	**$14.50**	**$15.50**	**$15.84**

Complete candle trimmings and No. 132 8-inch flint opalescent ball included in "not wired" and "wired" prices.

Complete fixture includes

Edison keyless socket ....each, **$0.34**
No. 132 8-inch F. O. ball.......... " .95
No. 445½ opal candle............. " .15

⅝-inch casing on stem, extra lengthening per foot, not wired, 45 cents; wired, 55 cents

No. 8893. Iron

Length, 36 inches over all; spread, 10 inches

	Not Wired.	Wired.	Complete as Shown Except Lamps.
2 gas, 1 electric,	**$19.50**	**$20.50**	**$21.00**

3¾x9-inch plain opalescent stalactite and No. 449 ivory candles included in "not wired" and "wired" prices.

Complete fixture includes

3¾-inch electric holder............each, **$0.13**
Edison key socket.... .... " .37
No. 417 9-inch F. O stalactite..... " 1.00
No. 449 ivory candles............. " .15

⅝-inch casing on stem, extra lengthening per foot, not wired, 45 cents; wired, 55 cents

WROUGHT IRON VESTIBULE AND HALL FIXTURES

No. 8894. Iron

Length, 36 inches over all; spread, 18 inches

	Not Wired.	Wired.	Complete as Shown Except Lamps.
1 gas, 2 electric	$13.00	$14.00	$15.00
1 " 1 "	10.50	11.00	11.37

No. 417, 7-inch opalescent stalactites and bowl in basket included in "not wired" and "wired" prices

Complete fixture includes

3¼-inch electric holders.................................each,	$0.13
Edison key sockets......................... .... "	.37
No. 417, 7-inch plain opalescent stalactite............... "	.75

⅞-inch casing on stem, extra lengthening per foot, not wired, 45 cents; wired 55 cents

No. 8895. Wrought iron

Length, 36 inches over all; spread, 14 inches

	Not Wired.	Wired.	Complete as Shown Except Lamps.
1 gas, 1 electric	$11.00	$11.50	11.84
1 " 2 "			
2 side arms	13.50	14.50	17.00

Complete fixture includes

Edison keyless sockets..............................each,	$0.34
Edison key sockets (on arms) .... "	.37
3¼-inch electric holders (on arms).................... "	.13
No. 417, 7-inch plain opalescent stalactite............ "	.75

⅞-inch casing on stem, extra lengthening per foot, not wired, 45 cents; wired, 55 cents

WROUGHT IRON VESTIBULE AND HALL FIXTURES

No. 8897. Wrought iron

Length, 36 inches over all; spread, 13 inches

	Not Wired.	Wired.	Complete as Shown Except Lamps.
1 gas, 1 electric	$10.50	$11.00	$11.34
1 " 2 " (made with 2 side arms)	13.00	14.00	16.50

Complete fixture includes

Edison keyless sockets	each,	$0.34
Edison key sockets (on arms)	"	.37
3¼-inch electric holders (on arms)	"	.18
No. 417 7-inch plain opalescent stalactite	"	.75

⅞-inch casing on stem, extra lengthening per foot, not wired, 45 cents; wired, 55 cents

No. 8896. Iron, dull black

Length, 42 inches over all

	Not Wired.	Wired.	Complete as Shown Except Lamp.
1 gas, 1 electric	$18.00	$19.00	$19.34

4x9-inch bevel plate glass included in "not wired" and "wired" prices

Complete fixture includes

Edison keyless socket ....each, $0.34

⅞-inch casing on stem, extra lengthening per foot, not wired, 45 cents; wired, 55 cents

NEWEL POST FIXTURES

No. 9035. Brushed brass

Height, 34 inches over all; base, 6 inches

	Not Wired.	Wired.	Complete as Shown Except Lamp.
1 gas, 1 electric	$10.00	$11.00	$11.37

Complete candle trimmings and 3¼x8-inch No. 9082 etched stalactite
included in "not wired" and "wired" prices

Complete fixture includes

Edison key sockets	each,	$0.37
No. 9082 8-inch etched stalactite	"	1.85
No. 447 ivory candle	"	.17
No. 448 ivory bobache	"	.21
No. 7 hexagon brass candle cup and stem	"	.25

No. 9034. Rich gilt

Height, 30 inches over all; base, 4½ inches

	Not Wired.	Wired.	Complete as Shown Except Lamp.
1 gas, 1 electric	$20.00	$20.50	$20.84

Complete candle trimmings and 3¼x6-inch
No. 422 opalescent ball included in "not
wired" and "wired" prices.

Complete fixture includes

Edison keyless socket	each,	$0.34
No. 422 3¼x6-inch P. O. ball	"	.65
No. 451 opal candle	"	.10
No. 452 crystal bobache	"	.10
No. 2 brass candle cup and stem	"	.25

No. 9033. Rich gilt

Height, 30 inches over all; base, 4½ inches

	Not Wired.	Wired.	Complete as Shown Except Lamp.
1 gas, 1 electric	$9.50	$10.50	$11.69

No. 4082 8-inch satin etched stalactite and
cast holder included in "not wired" and
"wired" prices.

Complete fixture includes

Edison keyless socket	each,	$0.34
No. 4082 8-inch stalactite	"	1.05
No. 3458 gas globe	"	.85

DESK AND WINDOW STANDARDS

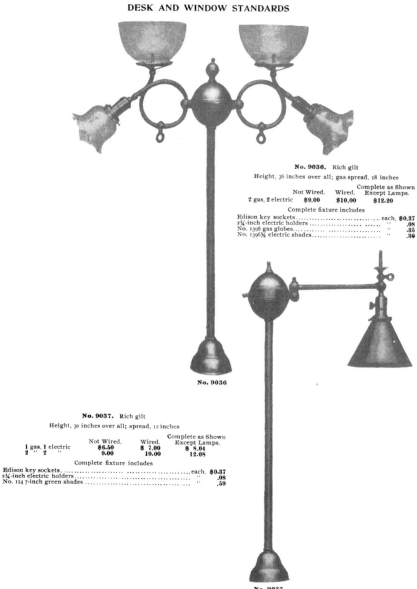

No. 9036. Rich gilt

Height, 36 inches over all; gas spread, 18 inches

	Not Wired.	Wired.	Complete as Shown Except Lamps.
2 gas, 2 electric	**$9.00**	**$10.00**	**$12.20**

Complete fixture includes

Edison key sockets	each,	**$0.37**
2¼-inch electric holders	"	**.08**
No. 1396 gas globes	"	**.35**
No. 1396½ electric shades	"	**.30**

No. 9036

No. 9037. Rich gilt

Height, 30 inches over all; spread, 12 inches

	Not Wired.	Wired.	Complete as Shown Except Lamps.
1 gas, 1 electric	**$6.50**	**$ 7.00**	**$ 8.04**
2 " 2 "	**9.00**	**10.00**	**12.08**

Complete fixture includes

Edison key sockets	each,	**$0.37**
2¼-inch electric holders	"	**.08**
No. 114 7-inch green shades	"	**.59**

No. 9037

No. 497

No. 493

No. 496

No. 495

No. 493. Rich gilt and satin
Height, 24 inches over all: base, 6 inches
Two Mascot cigar lighters included
Cigar lighter complete...$15.00

No. 495. Rich gilt and satin
Height, 40 inches over all; base, 6 inches

	Not Wired.	Wired.	Complete as Shown Except Lamps.
1 gas, 1 electric	**$12.00**	**$13.00**	**$13.34**

Mascot cigar lighter and No. 8768 6-inch etched ball included in "not wired" and "wired" prices
Complete fixture includes
Edison keyless socket.....................................each, **$0.34**
No. 8768 6-inch etched ball .... " **2.00**

No. 496. Brushed brass
Height, 8½ inches over all; base, 4⅛ inches
Complete as shown
1-light, gas... each, **$10.50**

No. 497. Titian bronze
Height, 15 inches over all; base, 3¾ inches
One-light cigar flame from cigarette
Complete as shown
Gas only.. each, **$15.00**

COMBINATION BRACKETS

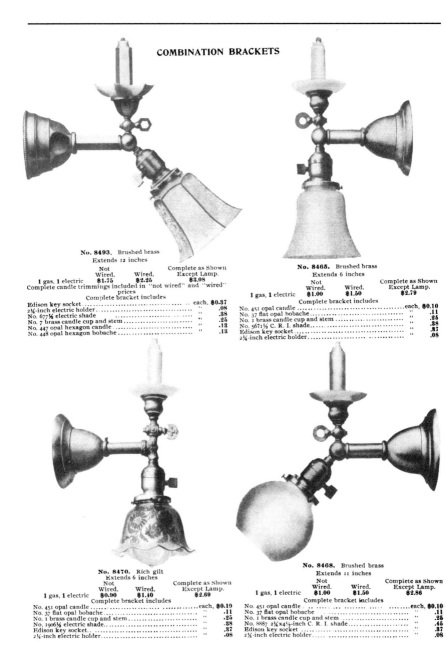

No. 8493. Brushed brass
Extends 12 inches

	Not Wired.	Wired.	Complete as Shown Except Lamp.
1 gas, 1 electric	$1.75	$2.25	$3.08

Complete candle trimmings included in "not wired" and "wired" prices

Complete bracket includes

Edison key socket	each,	$0.37
2¼-inch electric holder	"	.08
No. 677½ electric shade	"	.38
No. 7 brass candle cup and stem	"	.25
No. 447 opal hexagon candle	"	.13
No. 448 opal hexagon bobache	"	.13

No. 8465. Brushed brass
Extends 6 inches

	Not Wired.	Wired.	Complete as Shown Except Lamp.
1 gas, 1 electric	$1.00	$1.50	$2.79

Complete bracket includes

No. 451 opal candle	each,	$0.10
No. 37 flat opal bobache	"	.11
No. 1 brass candle cup and stem	"	.25
No. 5671½ C. R. I. shade	"	.38
Edison key socket	"	.37
2¼-inch electric holder	"	.08

No. 8470. Rich gilt
Extends 6 inches

	Not Wired.	Wired.	Complete as Shown Except Lamp.
1 gas, 1 electric	$0.90	$1.40	$2.69

Complete bracket includes

No. 451 opal candle	each,	$0.10
No. 37 flat opal bobache	"	.11
No. 1 brass candle cup and stem	"	.25
No. 1906½ electric shade	"	.38
Edison key socket	"	.37
2¼-inch electric holder	"	.08

No. 8468. Brushed brass
Extends 11 inches

	Not Wired.	Wired.	Complete as Shown Except Lamp.
1 gas, 1 electric	$1.00	$1.50	$2.86

Complete bracket includes

No. 451 opal candle	each,	$0.10
No. 37 flat opal bobache	"	.11
No. 1 brass candle cup and stem	"	.25
No. 8887 2⅜x4½-inch C. R. I. shade	"	.46
Edison key socket	"	.37
2¼-inch electric holder	"	.08

No. 8466. Brushed brass
Extends 6 inches

| 1 gas, 1 electric | Not Wired. **$3.25** | Wired. **$4.00** | Complete as Shown Except Lamp. **$5.12** |

Complete candle trimmings and 2¼-inch holder included in "not wired" and "wired" prices.

Complete bracket includes

Edison key socket..............................each, **$0.37**	
No. 9332 S. O. electric shade (4½ inches).............. "	.75
No. 7 brass candle cup and stem .... "	.25
No. 447 opal hexagon candle .... "	.13
No. 448 opal hexagon bobache .... "	.13

No. 8466½ indicates bracket made with gas light on left side and electric light on right side. Same price as No. 8466

No. 8473.
Brushed brass
Extends 6 inches

	Not Wired.	Wired.	Complete as Shown Except Lamp.
1 gas, 1 electric	**$2.75**	**$3.50**	**$4.40**

Complete candle trimmings included in "not wired" and "wired" prices

Complete bracket includes

Edison key socket...............................each, **$0.37**	
2¼-inch electric holder............................ "	.08
No. 8887 2¾x4½ C. R. I. shade.................... "	.45
No. 451 opal candle................................ "	.10
No. 37 flat opal bobache .... "	.11
No. 1 brass candle cup and stem .... "	.25

No. 8473½ indicates bracket with electric light on left side and gas light on right side. Same price as No. 8473

No. 8474. Rich gilt
Extends 7 inches

| 1 gas, 1 electric | Not Wired. **$1.65** | Wired. **$2.25** | Complete as Shown Except Lamps. **$3.08** |

Complete candle trimmings included in "not wired" and "wired" prices

Complete bracket includes

Edison key socket...............................each, **$0.37**	
2¼-inch electric holder .... "	.08
No. 9441⅛ electric shade .... "	.38
No. 451 opal candle............................... "	.10
No. 37 flat opal bobache.......................... "	.11
No. 1 brass candle cup and stem................... "	.25

No. 8474½ indicates bracket with gas light on right side and electric light on left side. Same price as No. 8474

No. 8469. Brushed brass
Extends 6 inches

| 1 gas, 1 electric | Not Wired. **$2.25** | Wired. **$3.00** | Complete as Shown Except Lamp. **$3.83** |

Complete candle trimmings included in "not wired" and "wired" prices.

Complete bracket includes

Edison key socket ....each, **$0.37**	
2¼-inch electric holder .... "	.08
No. 9441½ electric shade.......................... "	.38
No. 451 opal candle .... "	.10
No. 37 flat opal bobache .... "	.11
No. 1 brass candle cup and stem .... "	.25

No. 8469½ indicates bracket with electric light on left side and gas light on right side. Same price as No. 8469

211

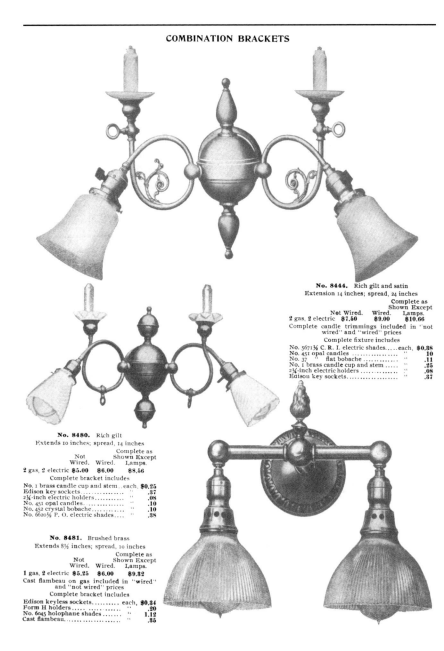

No. 8444. Rich gilt and satin

Extension 14 inches; spread, 24 inches

	Not Wired.	Wired.	Complete as Shown Except Lamps.
2 gas, 2 electric	$7.50	$9.00	$10.66

Complete candle trimmings included in "not wired" and "wired" prices

Complete fixture includes

No. 5671½ C. R. I. electric shades.....each,	$0.38
No. 451 opal candles	"	.10
No. 37 " flat bobache	"	.11
No. 1 brass candle cup and stem	"	.25
2¼-inch electric holders	"	.08
Edison key sockets..................	"	.37

No. 8480. Rich gilt

Extends 10 inches; spread, 14 inches

	Not Wired.	Wired.	Complete as Shown Except Lamps.
2 gas, 2 electric	$5.00	$6.00	$8.56

Complete bracket includes

No. 1 brass candle cup and stem..each,	$0.25
Edison key sockets	"	.37
2¼-inch electric holders...........	"	.08
No. 451 opal candles...........	"	.10
No. 452 crystal bobache...........	"	.10
No. 6620½ P. O. electric shades....	"	.38

No. 8481. Brushed brass

Extends 8½ inches; spread, 10 inches

	Not Wired.	Wired.	Complete as Shown Except Lamps.
1 gas, 2 electric	$5.25	$6.00	$9.32

Cast flambeau on gas included in "wired" and "not wired" prices

Complete bracket includes

Edison keyless sockets......... each,	$0.34
Form H holders....	"	.20
No. 6045 holophane shades	"	1.12
Cast flambeau..................	"	.35

COMBINATION BRACKETS

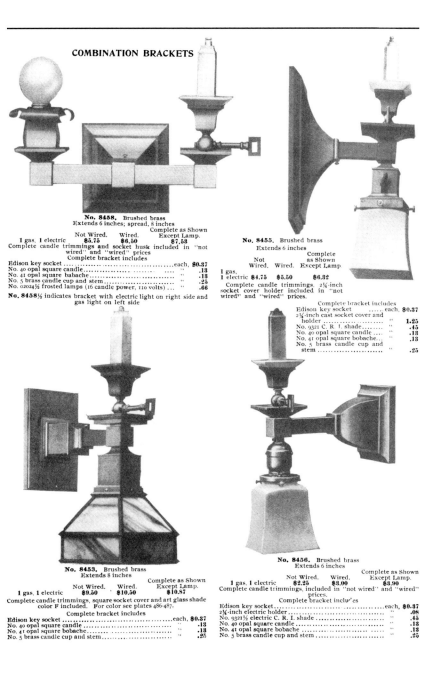

No. 8458. Brushed brass
Extends 6 inches; spread, 8 inches

	Not Wired.	Wired.	Complete as Shown Except Lamp.
1 gas, 1 electric	$5.75	$6.50	$7.53

Complete candle trimmings and socket husk included in "not wired" and "wired" prices

Complete bracket includes

Edison key socket	............each, $0.37
No. 40 opal square candle	" .13
No. 41 opal square babache	" .13
No. 5 brass candle cup and stem	" .25
No. 0202 4½ frosted lamps (16 candle power, 110 volts)	" .66

No. 8458½ indicates bracket with electric light on right side and gas light on left side

No. 8455. Brushed brass
Extends 6 inches

	Not Wired.	Wired.	Complete as Shown Except Lamp
1 gas, 1 electric	$4.75	$5.50	$6.32

Complete candle trimmings, 2¼-inch socket cover holder included in "not wired" and "wired" prices.

Complete bracket includes

Edison key socket	.....each, $0.37
2¼-inch cast socket cover and holder	" 1.25
No. 9321 C. R. I. shade	" .45
No. 40 opal square candle	" .13
No. 41 opal square bobache	" .13
No. 5 brass candle cup and stem	" .25

No. 8453. Brushed brass
Extends 8 inches

	Not Wired.	Wired.	Complete as Shown Except Lamp.
1 gas, 1 electric	$9.50	$10.50	$10.87

Complete candle trimmings, square socket cover and art glass shade color F included. For color see plates 486-487.

Complete bracket includes

Edison key socket	............each, $0.37
No. 40 opal square candle	" .13
No. 41 opal square bobache	" .13
No. 5 brass candle cup and stem	" .25

No. 8456. Brushed brass
Extends 6 inches

	Not Wired.	Wired.	Complete as Shown Except Lamp.
1 gas, 1 electric	$2.25	$3.00	$3.90

Complete candle trimmings, included in "not wired" and "wired" prices.

Complete bracket includes

Edison key socket	............each, $0.37
2¼-inch electric holder	" .08
No. 9321½ electric C. R. I. shade	" .45
No. 40 opal square candle	" .13
No. 41 opal square bobache	" .13
No. 5 brass candle cup and stem	" .25

213

COMBINATION BRACKETS

No. 8460. Brushed brass
Extends 6 inches; spread, 8 inches

	Not Wired.	Wired.	Complete as Shown Except Lamp.
1 gas, 1 electric	$4.75	$5.50	$6.40

Complete candle trimmings included in "not wired" and "wired" prices

Complete bracket includes

Edison key socket	each,	$0.37
2¼-inch electric holder	"	.08
No. 9321½ C. R. I. shade	"	.45
No. 40 opal square candle	"	.13
No. 41 opal square bobache	"	.13
No. 5 brass candle cup and stem	"	.25

No. 8460½ indicates bracket with gas light on left side and electric light on right side. Same price as No. 8460

No. 8449. Brushed brass
Extends 6 inches

	Not Wired.	Wired.	Complete as Shown Except Lamp.
1 gas, 1 electric	$7.75	$8.50	$9.16

Complete candle trimmings and No. 15161 art glass shade, color K glass included in "not wired" and "wired" prices

Complete bracket includes

Hubbell pull socket	each,	$0.66
No. 16151 shade only	"	5.00
No. 40 opal square candle	"	.13
No. 5 brass candle cup and stem	"	.25

No. 8457. Brushed brass
Extends 6 inches; spread, 10 inches

	Not Wired.	Wired.	Complete as Shown Except Lamps.
1 gas, 2 electric	$6.50	$8.00	$9.80

Complete candle trimmings included in "not wired" and "wired" prices

Complete bracket includes

Edison key sockets	each,	$0.37
2¼-inch electric holders	"	.08
No. 9321½ C. R. I. shades	"	.45
No. 40 opal square candle	"	.13
No. 41 opal square bobache	"	.13
No. 5 brass candle cup and stem	"	.25

No. 8471. Brushed brass

Extends 6 inches; spread, 8 inches

	Not Wired.	Wired.	Complete as Shown Except Lamp.
1 gas, 1 electric	$5.75	$6.50	$9.95

Complete candle trimmings, square, included in "not wired" and "wired" prices

Complete bracket includes

Edison key socket	each,	$0.37
2¼-inch electric holder	"	.08
No. 809 cut colonial shade	"	3 00
No. 40 opal square candle	"	.13
No. 41 opal square bobache	"	.13
No. 5½ brass candle cup and stem	"	.35

No. 8457

COMBINATION BRACKETS

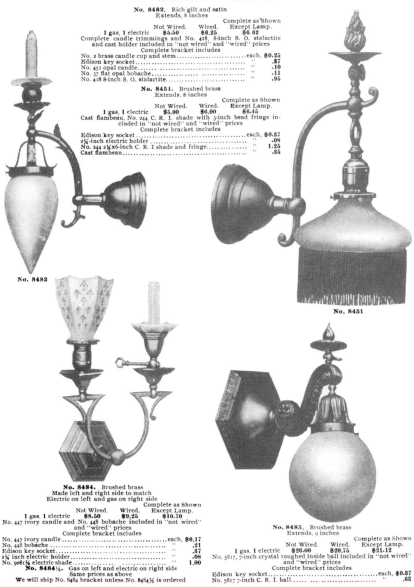

No. 8482. Rich gilt and satin
Extends, 8 inches

	Not Wired.	Wired.	Complete as Shown Except Lamp.
1 gas, 1 electric	$5.50	$6.25	$6.62

Complete candle trimmings and No. 418, 8-inch S. O. stalactite
and cast holder included in "not wired" and "wired" prices
Complete bracket includes

No. 2 brass candle cup and stem	each,	$0.25
Edison key socket	"	.37
No. 451 opal candle	"	.10
No. 37 flat opal bobache	"	.11
No. 418 8-inch S. O. stalactite	"	.95

No. 8451. Brushed brass
Extends, 8 inches

	Not Wired.	Wired.	Complete as Shown Except Lamp.
1 gas, 1 electric	$5.00	$6.00	$6.45

Cast flambeau, No. 244 C. R. I. shade with 3-inch bead fringe included in "not wired" and "wired" prices
Complete bracket includes

Edison key socket	each,	$0.37
2¼-inch electric holder	"	.08
No. 244 2½x6-inch C. R. I shade and fringe	"	1.25
Cast flambeau	"	.35

No. 8482

No. 8451

No. 8484. Brushed brass
Made left and right side to match
Electric on left and gas on right side

	Not Wired.	Wired.	Complete as Shown Except Lamp.
1 gas, 1 electric	$8.50	$9.25	$10.70

No. 447 ivory candle and No. 448 bobache included in "not wired"
and "wired" prices
Complete bracket includes

No. 447 ivory candle	each,	$0.17
No. 448 bobache	"	.21
Edison key socket	"	.37
2¼ inch electric holder	"	.08
No. 9081½ electric shade	"	1.00

No. 8484½. Gas on left and electric on right side
Same prices as above
We will ship No. 8484 bracket unless No. 8484½ is ordered

No. 8485. Brushed brass
Extends, 9 inches

	Not Wired.	Wired.	Complete as Shown Except Lamp.
1 gas, 1 electric	$20.00	$20.75	$21.12

No. 5817, 7-inch crystal roughed inside ball included in "not wired"
and "wired" prices
Complete bracket includes

Edison key socket	each,	$0.37
No. 5817 7-inch C. R. I. ball	"	.63

WROUGHT IRON COMBINATION BRACKETS

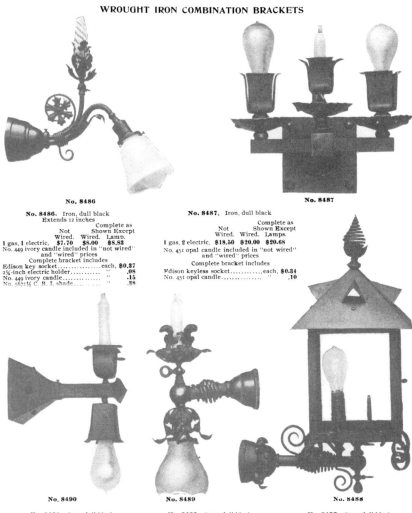

No. 8486

No. 8487

No. 8486. Iron, dull black
Extends 12 inches

	Complete as		
	Not	Shown	Except
	Wired.	Wired.	Lamp.
1 gas, 1 electric,	$7.70	$8.00	$8.88

No. 449 ivory candle included in "not wired"
and "wired" prices

Complete bracket includes

Edison key socket	each,	$0.37
2¼-inch electric holder	"	.08
No. 449 ivory candle	"	.15
No. 5671½ C. R. I. shade	"	.38

No. 8487. Iron, dull black

	Complete as		
	Not	Shown	Except
	Wired.	Wired.	Lamps.
1 gas, 2 electric,	$18.50	$20.00	$20.68

No. 451 opal candle included in "not wired"
and "wired" prices

Complete bracket includes

Edison keyless socket	each,	$0.34
No. 451 opal candle	"	.10

No. 8490

No. 8489

No. 8488

No. 8490. Iron, dull black

Extends 7 inches

	Complete as		
	Not	Shown	Except
	Wired.	Wired.	Lamp.
1 gas, 1 electric,	$9.20	$10.00	$10.34

Complete candle trimmings included in "not
wired" and "wired" prices

Complete bracket includes

Edison keyless socket	each,	$0.34
No. 451 opal candle	"	.10

No. 8489. Iron, dull black
Extends 6½ inches

	Complete as		
	Not	Shown	Except
	Wired.	Wired.	Lamp.
1 gas, 1 electric,	$5.20	$6.00	$7.25

Complete candle trimmings included in "not
wired" and "wired" prices

Complete bracket includes

Edison key socket	each,	$0.37
2¼-inch electric holder	"	.08
No. 451 opal candle	"	.10
No. 8950½ electric shade	"	.80

No. 8488. Iron, dull black

Extends 15 inches; height, 24 inches

	Complete as		
	Not	Shown	Except
	Wired.	Wired.	Lamp.
1 gas, 1 electric,	$16.00	$16.50	$16.84

Bevel plate glass included in "not wired"
and "wired" prices

Complete bracket includes

Edison keyless socket	each,	$0.34

CHURCH OR HALL FIXTURE

No. 9551. Rich gilt

Length, 90 inches over all

Upper tier spreads 60 inches
Lower tier spreads 36 inches

	Not Wired.	Wired.	Complete as Shown Except Lamps.
12 gas, 24 electric	$120.00	$135.00	$152.52
24 " 24 "	147.00	162.00	179.52
36 " 24 "	156.00	171.00	188.52

Complete candle trimmings included in "not wired" and "wired" prices

Complete fixture includes

Edison key sockets	each,	$0.37
2¼-inch electric holders	"	.08
No 1570½ electric shades	"	.28
No. 451 opal candles	"	.10
No. 37 flat opal bobache	"	.11
No. 1 brass candle cup and stem	"	.25

1-inch extra lengthening per foot, not wired, 45 cents; wired, 55 cents

No. 9551½ indicates that fixture is made with electric lights straight down for Tungsten lamps. Prices same as No. 9551.

CONSTRUCTION INFORMATION

The gas arms are only made for upper tier. When 12 gas and 24 electric fixture is ordered, the 12 gas arms on upper tier are trimmed with 1-light candle clusters; if 24 gas and 24 electric fixture is ordered, the 12 gas arms on upper tier are trimmed with a 2-light candle cluster, and if the fixture is ordered for 36 gas and 24 electric, the 12 gas arms on upper tier are trimmed with a 3-light candle cluster each, making the total of 36 gas candle lights.

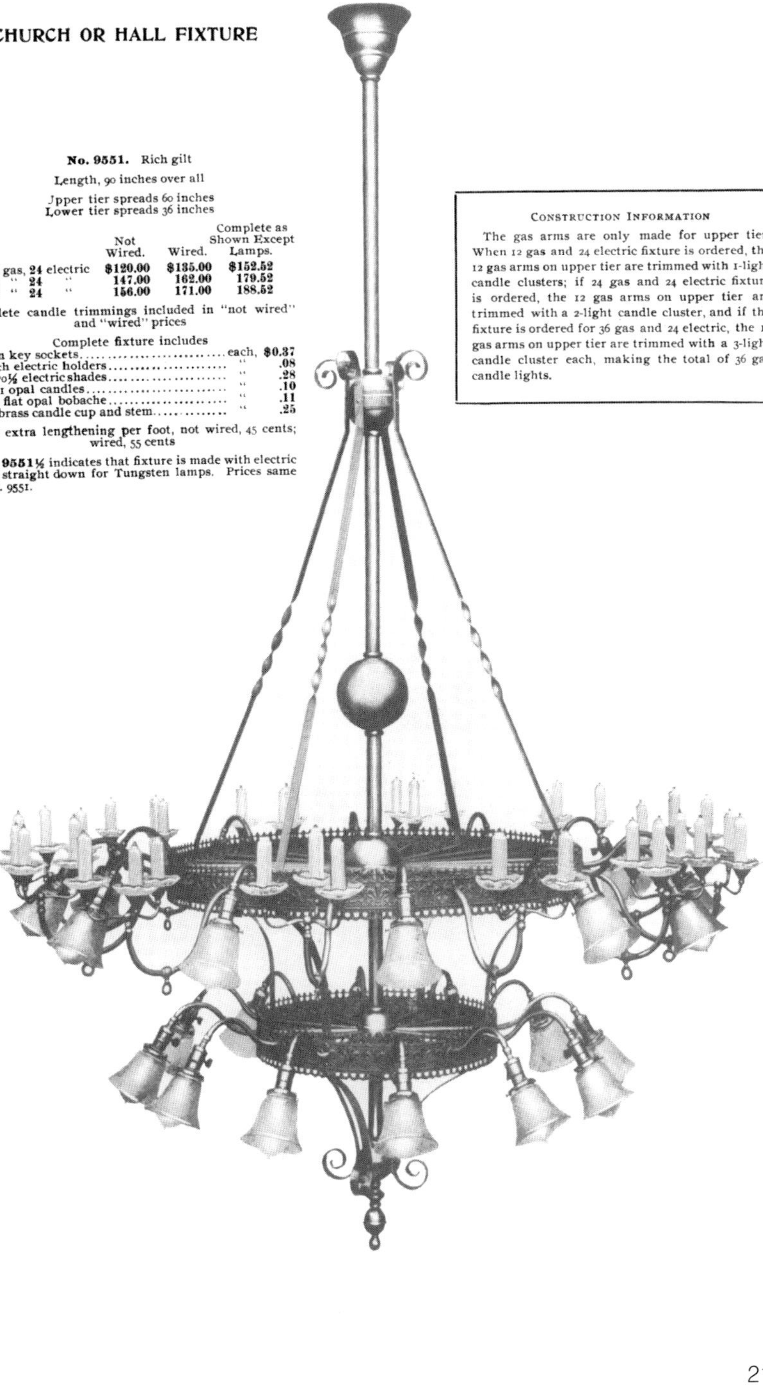

CHURCH OR HALL FIXTURE

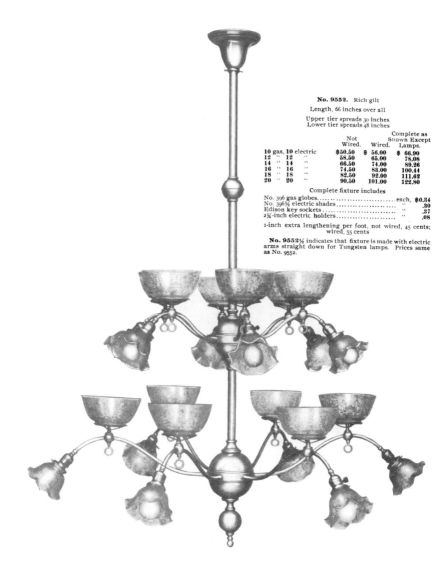

No. 9552. Rich gilt

Length, 66 inches over all

Upper tier spreads 30 inches
Lower tier spreads 48 inches

	Not Wired.	Wired.	Complete as Shown Except Lamps.
10 gas, 10 electric	$50.50	$ 56.00	$ 66.90
12 " 12 "	58.50	65.00	78.08
14 " 14 "	66.50	74.00	89.26
16 " 16 "	74.50	83.00	100.44
18 " 18 "	82.50	92.00	111.62
20 " 20 "	90.50	101.00	122.80

Complete fixture includes

No. 396 gas globes..........................each,		$0.34
No. 396½ electric shades.....................	"	.30
Edison key sockets..........................	"	.37
2¼-inch electric holders.....................	"	.08

1-inch extra lengthening per foot, not wired, 45 cents;
wired, 55 cents

No. 9552½ indicates that fixture is made with electric arms straight down for Tungsten lamps. Prices same as No. 9552.

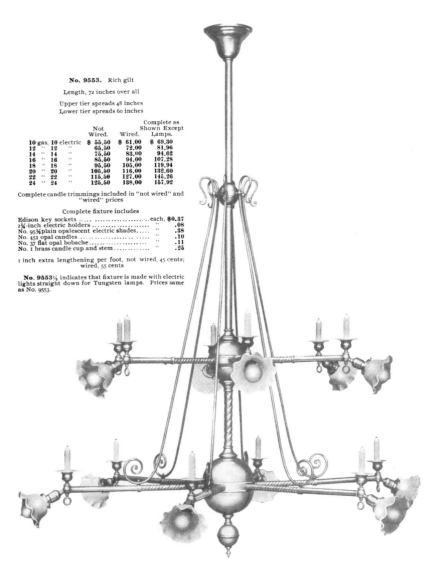

No. 9553. Rich gilt

Length, 72 inches over all

Upper tier spreads 48 inches
Lower tier spreads 60 inches

	Not Wired.	Wired.	Complete as Shown Except Lamps.
10 gas, 10 electric	$ 55.50	$ 61.00	$ 69.30
12 `` 12 ``	65.50	72.00	81.96
14 `` 14 ``	75.50	83.00	94.62
16 `` 16 ``	85.50	94.00	107.28
18 `` 18 ``	95.50	105.00	119.94
20 `` 20 ``	105.50	116.00	132.60
22 `` 22 ``	115.50	127.00	145.26
24 `` 24 ``	125.50	138.00	157.92

Complete candle trimmings included in "not wired" and "wired" prices

Complete fixture includes

Edison key sockets	each,	$0.37
2¼-inch electric holders	"	.08
No. 95½ plain opalescent electric shades	"	.38
No. 451 opal candles	"	.10
No. 37 flat opal bobache	"	.11
No. 1 brass candle cup and stem	"	.25

1 inch extra lengthening per foot, not wired, 45 cents; wired, 55 cents

No. 9553½ indicates that fixture is made with electric lights straight down for Tungsten lamps. Prices same as No. 9553.

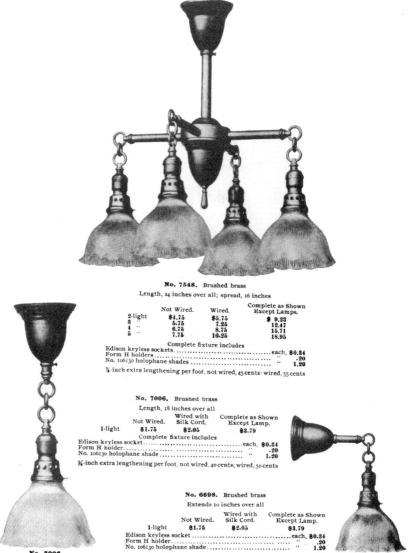

No. 7548. Brushed brass

Length, 24 inches over all; spread, 16 inches

	Not Wired.	Wired.	Complete as Shown Except Lamps.
2-light	$4.75	$5.75	$ 9.22
3 "	5.75	7.25	12.47
4 "	6.75	8.75	15.71
5 "	7.75	10.25	18.95

Complete fixture includes

Edison keyless sockets...........................each, $0.34
Form H holders....................................... " .20
No. 106130 holophane shades .... " 1.20
¾-inch extra lengthening per foot, not wired, 45 cents; wired, 55 cents

No. 7006. Brushed brass

Length, 18 inches over all

	Not Wired.	Wired with Silk Cord.	Complete as Shown Except Lamp.
1-light	$1.75	$2.05	$3.79

Complete fixture includes

Edison keyless socket...........................each, $0.34
Form H holder... .20
No. 106130 holophane shade 1.20
¾-inch extra lengthening per foot, not wired, 40 cents; wired, 50 cents

No. 6698. Brushed brass

Extends 10 inches over all

	Not Wired.	Wired with Silk Cord.	Complete as Shown Except Lamp.
1-light	$1.75	$2.05	$3.79

Edison keyless socket...........................each, $0.34
Form H holder... .20
No. 106130 holophane shade............................ " 1.20

No. 7006

No. 6698

TUNGSTEN FIXTURES

No. 6699. Brushed brass
Extends 10 inches over all

	Not Wired.	Wired with Silk Cord.	Complete as Shown Except Lamp.
1-light	$3.25	$3.55	$5.32

Stamped socket cover husk included in "not wired" and "wired" prices

Complete fixture includes

Edison key socket	each,	$0.37
Form H holder	"	.20
No. 106130 holophane shade	"	1.20

No. 7007. Brushed brass
Length, 18 inches over all

	Not Wired.	Wired with Silk Cord.	Complete as Shown Except Lamp.
1-light	$3.25	$3.55	$5.29

Stamped socket cover husk included in "not wired" and "wired" prices

Complete fixture includes

Edison keyless socket	each,	$0.34
Form H holder	"	.20
No. 106130 holophane shade	"	1.20

¾-inch extra lengthening per foot, not wired, 65 cents; wired, 75 cents

No. 7549. Brushed brass
Length, 24 inches over all; spread, 16 inches

	Not Wired.	Wired.	Complete as Shown Except Lamps.
2 light	$10.50	$11.50	$14.98
4 "	14.50	16.50	23.46

Stamped socket cover husk included in "not wired" and "wired" prices

Complete fixture includes

Edison keyless sockets	each,	$0.34
Form H holders	"	.20
No. 106130 holophane shades	"	1.20

¾-inch extra lengthening per foot, not wired, 75 cents; wired, 85 cents

ELECTRIC FIXTURE

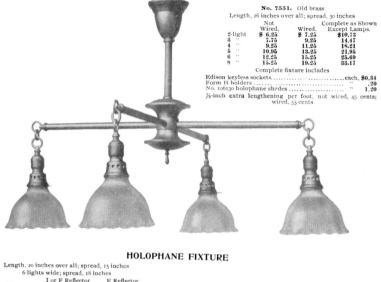

No. 7551. Old brass

Length, 26 inches over all; spread, 30 inches

	Not Wired.	Wired.	Complete as Shown Except Lamps.
2-light	$ 6.25	$ 7.25	$10.73
3 "	7.75	9.25	14.47
4 "	9.25	11.25	18.21
5 "	10.95	13.25	21.95
6 "	12.25	15.25	25.69
8 "	15.25	19.25	33.17

Complete fixture includes

Edison keyless sockets.................................each, $0.34
Form H holders .... "   .20
No. 106130 holophane shades .... " 1.20
⅝-inch **extra** lengthening per foot, not wired, 45 cents;
wired, 55 cents

HOLOPHANE FIXTURE

Length, 20 inches over all; spread, 15 inches

6-lights wide; spread, 18 inches

No.	I or F Reflector List.	E Reflector List.
50402	$ 9.10	$ 8.95
50403	11.85	11.60
50404	14.60	14.30
50405	17.35	16.95
50406	21.40	20.90
50602	9.60	9.10
50603	12.65	11.85
50604	15.65	14.60
50605	18.65	17.35
50606	22.95	21.40
50102	10.30	9.95
50103	13.65	13.15
50104	17.00	16.30
50105	20.35	19.50
50106	25.00	24.00
Switch, add	5.00	

Wired complete with special sockets, form H holders and
No. 106130 holophane shades included

Complete fixture includes

No. 106130 holophane shades.......... ....each, $1.20
Form H holders................................. "   .20

Fixtures are furnished wired (not assembled) unless ordered otherwise. Glassware, Electric Shade Holders, Sockets and Lamps not included unless mentioned.

Comfort obtained by the

" S-COMFORT" SYSTEM

of Indirect Illumination
(Patents Applied for)

TO LIGHT a room by some plan in which the source of light is concealed is acknowledged to be the most comfortable, aesthetic and perfect method. The initial expense and cost of maintenance has heretofore prevented its adoption for general use.

The development work by this company during the past year and the advent of the Tungsten lamp has resulted in the solving of these problems, and this very desirable method of indirect illumination is now commercially available.

In our "I-Comfort" (eye-comfort) system we combine with the highly efficient 60 and 100-watt Tungsten lamp or with upright, high grade, gas mantle burners, *a specially designed one-piece glass reflector with spiral and vertical corrugations, plated with pure silver, giving the most perfect reflecting surface known to science.*

By placing under the brilliant source of light this reflector (artistically incased) the light is reflected to the ceiling with the highest efficiency possible with any reflecting appliance known to-day. The diffused light reflected from the ceiling evenly distributed throughout the room, gives results that are surprising in efficiency, aesthetic effect, and eye-comfort.

Many eye troubles and headaches are caused by exposing the delicate organs of sight to the direct rays of brilliant modern light sources.

The "I-Comfort" system marks an epoch in interior illumination. It is so comfortable and pleasing that the present common methods seem barbaric by comparison after one has lived with and enjoyed the "I-Comfort" system for a time.

ESSENTIAL CONDITION

The ceiling must be light in color to make this system feasible. As a matter of fact, the majority of ceilings are light enough to be admirably adapted to this system.

The loss of light by absorption depends upon the color of the ceiling, which should be white or a light tint. It is not essential that the walls should be of a light color, although in such a case the absorption is less.

Where electrolier wall switches are used, or where both units will always be used, we advise the keyless sockets.

No. E401. Brushed brass
Single chain unit....each, **$11.00**

Elegantly simple design used in center of rooms up to 15x15 feet with 60 or 100 watt lamps.

Two or more in larger rooms or where very brilliant illumination is required.

E401. This chain unit is furnished complete wired and with key or keyless socket as desired and with blind insulating joint for ⅜-inch gas pipe. The stem is so arranged that fixture can be readily attached whether the pipe comes even with the ceiling or extends 1½ to 1¾ inches.

No. E402. Brushed brass
Double chain unit ....each. **$27.50**

Used in center of large rooms or where one unit would prove insufficient

E402 consists of two units, same as E401, except with ceiling fixture similar to cut shown. The design of the ceiling fixture has been changed to give a more artistic appearance. By use of a body of novel construction, the arms can be placed directly against ceiling and after wires are connected the canopy is fastened in place by an ornamental bolt.

No. E315. Brushed brass
Each....................**$10.00**

An adaptable unit to be used on fixtures or wherever a pendant socket is already in place on or a few inches from the ceiling.

E315. These are ordinarily furnished with the top of the reflector 16 inches below the top of the attachment plug. Furnished with shorter chain where so specified.

"I-COMFORT" ADAPTABLES

No. E300. Brushed brass, adaptable
Each....................**$5.75**

For use on fixtures already in place, on 45 degree arms of regular electric or combination fixtures.

The ball fitting is so arranged that the unit may be attached in a very few moments without rewiring of fixture.

E300 consists of equipment as in E305, together with key or keyless socket, stem, separable angle ball. Wired complete ready for installation.

No. E305. Brushed brass, adagtable
Each.................... **$4.25**

For use on combination or electric fixtures already in use or to be made where the sockets stand perpendicular. Fits all standard sockets.

E305 consists of a casing or receptacle made with a spinning which fits snugly over an upright socket and one of our E100 reflectors. These are designed for use either on old fixtures with upright sockets or for use on new fixtures.

No. E310. Brushed brass, adaptable
Each....................**$5.50**

For use on combination fixtures, the unit being attached to gas nipple. Current being carried from electric socket. Give distance gas jet to electric socket.

E310 consists of equipment the same as E305, in addition to key or keyless socket as desired, with blind attachment cap to go on gas opening and with side opening so that electric cord can be carried through same. Socket is wired and we furnish 18 inches of silk covered cord and attachment plug.

> Above "I-Comfort System" fixtures are furnished wired with key or keyless socket, blind insulating joints, ready for installation, less lamps unless ordered otherwise.

Fixtures are furnished wired (not assembled) unless ordered otherwise. Glassware, Electric Shade Holders, Sockets and Lamps not included unless mentioned.

ART DOME SHADES

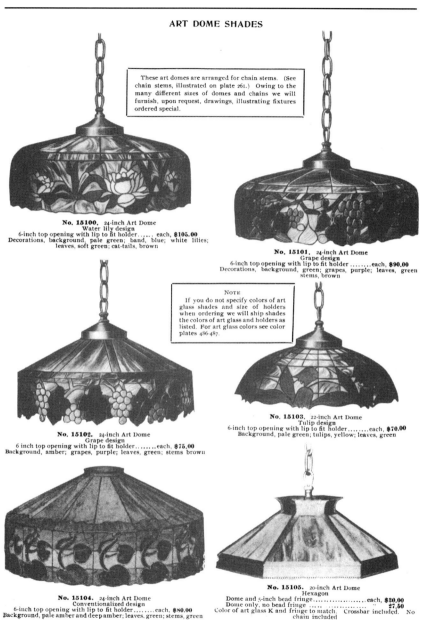

These art domes are arranged for chain stems. (See chain stems, illustrated on plate 261.) Owing to the many different sizes of domes and chains we will furnish, upon request, drawings, illustrating fixtures ordered special.

No. 15100. 24-inch Art Dome
Water lily design
6-inch top opening with lip to fit holder..... each, **$105.00**
Decorations, background, pale green; band, blue; white lilies; leaves, soft green; cat-tails, brown

No. 15101. 24-inch Art Dome
Grape design
6-inch top opening with lip to fit holder........each, **$90.00**
Decorations, background, green; grapes, purple; leaves, green stems, brown

NOTE
If you do not specify colors of art glass shades and size of holders when ordering we will ship shades the colors of art glass and holders as listed. For art glass colors see color plates 486-487.

No. 15102. 24-inch Art Dome
Grape design
6 inch top opening with lip to fit holder.......each, **$75.00**
Background, amber; grapes, purple; leaves, green; stems brown

No. 15103. 22-inch Art Dome
Tulip design
6-inch top opening with lip to fit holder........each, **$70.00**
Background, pale green; tulips, yellow; leaves, green

No. 15104. 24-inch Art Dome
Conventionalized design
6-inch top opening with lip to fit holder........each, **$80.00**
Background, pale amber and deep amber; leaves, green; stems green

No. 15105. 20-inch Art Dome
Hexagon
Dome and 5-inch bead fringe..................each, **$30.00**
Dome only, no bead fringe...... .... " **27.50**
Color of art glass K and fringe to match. Crossbar included. No chain included

225

ART DOME SHADES

No. 15106. 24-inch Art Dome
Wild rose design
6-inch top opening with lip to fit holder.......each, **$90.00**
Background, pale green; green leaves; pale amber stripes; pink roses

No. 15107. 24-inch Art Dome
Grape design
6-inch top opening with lip to fit holder.......each, **$105.00**
Background, pale olive green; grapes, red and green; leaves, green and green stems

No. 15108. 20-inch Art Dome
Apple blossom design
6-inch top opening with lip to fit holder........each, **$75.00**
Background, pale blue; border, pale green; pink apple blossoms; green leaves and stems

No. 15109. 22-inch Art Dome
Grape design
6-inch top opening with lip to fit holder.......each, **$80.00**
Background, greenish amber; green leaves; purple and green grapes

No. 15110. 20-inch Art Dome
Grape design
6-inch top opening with lip to fit holder, each, **$65.00**
Background, red and green; green leaves; purple grapes

These art domes are arranged for chain stems illustrated on plate 255.) Owing to the many different sizes of domes and chains, we will furnish upon request, drawings, illustrating fixtures ordered special.

If you do not specify colors of art glass shades and size of holders when ordering we will ship shades the colors of art glass and holders as listed. For art glass colors see color plates 486-487.

No. 15111. 20-inch Art Dome
Conventionalized design
6-inch top opening with lip to fit holder, each, **$60.00**
Background, pale amber and red; green leaves

No. 15112. 16-inch Art Dome
Conventionalized design
Each.. $55.00
Pale green and blue; peacock colors

No. 15113. 17-inch Art Dome
Conventionalized design
Each.. $30.00
Pale green, amber and red

ART DOME SHADES

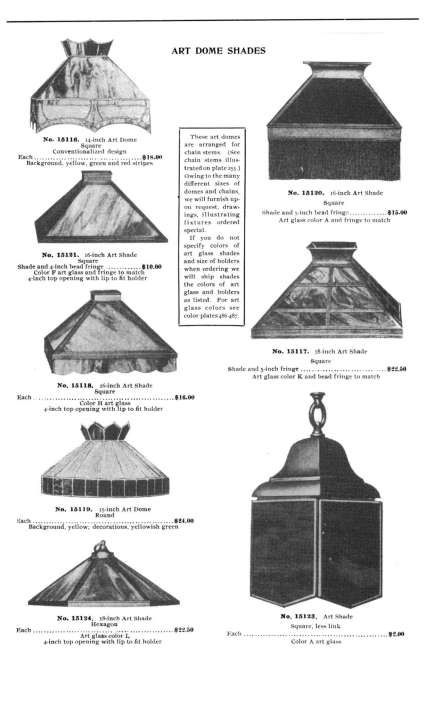

No. 15116. 14-inch Art Dome
Square
Conventionalized design
Each **$18.00**
Background, yellow, green and red stripes

No. 15121. 16-inch Art Shade
Square
Shade and 4-inch bead fringe **$10.00**
Color F art glass and fringe to match
4-inch top opening with lip to fit holder

No. 15118. 16-inch Art Shade
Square
Each **$16.00**
Color H art glass
4-inch top opening with lip to fit holder

No. 15119. 15-inch Art Dome
Round
Each **$24.00**
Background, yellow; decorations, yellowish green

No. 15124. 18-inch Art Shade
Hexagon
Each **$22.50**
Art glass color L
4-inch top opening with lip to fit holder

These art domes are arranged for chain stems. (See chain stems illustrated on plate 255.) Owing to the many different sizes of domes and chains, we will furnish upon request, drawings, illustrating fixtures ordered special.

If you do not specify colors of art glass shades and size of holders when ordering we will ship shades the colors of art glass and holders as listed. For art glass colors see color plates 486-487.

No. 15120. 16-inch Art Shade
Square
Shade and 5-inch bead fringe **$15.00**
Art glass color A and fringe to match

No. 15117. 18-inch Art Shade
Square
Shade and 5-inch fringe **$22.50**
Art glass color K and bead fringe to match

No. 15123. Art Shade
Square, less link
Each **$2.00**
Color A art glass

227

ART DOME SHADES

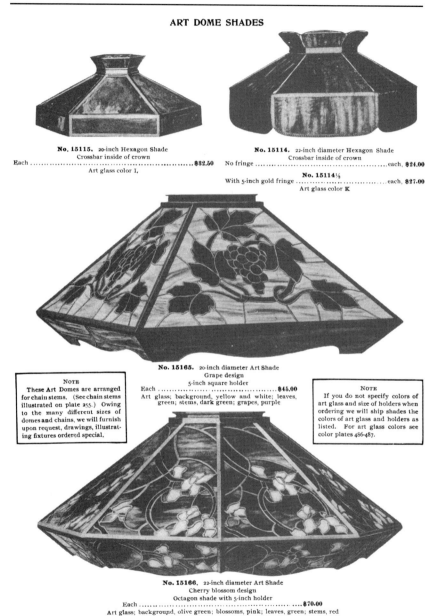

No. 15115. 20-inch Hexagon Shade
Crossbar inside of crown
Each **$32.50**
Art glass color I,

No. 15114. 22-inch diameter Hexagon Shade
Crossbar inside of crown
No fringe .... each, **$24.00**

No. 15114½
With 5-inch gold fringe .... each, **$27.00**
Art glass color **K**

No. 15165. 20-inch diameter Art Shade
Grape design
5-inch square holder
Each **$45.00**
Art glass; background, yellow and white; leaves,
green; stems, dark green; grapes, purple

NOTE
These Art Domes are arranged
for chain stems. (See chain stems
illustrated on plate 255.) Owing
to the many different sizes of
domes and chains, we will furnish
upon request, drawings, illustrating fixtures ordered special.

NOTE
If you do not specify colors of
art glass and size of holders when
ordering we will ship shades the
colors of art glass and holders as
listed. For art glass colors see
color plates 486-487.

No. 15166. 22-inch diameter Art Shade
Cherry blossom design
Octagon shade with 5-inch holder
Each **$70.00**
Art glass; background, olive green; blossoms, pink; leaves, green; stems, red

When ordering state number of shade, colors and size of holders wanted

ART DOME SHADES

No. 15163. 20 inch diameter Art Shade
Cherry design
With 5-inch square holder............................... each, **$24.00**
Art glass; background, yellow and white; leaves, green; cherries, red

No. 15164. 20-inch diameter Art Shade
Conventional morning glory design
With 5-inch square holder ....each, **$40.00**
Art glass; background, yellow and green; leaves, green; pink and white flowers

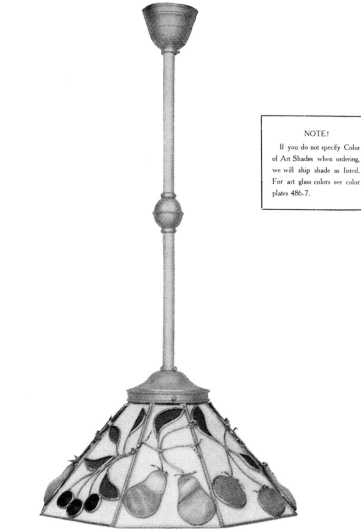

NOTE!

If you do not specify Color
of Art Shades when ordering,
we will ship shade as listed.
For art glass colors see color
plates 486-7.

7922. Brushed Brass.
Length 36 inches over all.   Spread 18 inch shade.

	Not wired	Wired	Complete, as shown, except lamps
3 light	**$45.00**	**$46.50**	**$48.48**
4 light	**45.50**	**47.50**	**50.14**

With 18 inch Art Shade.   Background Color K art glass, pears Color D, apples Color G, cherries **Color E**, leaves **Color L** art glass, included in not wired and wired prices.
Complete fixture includes Hubbell pull sockets.   Each...**66c**

7923. Brushed Brass.
Same as 7922, only with 0560 chain stem, see page 261

	Not wired	Wired	Complete, as shown, except lamps
3 light	**$50.50**	**$52.00**	**$53.98**
4 light....................	**51.00**	**53.00**	**55.64**
Extra chain, per ft.......	**1.13**	**1.35**	

DINING ROOM FIXTURES

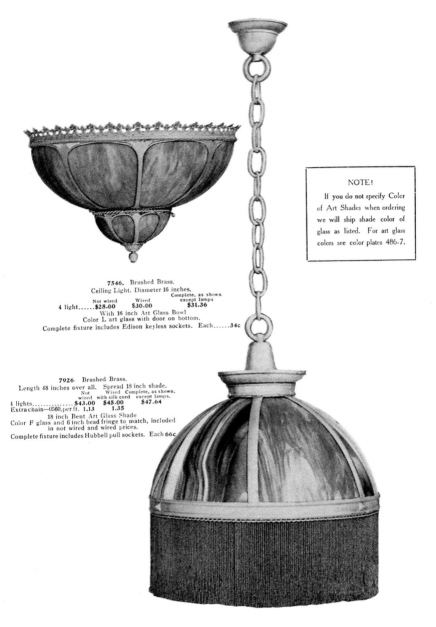

7546. Brushed Brass.
Ceiling Light. Diameter 16 inches.

	Not wired	Wired	Complete, as shown except lamps
4 light	$28.00	$30.00	$31.36

With 16 inch Art Glass Bowl
Color L art glass with door on bottom.
Complete fixture includes Edison keyless sockets. Each......34c

7926. Brushed Brass.
Length 48 inches over all. Spread 18 inch shade.

	Not wired with silk cord	Wired	Complete, as shown except lamps.
4 lights	$43.00	$45.00	$47.64
Extra chain—0560, per ft.	1.13	1.35	

18 inch Bent Art Glass Shade
Color F glass and 6 inch bead fringe to match, included in not wired and wired prices.
Complete fixture includes Hubbell pull sockets. Each 66c

231

NOTE!

If you do not specify Color of Art Glass when ordering we will ship shade color G glass and bead fringe to match. For art glass colors see color plates 486-7.

7929. Brushed Brass.
Length 48 inches over all. Spread 18 inch shade.

	Not wired	Wired	Complete, as shown, except lamps
4 lights,	$52.00	$54.00	$56.64
Extra chain, per ft.	1.13	1.35	

With 18 inch Bent Art Glass Shade
Color G glass and 6 inch bead fringe to match, included in not wired and wired prices.
Complete fixtures includes Hubbell pull sockets. Each 66c

7547. Rich Gilt.
Ceiling Light. Diameter 16 inches.

Complete, as shown, except lamps

	Not wired	Wired	
4 lights.........	$28.00	$30.00	$31.36

16 inch Art Glass Bowl
Color B with door on bottom, included in not wired and wired prices.
Complete fixture includes Edison keyless sockets. Each......34c

7930. Brushed Brass.
Length 48 inches over all. Spread 22 inch shade.

Complete, as shown, except lamps

	Not wired	Wired	
4 lights.....................	$40.00	$41.50	$44.14
5 lights.....................	40.50	42.50	45.80
6 lights.....................	41.00	43.50	47.46

22 inch Bent Art Glass Shade
Color B glass and 6 inch bead fringe, included in not wired and wired prices.
Complete fixture includes Hubbell pull sockets. Each..........66c

7931. Brushed Brass.
Same as 7930, only with 0560 chain stem, see page 261.

Complete, as shown, except lamps

	Not wired	Wired	
4 lights.....................	$45.00	$47.00	$49.64
5 lights.....................	45.50	48.00	51.30
6 lights.....................	46.00	49.00	52.96
Extra chain per ft..........	1.13	1.35	

BENT ART GLASS GLASSWARE

All bent glass illustrated in this catalogue can be furnished in the various colors shown on these pages. Red, pink, yellow and green in each article usually in stock. Other colors, see color plates 486-7.

44-211. Electric Ball.
Color K.
3¼x6 inch. Each............$ 6.75
3¼x8 inch. Each............ 12.00

43-543. Stalactite.
Color A.
3¼x7 inch.
Each **$4.25**

42-542. Stalactite.
Color F.
3¼x7½ inch. Each....**$6.00**

48-548. Flame.
Color E.
3¼x8½ inch. Each.....**$9.00**

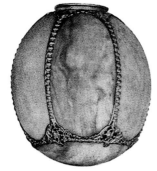

51-212. Electric Ball.
Color, Yellow K, **Green C**.
3¼x9 inch. Each.....................**$10.50**
Bottom opens on hinge.

50-210. Stalactite.
Color A.
4x9 inch. Each........**$7.50**

49-230. Stalactite.
Color G.
Each **$9.00**
5 inch holder, 9 inches high.

41-541. Stalactite.
Color G.
Each.......................................$18.00
8 inch holder, 8 inches high.

40-540. Stalactite.
Color A.
3¼x7 inch. Each....**$4.50**

38-211. Electric Ball.
Color K.
3¼x6 inch. Each..................$ 6.75
3¼x8 inch. Each................. 12.00

234

BENT ART GLASSWARE FOR ELECTRIC

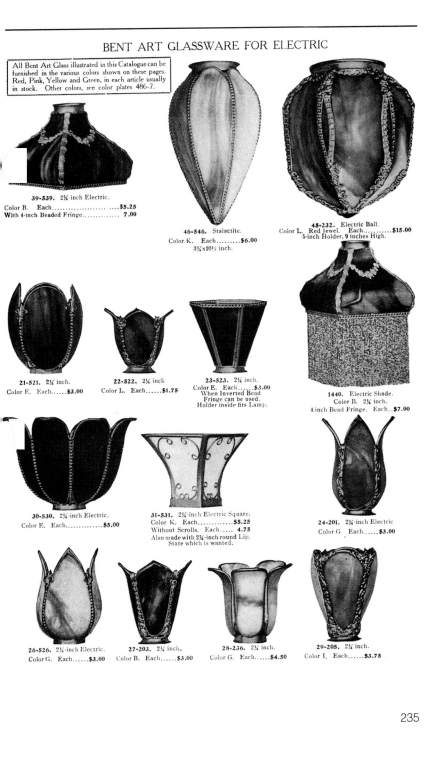

All Bent Art Glass illustrated in this Catalogue can be furnished in the various colors shown on these pages. Red, Pink, Yellow and Green, in each article usually in stock. Other colors, see color plates 486-7.

39-539. 2¼-inch Electric.
Color B. Each.................\$5.25
With 4-inch Beaded Fringe.............. **7.00**

46-546. Stalactite.
Color K. Each.........\$6.00
3¼x10½ inch.

45-232. Electric Ball.
Color L. Red Jewel. Each..........\$15.00
5-inch Holder, 9 inches High.

21-521. 2¼ inch.
Color E. Each......\$3.00

22-522. 2¼ inch.
Color L. Each......\$1.75

23-523. 2¼ inch.
Color E. Each......\$3.00
When Inverted Bead Fringe can be used. Holder inside fits Lamp.

1440. Electric Shade.
Color B. 2¼ inch.
4-inch Bead Fringe. Each..\$7.00

30-530. 2¼-inch Electric.
Color E. Each..............\$5.00

31-531. 2¼-inch Electric Square.
Color K. Each..............\$5.25
Without Scrolls. Each..... **4.75**
Also made with 2¼-inch round Lip. State which is wanted.

24-201. 2¼-inch Electric
Color G. Each......\$3.00

26-526. 2¼-inch Electric.
Color G. Each......\$3.00

27-203. 2¼ inch.
Color B. Each......\$3.00

28-236. 2¼ inch.
Color G. Each......\$4.50

29-205. 2¼ inch.
Color I. Each......\$3.75

34-222. 2¼ inch.
Color A.
Each $6.00

35-535. 2¼ inch.
Color F.
Each $2.50

36-536. 2¼ inch.
Color G.
Each $3.50

37-537. 2¼ inch.
Color E.
Each $3.00

32-532. 2¼ inch.
Color F.
Each $2.25

33-533. 3¼ inch.
Color, Pink G, Green C
6 inch. Each..........$10.00

18-518. Dome.
Color E.
3¼ x10 inch. Each.............................$5.50
4 x12 inch. Each............................. 6.50

NOTE!
Mica Protector
Linings
for Candelabra
Shades, can
be furnished
when ordered,
from
85c. to $2.25
per dozen.

1898. Cuirass No. 14 Lining.
Gold. Doz............$15.00
Holders Extra.
Cuirass Only.
Silver.
Doz. $10.00
Gold,
Doz. $12.00

4-14. Cuirass with No. 14 Lining.
Silver. Doz.............. $16.50
Gold. Doz................. 18.50
Holders Extra.

1245. Electric Art Shade.
Color E, Red.
Each $4.00
Holder inside, which clasps over lamp.

430. Linen Shades, white lined, 7 inch,
with clasp holder to fit Electric Lamp. Green,
Red, Orange, Light Blue, Pink. Doz.....$10.50

14. Linen Shades,
Green, Red, Pink, White, Yellow, Blue,
Lavender. Doz $3.00
Holders Extra.

48. Celluloid Shades, 7 inch.
Yellow, Pink, Blue, Red, Light Green
Doz ....$ 6.
98. Dark Green. Doz...........10.
White Lined.

No.6. CandleShade
Holder to fit over
Electric Lamps.
Doz..........$1.75

No.30. Universal Candle Shade Holder, to
fit Electric Lamp in any Position.
Doz.................................$1.75

No.19. Candle Shade
Holder, Clasps on
Candle.
Doz 75c

No.20. Extension
Candle Shade
Holder, with
Clasp on Candle.
Doz......$1.00

No.26. Loaded Candle
Shade Holder, Nickle
Rests on Candle.
Doz..............$1.50

236

WILLIAMSON'S TEPLITZ GLASS

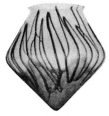

6907. Stalactite.
Red and Blue Veins, Green and Blue Veins.
3¼ x 6 inch. Each..............$2.75

7054. Stalactite.
Blue and Green, Red and Yellow.
3¼ x 7 inch. Each..............$3.00

7591. 2¾ inch.
Red. Each.. ....$1.50
Green. Each.................... 1.50

7588. 2¾ inch.
Green. Each.......$1.75

7595. 2¾ inch.
Canary. Each........$2.00

7594. 2¾ inch.
Red. Each............$1.75

7589. 2¾ inch.
Green. Each............$1.60
Red. Each.............. 1.60

7590. 2¾ inch.
ed. Each $2.00

7596. 2¾ inch.
Canary. Each $1.75

7598. 2¾ inch.
Green and Blue Veins.
2¾ x 7 inches. Each....................$1.65

6098. 2¾ inch.
Red, Pink, Yellow, Green, **Blue.**
Each.................$1.00

6909. Stalactite.
Red and Green.
3¼ x 8 inch. Each $3.00

7052. Stalactite.
Red and Green, Green and Red.
3¼ x 8 inch. Each $2.75

7065. Stalactite.
Red and Yellow, Green and Red, Red and Green, Red and Red.
3¼ x 7½ inch. Each............$3.00

237

WILLIAMSON'S TEPLITZ GLASS

7110. Ball.
Ruby and Yellow, Yellow and Gold, Ruby and Green, Green and Red.
3¼ x 9 inch. Each.............................$10.00

7066. Ball.
Blue and Yellow, Green and Red, Blue and Green.
3¼ x 6 inch. Each.............$3.00

2026. Stalactite.
Opalescent.
3¼ x 8 inch. Each..$1.25

7067. Stalactite.
Blue and Yellow, Green and Red, Blue and Red.
3¼ x 7½ inch. Each............$3.25

7063. Stalactite.
Red and Yellow, Blue and Green.
3¼ x 8 inch. Each........$3.00
7064. Stalactite.
Dark Red, Dark Green.
3¼ x 8 inch. Each.......$3.50

7034. Stalactite.
Red and Blue Veins, Green and Red Veins.
3¼ x 6½ in. Each. $3.00

7027. Stalactite.
Red and Green, Green and Yellow.
4¼ x 7½ in. Each. $2.75

403. Bright Finish. Blue, Yellow, Amber. Each.............$11.00.   Purple. Each.............$11.50
404. Satin Dull Finish. Blue, Yellow, Amber. Each.......... 12.00.   Purple. Each............. 12.50

238

5823. 4 inch.
Opalescent. Doz...............**$5.00**

2040. 4 inch.
Ruby and Pink. Doz..........**$11.50**
Blue, Opalescent, Amber.
etc. Doz...................... 6.00

6517. 4 inch.
Straw Opalescent. Doz........**$12.00**

5823½. 2¼ inch.
Opalescent. Doz...............**$4.50**

2040½. 2¼ inch.
Ruby and Pink. Doz.......**$10.50**
Blue, Opalescent, Amber. Doz. **5.50**

6517½. 2¼ inch.
Straw Opalescent. Doz......**$10.00**

413. 4 inch.
Ruby or Pink. Doz...........**$11.50**
Blue, Opalescent. etc. Doz.... 6.00

513. 4 inch. Satin.
Assorted colors. Doz.........**$15.00**

95. 4 inch.
Straw Opalescent. Doz **$7.50**
Plain Opalescent. Doz......... 6.00

413½. 2¼ inch.
Ruby or Pink. Doz...........**$10.50**
Blue, Opalescent, etc. Doz... **5.50**

513½. 2¼ inch. Satin.
Assorted colors. Doz.........**$10.00**

95½. 2¼ inch.
Straw Opalescent. Doz........**$6.00**
Plain Opalescent. Doz......... **4.50**

93½. 2¼ inch.
Ruby. Doz...................**$10.50**

94½. 2¼ inch.
Straw Opalescent. Doz........**$5.50**

3453½. 2¼ inch.
Straw Opalescent. Doz........**$8.50**
Plain Opalescent. Doz......... 7.50

COLORED GAS AND ELECTRIC GLOBES

6716. 4 inch.
Ruby, Blue, Citron, Orange.
Dozen............................$14.50

6878. 4 inch.
Etched and Assorted, Colored Edges
Dozen............................$14.50

1090. 4 inch
Assorted, Colored Tops, W. A.
Dozen............................$10.00

6716. 2¼ inch.
Ruby, Blue, Citron, Orange.
Dozen..................$12.00

6878½. 2¼ inch.
Etched and Assorted,
Colored Edges.
Dozen...................$12.00

1090½. 2¼ inch.
Assorted, Colored Tops, W. A.
Dozen...................$8.50

287. 4 inch.
Ruby, Blue, Citron, Orange, W. A.
Dozen........................$16.00

325. 4 inch.
Ruby, Pink, Blue, Citron.
Dozen..........................$12.00

9112. 4 inch.
Assorted Colors.
Dozen........................$30.00

287½. 2¼ inch.
Ruby, Blue, Citron,
Orange, W. A.
Dozen..............$13.50

325½. 2¼ inch.
Ruby, Pink, Blue, Citron.
Dozen..............$10.50

9112½. 2¼ inch.
Assorted Colors, Etched.
Dozen $24.00

6715. 4 inch.
Ruby, Blue, Citron, Orange, W. A.
Dozen..........................$16.00

6715½. 2¼ inch.
Ruby, Blue, Citron, Orange,
W. A.
Dozen $13.50

799. 4 inch.
Ruby....................Dozen, $12.00
Blue....................Dozen, 6.00
Green ....Dozen, 6.00

2423. 4 inch.
Straw Opalescent. Dozen....$6.00
Plain Opalescent. Dozen **5.00**

413T. 4 inch.
Ruby or Pink. Dozen........$11.50
Blue, Opalescent. Dozen.... 6.00

6620½. 2¼ inch.
Straw Opalescent.
Dozen......$5.00
Plain Opalescent.
Dozen......$4.50

4920½. 2¼ inch.
Twist Opalescent.
Dozen..................$4.50

2423½. 2¼ inch.
Straw Opalescent.
Dozen..........$5.50
Plain Opalescent.
Dozen..........$4.25

413½T. 2¼ inch.
Ruby or Pink.
Dozen........$10.50
Blue Opalescent.
Dozen..........$5.50

433. 3¼x10 inch.
Opalescent Twist. Dozen.....................$12.00
433½. 4x12 inch.
Dozen.. 13.50

430. Dome. 3¼x10 inch.
Flint Opalescent. Dozen.......................$12.00
Straw Opalescent. Dozen...................... 13.50
430½. 4x12 inch.
Flint Opalescent. Dozen 13.50
Straw Opalescent. Dozen...................... 15.00

4892. 3¼x7 inch.
Flint Opalescent. Doz..$13.50
Straw Opalescent. Doz.. 16.50
Ruby. Dozen 21.00
Pink Opalescent..Doz.. 21.00

5209. 5x9 inch. Stalactite.
Pink. Dozen..................$27.00
Ruby. Dozen................. 27.00
Opalescent. Dozen............ 15.00

6652. 3¼x7 inch.
Straw Opalescent.
Dozen.......$13.50
Flint Opalescent.
Dozen.......$12.00
Roughed inside.
Dozen.......$13.50

COLORED ELECTRIC BOWLS, STALACTITES AND BALLS

2160.
Crystal, Roughed Inside.

10 inch.	Doz.	**$22.50**
12 inch.	Doz.	**27.00**
14 inch.	Doz.	**36.00**
16 inch.	Doz.	**72.00**

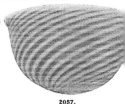

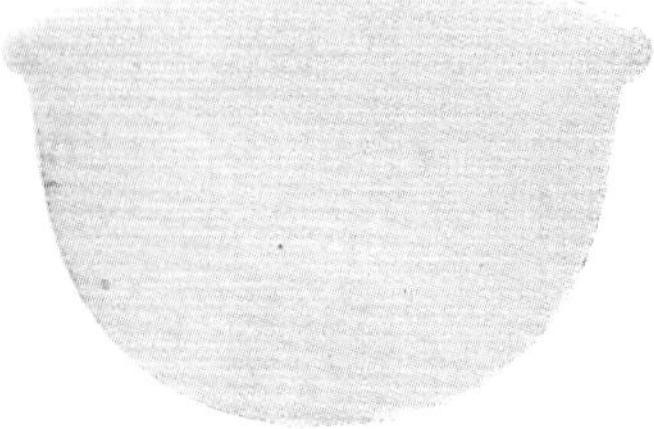

427. Flint, Opalescent.

10 in.	Doz..$30.00	12 in.	Doz..$36.00
14 in.	Doz.. 60.00	16 in.	Doz.. 81.00

Straw Opalescent.

10 in.	Doz..$36.00	12 in.	Doz.$ 45.00
14 in.	Doz.. 63.00	16 in.	Doz. 108.00

2057.
Flint, Opalescent, Twist.

10 inch.	Doz.	**$30.00**
12 inch.	Doz.	**36.00**
14 inch.	Doz.	**60.00**
16 inch.	Doz.	**81.00**

311. Ruby or Pink.

3¼ x 6 inch.	Doz.	**$12.50**
3¼ x 7 inch.	Doz.	**18.00**
3¼ x 8 inch.	Doz.	**22.50**

509. 3¼ x 6 in. Crystal, Roughed. Doz.$12.00
512. 4 x 8 in. Crystal, Roughed. Doz.... 18.00
Assorted Colors: Satin Red, Ivory, Sea Green,
Canary, Blue, Pink.

509. 3¼ x 6 inch. Doz. **$15.00**
512. 4 x 8 inch. Doz. **21.00**

132. Flint Opalescent Ball.

3¼ x 6 inch.	Doz.	**$ 7.50**
3¼ x 7 inch.	Doz.	**9.00**
3¼ x 8 inch.	Doz.	**11.25**

6095. 3¼ x 7 inch.

Pink.	Doz.	**$24.00**
Ruby.	Doz.	**24.00**
Orange.	Doz.	**24.00**
Citron.	Doz.	**20 00**
Opal.	Doz.	**13.50**

3632. 3¼ x 8 inch.
Ruby. Doz. **$24.00**

9243. 3¼ x 8 inch.
Ruby. Doz. **$24.00**
Opal. Doz. **15.00**
Lettering: Fire Escape,
Stairs, etc. Each **$1.25**

505. 3¼ x 8 inch.
Assorted colors: Ruby,
Pink, Canary, Blue, Green,
Roughed and Ivory
Dozen **$18.00**

2158.
3¼ x 8
inch.
Ruby or
Pink.
Dozen
$16.50

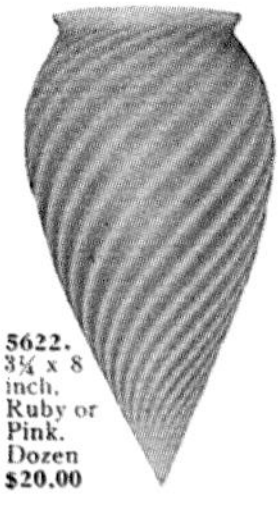

5622.
3¼ x 8
inch.
Ruby or
Pink.
Dozen
$20.00

4518.
3¼ x 8
inch.
Ruby or
Pink.
Dozen
$15.00

5862.
3¼ x 6½ inch.
Ruby.
Doz..... **$15.00**
Pink.
Doz..... **$15.00**
Opalescent.
Doz..... **$9.00**

GREEN, WHITE LINED ELECTRIC GLASSWARE

8518.
2¼x7 inch.
Green Side Shade, white lined.
Dozen...................**$9.00**

8516. 2¼x6 inch.
Green Side Shade, white lined.
Dozen...............**$7.50**

8517. 2¼x6 inch.
Green Side Shade, white lined
Dozen..............**$7.50**

8515. 2¼x5 inch.
Green Side Shade, white lined.
Dozen..............**$9.00**

470.
2¼x6 inch.
Green Side Shade, white lined.
Dozen...**$9.00**

115. 3¼x8 inch.
Green Reading Shade, white lined.
Dozen...................**$22.50**
Ground glass bottom.

511. 3¼x10 inch.
Green, white lined. Dozen.................**$11.00**
Yellow, pink, maroon, white lined. Dozen.... **15.00**
Red, white lined. Dozen...................... **18.00**

114. 2¼x7 inch.
Green, white lined.
Dozen.........................**$7.00**

514. 2¼x7 inch.
Green, white lined. Dozen....**$ 6.75**
Maroon, pink, yellow, white lined. Dozen............... **10.00**
Red, white lined **11.00**

113. 3¼x16 inch.
Green, white lined.
Dozen....................................**$12.00**
113½. 2¼x10 inch.
Dozen.................................... **12.00**

434. 10 inch. Closed top.
Green, white lined. Dozen.....................**$15.00**

309. 3¼x10 inch.
Green, white lined. Dozen.....................**$13.50**

243

BEAD LAMP COVERS AND CANDLES AND HOLDERS

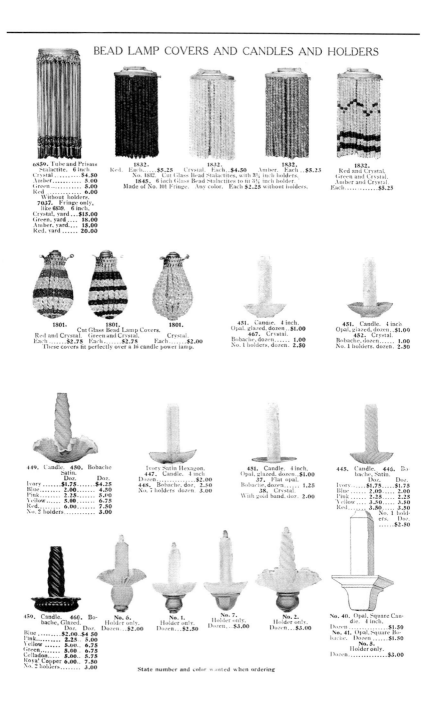

6859. Tube and Prisms
Stalactite. 6 inch.
Crystal $4.50
Amber 5.00
Green 5.00
Red 6.00
Without holders.
7037. Fringe only,
like 6859. 6 inch.
Crystal, yard ...$15.00
Green, yard 18.00
Amber, yard.... 18.00
Red, yard 20.00

1832.
Red. Each......$5.25   Crystal. Each..$4.50   Amber. Each..$5.25
No. 1832. Cut Glass Bead Stalactites, with 3½ inch holders.
1845. 6 inch Glass Bead Stalactites to fit 3½ inch holder.
Made of No. 101 Fringe. Any color. Each $2.25 without holders.

1832.
Red and Crystal,
Green and Crystal,
Amber and Crystal.
Each............$5.25

1801.   **1801.**   **1801.**
Cut Glass Bead Lamp Covers.
Red and Crystal.   Green and Crystal.   Crystal.
Each ......$2.75   Each......$2.75   Each......$2.00
These covers fit perfectly over a 16 candle power lamp.

451. Candle. 4 inch.
Opal. glazed, dozen..$1.00
467. Crystal.
Bobache, dozen...... 1.00
No. 1 holders, dozen. 2.50

451. Candle. 4 inch.
Opal, glazed, dozen...$1.00
452. Crystal.
Bobache, dozen...... 1.00
No. 1 holders, dozen. 2.50

449. Candle. **450.** Bobache
Satin.
	Doz.	Doz.
Ivory.......	$1.75	$4.25
Blue.......	2.00	4.50
Pink.......	2.25	5.00
Yellow	5.00	6.75
Red.......	6.00	7.50
No. 2 holders		3.00

Ivory Satin Hexagon.
447. Candle. 4 inch
Dozen.............$2.00
448. Bobache, doz. 2.50
No. 7 holders dozen. 3.00

451. Candle. 4 inch.
Opal, glazed, dozen...$1.00
37. Flat opal.
Bobache, dozen...... 1.25
38. Crystal.
With gold band, doz. 2.00

448. Candle. **446.** Bobache, Satin.
	Doz.	Doz.
Ivory.......	$1.75	$1.75
Blue	2.00	2.00
Pink	2.25	2.25
Yellow	3.50	3.50
Red.......	3.50	3.50
No. 1 holders.		Doz.
		$2.50

459. Candle. **460.** Bobache, Glazed.
	Doz.	Doz.
Blue	$2.00	$4.50
Pink.......	2.25	5.00
Yellow	5.00	6.75
Green.......	5.00	6.75
Celladon....	5.00	5.75
Roya' Copper	6.00	7.50
No. 2 holders		3.00

No. 6.
Holder only.
Dozen...$2.00

No. 1.
Holder only.
Dozen...$2.50

No. 7.
Holder only.
Dozen...$3.00

No. 2.
Holder only.
Dozen...$3.00

No. 40. Opal, Square Candle. 4 inch.
Dozen $1.50
No. 41. Opal, Square Bobache. Dozen $1.50
No. 5.
Holder only.
Dozen..............$3.00

State number and color wanted when ordering

244

IMPORTED BEAD FRINGE

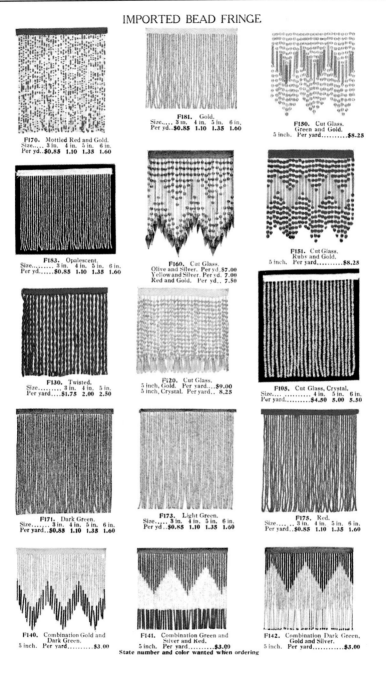

F170. Mottled Red and Gold.
Size.... 3 in. 4 in. 5 in. 6 in.
Per yd..$0.85 1.10 1.35 1.60

F181. Gold.
Size.... 3 in. 4 in. 5 in. 6 in.
Per yd..$0.85 1.10 1.35 1.60

F150. Cut Glass.
Green and Gold.
5 inch. Per yard.........$8.25

F183. Opalescent.
Size........ 3 in. 4 in. 5 in. 6 in.
Per yd.....$0.85 1.10 1.35 1.60

F160. Cut Glass.
Olive and Silver. Per yd..$7.00
Yellow and Silver. Per yd. 7.00
Red and Gold. Per yd.. 7.50

F151. Cut Glass.
Ruby and Gold.
5 inch. Per yard.........$8.25

F130. Twisted.
Size........ 3 in. 4 in. 5 in.
Per yard....$1.75 2.00 2.50

F120. Cut Glass.
5 inch, Gold. Per yard....$9.00
5 inch, Crystal. Per yard.. 8.25

F105. Cut Glass, Crystal.
Size.... 4 in. 5 in. 6 in.
Per yard.........$4.50 5.00 5.50

F171. Dark Green.
Size....... 3 in. 4 in. 5 in. 6 in.
Per yard..$0.85 1.10 1.35 1.60

F173. Light Green.
Size.... 3 in. 4 in. 5 in. 6 in.
Per yd..$0.85 1.10 1.35 1.60

F175. Red.
Size.... 3 in. 4 in. 5 in. 6 in.
Per yard..$0.85 1.10 1.35 1.60

F140. Combination Gold and
Dark Green.
5 inch. Per yard.........$3.00

F141. Combination Green and
Silver and Red.
5 inch. Per yard.........$3.00

F142. Combination Dark Green,
Gold and Silver.
5 inch. Per yard.........$3.00

State number and color wanted when ordering

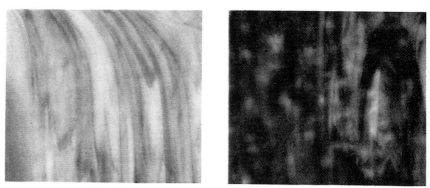

Color A   Color B

We have endeavored to represent the various colors in Art Glass
which we can furnish.

Color C   Color D

When ordering by letter it should be remembered that the colors vary somewhat, but it will
be our effort to furnish same as near above colors as possible.

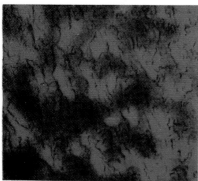

Color E   Color F

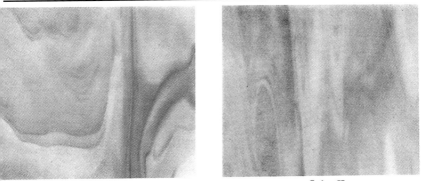

Color G   Color H

We have endeavored to represent the various colors in Art Glass
which we can furnish.

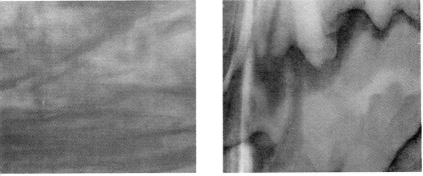

Color I   Color J

When ordering by letter it should be remembered that the colors vary somewhat, but it will
be our effort to furnish same as near above colors as possible.

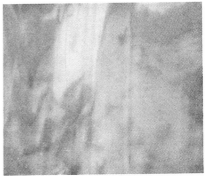

Color K   Color L

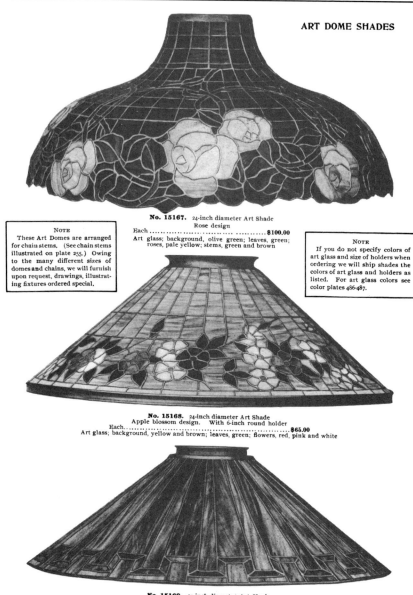

No. 15167. 24-inch diameter Art Shade
Rose design

Each **$100.00**
Art glass; background, olive green; leaves, green;
roses, pale yellow; stems, green and brown

NOTE
These Art Domes are arranged for chain stems. (See chain stems illustrated on plate 255.) Owing to the many different sizes of domes and chains, we will furnish upon request, drawings, illustrating fixtures ordered special.

NOTE
If you do not specify colors of art glass and size of holders when ordering we will ship shades the colors of art glass and holders as listed. For art glass colors see color plates 486-487.

No. 15168. 24-inch diameter Art Shade
Apple blossom design. With 6-inch round holder

Each **$65.00**
Art glass; background, yellow and brown; leaves, green; flowers, red, pink and white

No. 15169. 24-inch diameter Art Shade
Grecian design. With 5-inch round holder

Each **$32.00**
Art glass; background, panels, light and dark yellow alternate; green decoration

When ordering state number of shade, colors and size of holders wanted

248

ART DOME SHADES

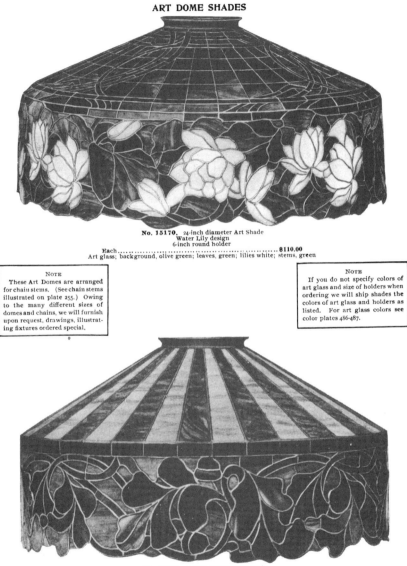

No. 15170. 24-inch diameter Art Shade
Water Lily design
6-inch round holder

Each..**$110.00**
Art glass; background, olive green; leaves, green; lilies white; stems, green

NOTE

These Art Domes are arranged for chain stems. (See chain stems illustrated on plate 255.) Owing to the many different sizes of domes and chains, we will furnish upon request, drawings, illustrating fixtures ordered special.

NOTE

If you do not specify colors of art glass and size of holders when ordering we will ship shades the colors of art glass and holders as listed. For art glass colors see color plates 486-487.

No 15171. 20-inch diameter Art Shade
Oak Leaf design
5-inch round holder

Each..**$77.00**
Art glass; background, top panels, yellow and white; alternate flowers, dark red; leaves and stems green

When ordering state number of shade, colors and size of holders wanted

ART DOME SHADES

No. 15172. 20-inch diameter Art Shade
Nasturtion design
5-inch square holder
Each $28.00
Art glass; background, green and yellow; flowers, yellow; leaves,
olive green; stems, blueish green

No. 15173. 20-inch diameter Art Shade
Wild Rose design
5-inch square holder
Each $25.00
Art glass; background, olive green; leaves, green; stems, red;
flowers, pink and white

When ordering state number of shade, colors and size of holders wanted

ART DOME SHADES

No. 15174. 22-inch diameter Art Shade
Rose design
6-inch round holder

Each...**$65.00**

Art glass; background, yellow and brown; stripes, green and red;
leaves, green; roses, red

No. 15175. 22-inches diameter Art Shade
Grape design
6-inch square holder

Each...**$45.00**

Art glass; background, yellow and brown; leaves, green; grapes,
purple; stems, dark green

When ordering state number of shade, colors and size of holders wanted

ART DOME SHADES

No. 15176. 18-inch diameter Art Shade
Geometric design
5-inch square holder
Each **$23.00**
Art glass; background, olive green; decorations, blue and white

No. 15177. 21-inch diameter Art Shade
Grape design
6-inch square holder
Each **$40.00**
Art glass; background, yellow and white; leaves, green; grapes, purple; stems, dark green

When ordering state number of shade, colors and size of holders wanted

ART DOME SHADES

No. 15178. 21-inch diameter Art Shade
Water lily design
4-inch round holder

Each **$85.00**

Art glass; background, blue and white; lilies, white; leaves, green;
cat-tails, brown

NOTE

These Art Domes are arranged for chain stems. (See chain stems illustrated on plate 255.) Owing to the many different sizes of domes and chains, we will furnish upon request, drawings, illustrating fixtures ordered special.

NOTE

If you do not specify colors of art glass and size of holders when ordering we will ship shades the colors of art glass and holders as listed. For art glass colors see color plates 486-487.

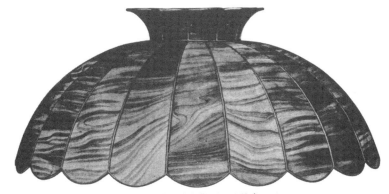

No. 15179. 20-inch diameter Art Shade
Crossbar inside of crown

Each **$65.00**

Art glass, color K

When ordering state number of shade, colors and size of holders wanted

ART DOME SHADES

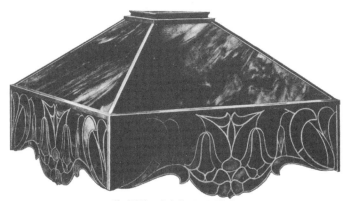

No. 15181. 20-inch diameter Art Shade
Bluebell design
5-inch square top holder, with lip
Each. **$38.00**
Art glass; background, variegated blue and green;
decorations, blue

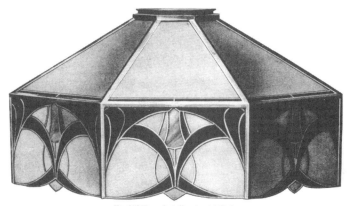

No. 15180. 22-inch diameter Art Shade
Conventionalized design
5½-inch octagon holder, with lip
Each.. **$32.00**
Art glass; background, opalescent;
decorations, red and green

When ordering state number of shade, colors and size of holders wanted

STAPLE GLASSWARE

No. 5817. Ball

	Crystal Roughed Inside Dozen	Straw or Flint Opalescent Dozen
6-inch	$ 3.50	$ 5.25
7 "	4.25	6 50
8 "	6.00	8.00
10 "	15.00	18.00
12 "	20.00	24.00
14 "	60 00	
16 "	100.00	
18 "	170.00	
20 "	450.00	

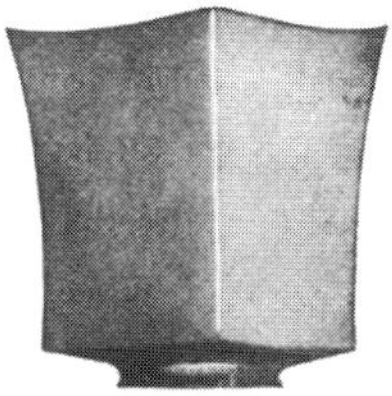

No. 9321½. 2¼-inch

	Dozen
Crystal roughed inside	$4.00
Straw opalescent	8.00
Pearl "	7.50

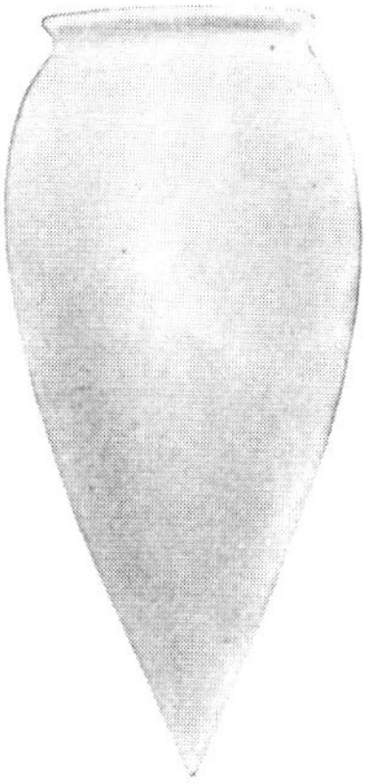

No. 6088. Stalactite

			Dozen
3¼x7-inch	straw	opalescent	$10.00
3¼x8 "	"	"	12.00
3¼x9 "	"	"	15.00
3¼x7 "	pearl	"	8.25
3¼x8 "	"	"	10.00
3¼x9 "	"	"	12 00
3¼x7 "	C. R. I.	"	9.00
3¼x8 "	"	"	11.00
3¼x9 "	"	"	13.50

No. 7005. Mushroom Dome
Ground Inside

	Crystal Dozen	Straw or Flint Opalescent Dozen
10-inch fits 8-inch holder	$15.50	$24.00
12 " " 10 " "	22.00	28.00
14 " " 12 " "	26.00	32.50

No. 94

	Dozen
2¼-inch C. R. I.	$4.50

No. 258. Crystal Roughed Inside

	Dozen
2¼-inch	$7.00

No. 5671½

	Dozen
2¼-inch crystal roughed inside	$3.00
Straw or flint opalescent	4.25

No. 244. 2¼x7

	Dozen
Crystal roughed inside	$ 4 00
Straw or flint opalescent	5.50
Green plate	10.50
Opal	4.00
Ruby or orange, roughed inside	7.00

No. 3453½. 2¼-inch Bevel Top

	Dozen
Crystal roughed inside	$5.00
Straw or flint opalescent	7.50

No. 180. 4-inch Square Gas Globe

	Dozen
Straw or flint opalescent	$8.00
Crystal roughed inside	6.00

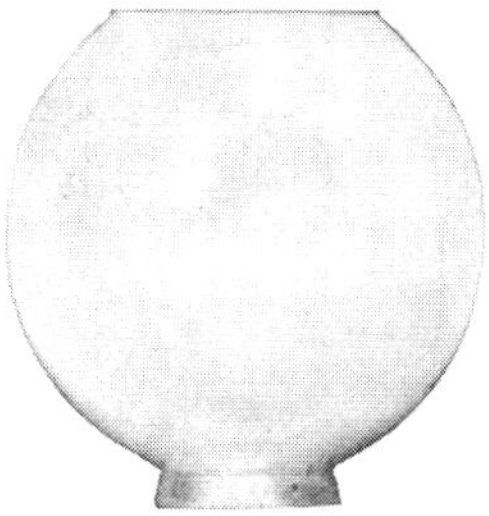

No. 8887. 2¼-inch

	4½-inch Dozen	5½-inch Dozen
Crystal roughed inside	$2.00	$3.50
Plain or flint opalescent	4.00	5.00

Unless otherwise specified we will ship crystal roughed inside glassware

Order by Catalogue numbers

ELECTRIC SHADES

No. 657½. Sand blast
2¼-inch.....................dozen, $2.65
No. 657. Gas to match
Dozen..................................$4.00

No. 396½. White acid
2¼-inch.....................dozen, $3.50
No. 396. Gas to match
Dozen..................................$4.00

No. 6043½. Etched
2¼-inch.....................dozen, $6.75
No. 6043. Gas to match
Dozen..................................$7.50

No. 6566½. White acid
2¼-inch.....................dozen, $5.00
No. 6566. Gas to match
Dozen..................................$5.50

No. 615½. Etched
2¼-inch.....................dozen, $6.50
No. 615. Gas to match
Dozen..................................$7.50

No. 9441½.
White acid. Clear
2¼-inch.....................dozen, $4.50
No. 9441. Gas to match
Dozen..................................$5.00

No. 9178½. Etched
2¼-inch.....................dozen, $8.00
No. 9178. Gas to match
Dozen..................................$9.00

No. 1570½. White acid
2¼-inch.....................dozen, $3.25
No. 1570. Gas to match
Dozen..................................$3.50

No. 9440½. White acid
2¼-inch.....................dozen, $4.00
No. 9440. Gas to match
Dozen..................................$4.50

No. 9434½. White acid
2¼-inch.....................dozen, $4.25
No. 9434. Gas to match
Dozen..................................$4.75

No. 1661½. White acid
2¼-inch.....................dozen, $4.00
No. 1661. Gas to match
Dozen..................................$4.50

No. 453½. White acid
2¼-inch.....................dozen, $4.00
No. 453. Gas to match
Dozen..................................$4.75

No. 2956½. White acid
2¼-inch.....................dozen, $4.00
No. 2956. Gas to match
Dozen..................................$4.50

No. 2735½. White acid
2¼-inch.....................dozen, $4.80
No. 2735. Gas to match
Dozen..................................$5.25

No. 1906½. White acid. Clear
2¼-inch.....................dozen, $4.50
No. 1906. Gas to match
Dozen..................................$5.00

Order by Catalogue numbers

PRESSED GLASSWARE

No. 51½. Pressed
2¼-inch..........................dozen, $3.00

No. 42½. Crystal
2¼-inch.......................dozen, $3.10
No. 42. Gas to match........ " 3.60

No. 50½ Pressed
2¼-inch..........................dozen, $4.25

No. 167½C
2¼-inch..........................dozen, $3.00

No. 49½. Square. Clear line
2¼-inch...................... .....dozen, $3.25
No. 49. Gas to match........ " 5.00

No. 418. Stalactite. Crystal pressed
3¾x7-inch........................dozen, $7.50
3¾x9 " .... " 9.00

No. 46½. Pressed star
2¼-inch..........................dozen, $5.00
No. 46. Gas to match....... " 6.25

No. 48½. Pressed
2¼-inch..........................dozen, $3.00
No. 48. Gas to match........ " 3.50

No. 45½.
2¼ inch..........................dozen, $3.25

No. 44½. Crystal
2¼-inch..........................dozen, $3.25
No. 44. Gas to match....... " 3.75

No. 47½. Pressed
2¼-inch..........................dozen, $3.00

Order by Catalogue numbers

TUNGSTEN GLASSWARE

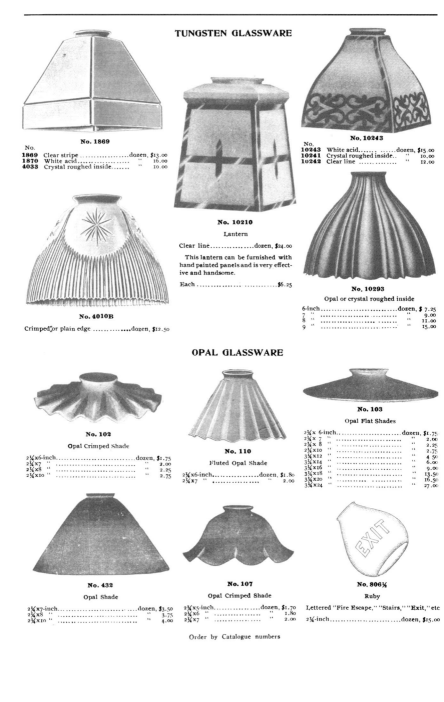

No. 1869

No.
1869 Clear stripe .... dozen, $13.00
1870 White acid .... " 16.00
4033 Crystal roughed inside ...... " 10.00

No. 4010B

Crimped or plain edge .... dozen, $12.50

No. 10210
Lantern

Clear line .... dozen, $24.00

This lantern can be furnished with hand painted panels and is very effective and handsome.

Each $6.25

No. 10243

No.
10243 White acid .... dozen, $15.00
10241 Crystal roughed inside .. " 10.00
10242 Clear line .... " 12.00

No. 10293
Opal or crystal roughed inside

6-inch .... dozen, $ 7.25
7 " .... " 9.00
8 " .... " 11.00
9 " .... " 15.00

OPAL GLASSWARE

No. 102
Opal Crimped Shade

2¼x6-inch......................... dozen, $1.75
2¼x7 " .... " 2.00
2¼x8 " .... " 2.25
2¼x10 " .... " 2.75

No. 110
Fluted Opal Shade

2¼x6-inch................. dozen, $1.80
2¼x7 " .... " 2.00

No. 103
Opal Flat Shades

2¼x 6-inch........................ dozen, $1.75
2¼x 7 " .... " 2.00
2¼x 8 " .... " 2.25
2¼x10 " .... " 2.75
3¼x12 " .... " 4.50
3¼x14 " .... " 6.00
3¼x16 " .... " 9.00
3¼x18 " .... " 13.50
3¼x20 " .... " 16.50
3¼x24 " .... " 27.00

No. 432
Opal Shade

2¼x7-inch........................ dozen, $3.50
2¼x8 " .... " 3.75
2¼x10 " .... " 4.00

No. 107
Opal Crimped Shade

2¼x5-inch................. dozen, $1.70
2¼x6 " .... " 1.80
2¼x7 " .... " 2.00

No. 806½
Ruby

Lettered "Fire Escape," "Stairs," "Exit," etc

2¼-inch........................ dozen, $15.00

Order by Catalogue numbers

GLASSWARE

No. 9189. White acid
2¼-inch .... dozen, $7.00

No. 1864. White acid
2¼-inch .... dozen, $8.50

No. 1865. White acid
2¾-inch .... dozen, $8.00

No. 9191. Roughed outside. Clear stripe
2¼-inch .... dozen, $6.25

No. 9910. Clear edge ball
3¼x7-inch .... dozen, $10.50

No. 9972½. Grecian etched
2¼-inch .... dozen, $8.50

No. 9589½. Grecian etched
2¼-inch .... dozen, $10.00

No. 2540. Black stripe
3¼x6¾-inch .... dozen, $36.00

No. 9590. Grecian
2¼-inch .... dozen, $6.00

No. 4501½. Crystal roughed, with clear lines
2¼-inch .... dozen, $12.50

No. 2536. Black stripe
2¼-inch .... dozen, $18.00

No. 9836½. Straw opalescent
Roughed outside
2¼-inch .... dozen, $10.00

Order by Catalogue numbers

259

No. 9815½. Plain. Crystal roughed inside
Dozen $7 50

No. 10069½. Double Rib
Dozen $4.50

No. 1948. Square Stalactite
Plain
Crystal roughed inside
3¼x6-inch........dozen, $ 9.00
3¼x7 " .... " 11.00

No. 238. Square Ball. Crystal roughed inside
3¼x6-inch.............................dozen, $ 7.50
3¼x7 " .... " 9.00
3¼x8 " .... " 13.50

No. 180B. Plain. Crystal roughed inside
7-inch... ....dozen, $ 8.00
8 " .... " 12 00

No. 10018½. Clear line
Dozen...............................$6.50

No. 10090. Clear line
Dozen.............................$12 00

No. 8884½. Clear line
Dozen...............................$16.00

No. 4780. Plain. Crystal roughed inside
Dozen...............................$7.50

No. 9999½. Clear line
Dozen...............................$7.00

Order by Catalogue numbers

No. 9896½. Clear line. Umbrella
Dozen...............................$7.50

CUT AND ETCHED GLASSWARE

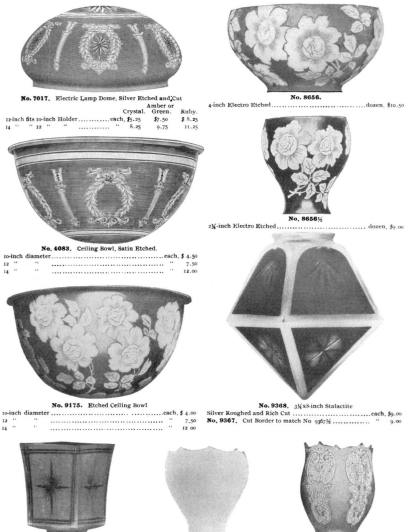

No. 7017. Electric Lamp Dome, Silver Etched and Cut

	Amber or		
	Crystal.	Green.	Ruby.
12-inch fits 10-inch Holder............each, $5.25		$7.50	$ 8.25
14 " " 12 " " .... " 8.25		9.75	11.25

No. 4083. Ceiling Bowl, Satin Etched.

10-inch diameter.......................................each, $ 4.50
12 " " .... " 7.50
14 " " .... " 12.00

No. 9175. Etched Ceiling Bowl

10-inch diameter............................. ....each, $ 4.00
12 " " .... " 7.50
14 " " .... " 12 00

No. 8656.

4-inch Electro Etched..dozen, $10.50

No. 8656½

2¼-inch Electro Etched.................................... dozen, $9.00

No. 9368. 3¼x8-inch Stalactite

Silver Roughed and Rich Cut ....each, $9.00
No. 9367. Cut Border to match No 9367½............. " 9.00

No. 9367½. 2¼-inch Silver Roughed
and Rich Cut...............dozen, $45.00
No. 9368½. Silver Roughed and Rich
Cut, Frosted Border to match 9368,
Dozen.............................. 45.00

No. 8950½. 2¼-inch Silver
Roughed, Bevel Top..dozen, $9.50

No. 9115½. 2¼-inch Electro Etched,
Cut Top ....dozen, $12.00

Order by Catalogue numbers

261

No. 6578. Stalactite

Silver etched and cut

3¼x7 inch..........dozen, $19.50

No. 870C. Roughed and cut ceiling bowl

10-inch diameter	....	each,	$ 9.00
12 " "	....	"	11.00
14 " "	....	"	15.00

No. 9086. Ball

Electro etched and cut

3¼x6 inch....................dozen, $45.00

No. 9082. Stalactite
3¼x7-inch electro etched........dozen, $16.00

No. 292.
3½x6-inch cut star.......... dozen, $15.00

No. 8780. Stalactite
Crystal roughed and cut star
3¼x7-inch ....dozen, $18.00

No. 9083. Ball
3¼x6-inch electro etched........ dozen, $18.00

No. 4081. Ball, 3¼-inch Holder

6-inch satin etched	.........dozen,	$13.50
7 " " "	.... "	18.00
8 " " "	.... "	21.00

No. 8770. Ball
Crystal roughed and cut star

3¼x6-inch	.... dozen,	$16.00
3¼x8 "	.... "	25.00

Order by Catalogue numbers

COLONIAL CUT GLASSWARE

No. 10139. Ball

3¼x6-inch	dozen,	$30.00
3¼x7 "	"	45.00
3¼x8 "	"	45.00
4x10 "	"	65.00

No. 9170. Bowl

10-inch diameter	each,	$ 8.00
12 " "	"	12.00
14 " "	"	16.00

No. 9917½

2¼x7-inch......................dozen, $22.00

No. 10111½

2¼-inch.....................dozen, $30.00

No. 10141

3¼x4½-inch	dozen,	$15.00
3¼x5½ "	"	18.00

COLONIAL PRISMS

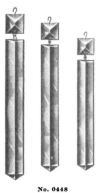

No. 0448

No. 0448½. Colonial Square Chain

18-inch lengths	each,	$1.50
24 " "	"	2.00
30 " "	"	2.75

Graduated

No. 0448. Colonial Prisms

	Dozen	Per 100
3-inch	$1.25	$ 9.00
4 "	1.75	12.50
5 "	2.20	17.50
6 "	3.50	25.00
7 "	5.00	35.00
8 "	6.00	50.00

Fixtures and candle sticks may be decorated with above prisms, etc., furnishing at once a beautiful and striking appearance

Order by Catalogue numbers

HOLOPHANE GLOBES AND REFLECTORS

The Holophane System

The Holophane System of Illumination is based upon well-known optical laws. Glass of particular quality is molded into globes, the faces of which are made up of tiny prisms, which are calculated with the greatest exactness to reflect, diffuse and deflect light rays so that these rays are redirected into useful directions and the intrinsic brilliancy of the light sources greatly reduced. These results are accomplished at the minimum loss through absorption because of the peculiar high grade glass employed. All Holophane Globes and Reflectors are constructed upon variations of this principle, the various results obtained by different globes and reflectors being due to variations in the size, shape, position and kind of prisms employed.

Holophane Globes are made in three classes as shown in the following diagrams:

Class A. Concentrating   **Class B.** Distributing   **Class C.** Sideways

Class A Globes throw the maximum light directly downward. Class B Globes throw the maximum of light downward at an angle of 45°. Class C Globes throw a maximum illumination at from 10° to 15° below the horizontal.

Holophane Reflectors are also made in three classes, identified as Form E, Form F and Form I, which may be diagrammed thus:

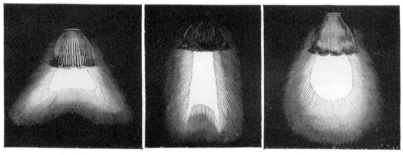

Form E   **Form F**   **Form I**

Although Holophane is constructed upon the principle of the optical prism, our product should not be confounded with the so-called "prism glass." The Holophane System is protected by letters patent and no imitation, unless it be an infringement upon our rights, can be made to give the results we advertise. In all cases the claims made for Holophane Globes and Reflectors are supported by photometric measurements made by the Electrical Testing Laboratories whose tests are published in Holophane Company's data book.

General Suggestions

The prospective purchaser of Holophane Globes and Reflectors is particularly requested to read and be guided by the following general suggestions as to the selection and application of our goods. We have no hesitation in saying that whenever, in the past, the Holophane product has failed to give complete satisfaction, it has been because of misunderstanding or carelessness in the selection of the proper Globe or Reflector or because of error in installing same.

(1) Never use a pendant Holophane Globe for an upright or *vice versa*. Both classes are identified by proper labels, so that there is no excuse for this mistake. When the wrong globe is used, it throws the light toward the ceiling, thus giving the exact reverse of the desired distribution.

(2) In all cases use lamps *at least* as large as those recommended. Lamps of smaller candlepower than are recommended give a dim and unsatisfactory light. If it is planned to use small lamps, select Globes or Reflectors designed for such lamps.

(3) Be careful in every case to use the holder recommended. A comparatively slight variation of the relative positions of lamps and Globes or Reflectors may entirely change the form of light distribution.

(4) Be sure you get the genuine Holophane. The so-called "prism glass" offered in substitution is not scientifically designed and does not give the illuminating results of Holophane. Our claims are supported by photometric tests of the Electrical Testing Laboratories.

(5) If in doubt as to the proper Globe or Reflector to use for any specific purpose, consult us. The Engineering Department, Holophane Company, is maintained to assist customers to select and place the proper Globe or Reflector. This Department will also lay out and submit complete specifications for lighting installations of any size. Our wide experience in this work enables us to serve owners, builders and architects as consulting illuminating engineers with complete satisfaction. Such service is rendered without charge.

(6) Each photometric data on any Holophane Globe or Reflector will be supplied on request. Considerable data of this nature is contained in our data book, but blue prints of photometric tests made by the Electrical Testing Laboratories on every Holophane Globe and Reflector are available to all.

Order by Catalogue numbers

HOLOPHANE REFLECTORS

For Tungsten, Tantalum, Gem and Meridian Lamps.

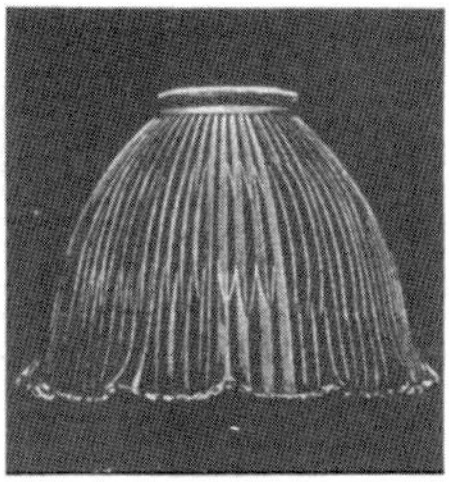

Extensive Type

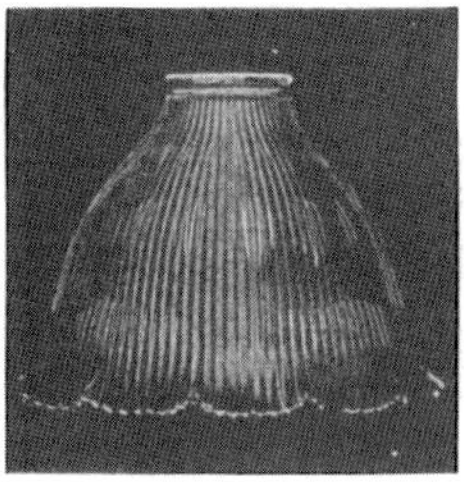

Intensive Type

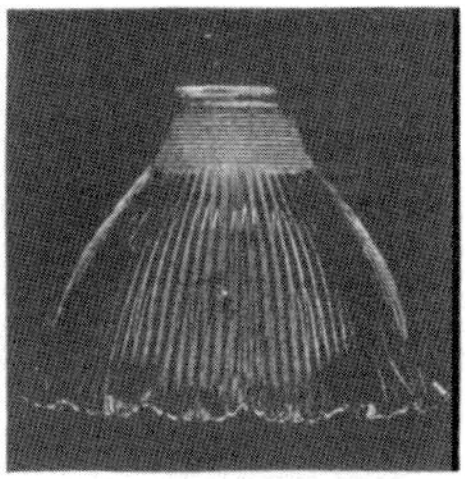

Focusing Type

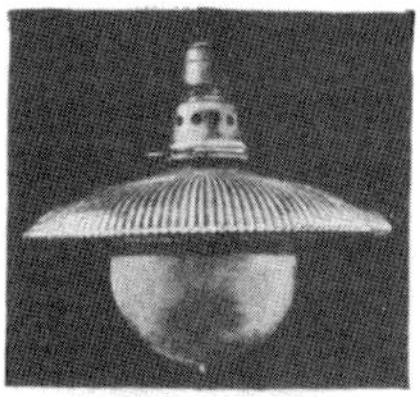

Form S

Table of Use of Holophane Reflectors on High Efficiency Lamps.

Lamps: Gem Watts	Tantalum Watts	Tungsten Watts	Reflectors: Extensive Type Number	Intensive Type Number	Focusing Type Number	Form Holder
40, 50	40	25	106225 E-3	106125 I-3	106325 F-3	O
80		40	106230 E-5	106130 I-5	106330 F-5	H
100	80	60	106250 E-7	106150 I-7	106350 F-7	H
125		100	106280 E-9	106180 I-9	106380 F-9	H
187			Bowl Type Reflector	4-B	106081	H
250			" " "	5-B	106111	H
		250	" " "	6-B	106121	A
Meridian Type Lamps						
No. 1	No. 1	No. 1		S-1	106008	H
No. 2	No. 2	No. 2		S-2	106010	H

No.	Form No.	Holder	Width	Height	Packed to a Box	Standard Pkg.	List Price Each
106125	I-3	O	....	....	20	60	$0.65
106130	I-5	H	7	4¾	10	40	.70
106150	I-7	H	7¼	5 11/16	10	40	.85
106180	I-9	H	7 13/16	6 1/16	10	40	1.05
106225	E-3	O	....		20	60	60
106230	E-5	H	6⅜	4 7/16	10	40	.65
106250	E-7	H	6¾	5	10	40	.70
106280	E-9	H	7⅝	5 11/16	10	40	.95
106325	F-3	O	....	....	20	60	65
106330	F-5	H	7¼	4¾	10	40	.70
106350	F-7	H	8	5½	10	40	.85
106380	F-9	H	8¼	6 3/16	10	40	1.05
106181	B-4	H	9⅜	6⅜	10	40	1.20
106111	B-5	H	10⅝	7 1/16	10	30	1.50
106121	B-6	A	10⅝	8 7/16	6	12	2.45
106008	S-1	H	8¼	1⅝	20	60	.45
106010	S-2	H	10⅛	2¼	20	40	.65

Order by Catalogue numbers

HOLOPHANE GLOBE REFLECTORS AND HOLDERS

Globes for Air Hole Mantel Burners

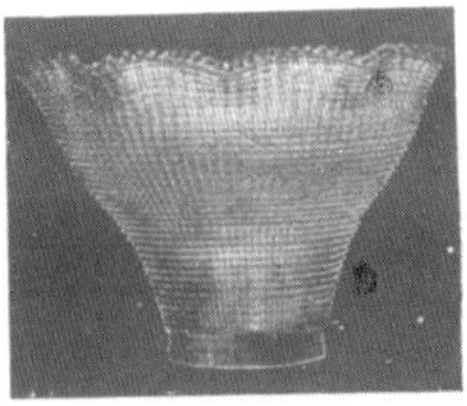

No. 2481. Class A. (¼ scale)

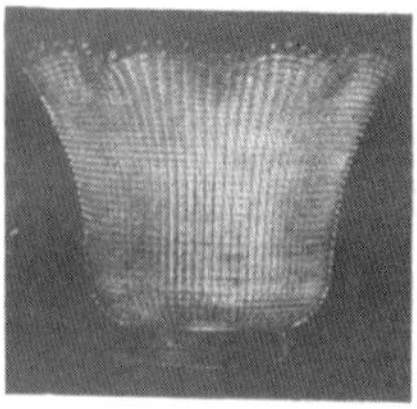

No. 2811. Class B. (¼ scale)

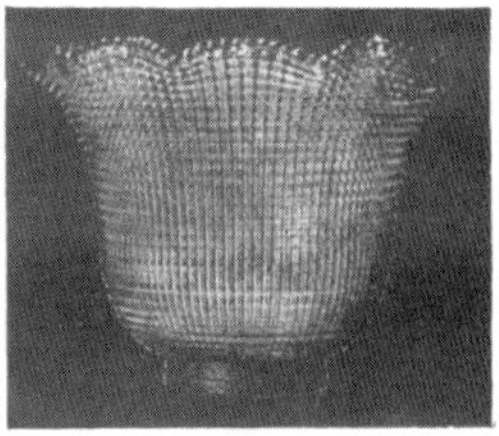

No. 2711. Class C. (¼ scale)

These globes are designed for the Welsbach Universal, Lindsay and other air hole burners. They will fit any standard gallery burner, the neck of the globe slipping over the basket and resting on the ridge outside. The globe should be used with the short or Fi. type of air hole chimney. Similar shapes can be furnished for small neck gallery burners.

No.	Class.	Diameter Inside of Neck.	Diameter Outside of Neck.	Width.	Height.	Std. Pkg.	List Price per 100.
2481	A	2 1/16	2⅜	6⅛	4½	50	$100.00
2811	B	2 1/16	2⅜	6	4½	50	100.00
2711	C	2 1/16	2⅜	6⅛	5	40	112.00

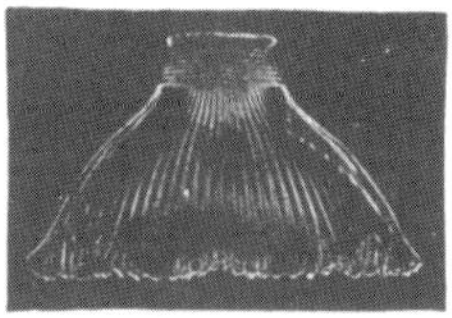

No. 2621

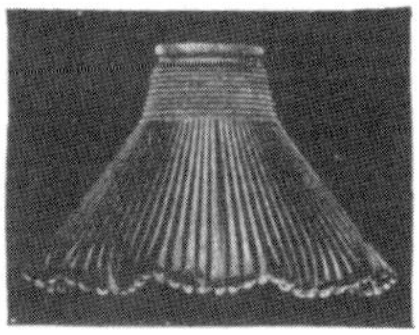

No. 2631

Prices and Data on Small Concentrating Reflectors, 1⅝-inch Neck

No.	Neck.	Width.	Height.	Lamps Recommended.	Std. Pkg.	List Price per 100.
2621	1⅝	6	3¾	8 to 16 c. p.	90	$71.00
2631	1⅝	5½	3½	8 to 16 c. p.	120	71.00

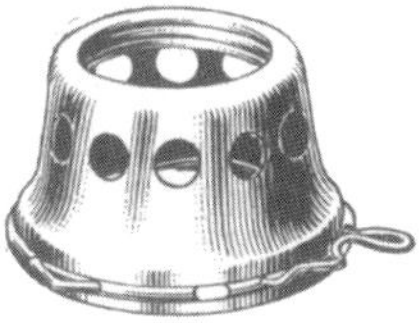

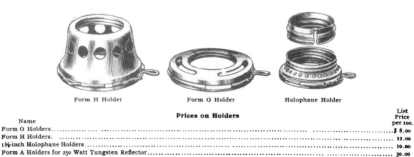

Form H Holder

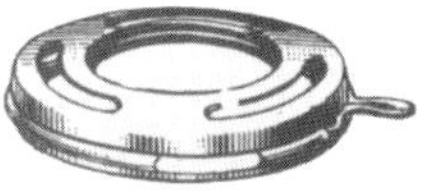

Form O Holder

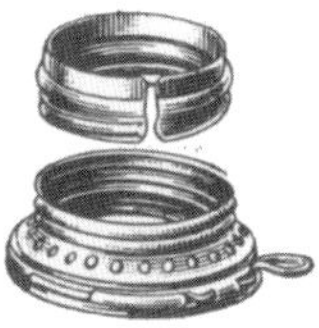

Holophane Holder

Prices on Holders

Name	List Price per 100.
Form O Holders	$8.00
Form H Holders.	12.00
1⅝-inch Holophane Holders	10.00
Form A Holders for 250 Watt Tungsten Reflector	30.00

Order by Catalogue numbers

HOLOPHANE REFLECTORS

Reflectors, 2¼-inch Neck

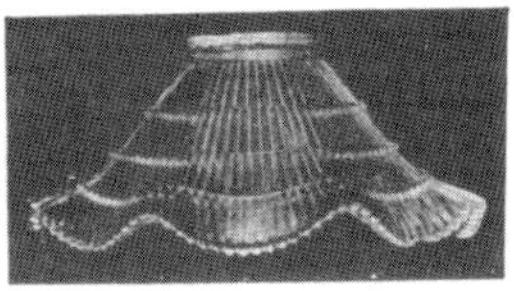

No. 9004

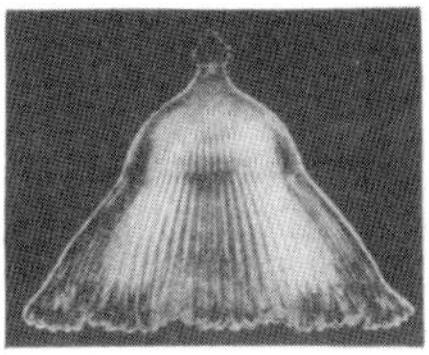

No. 2506

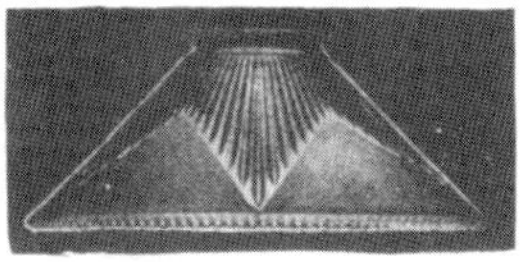

No. 9097

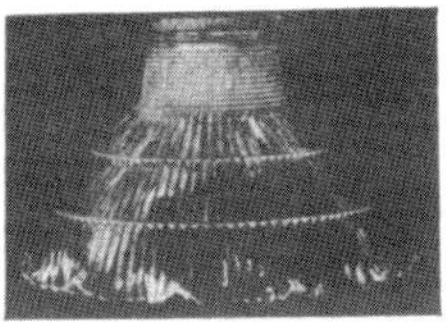

No. 9623

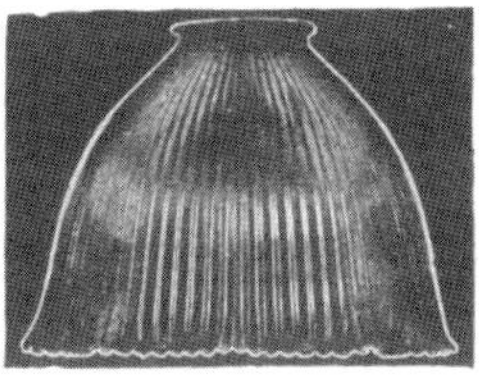

No 7381

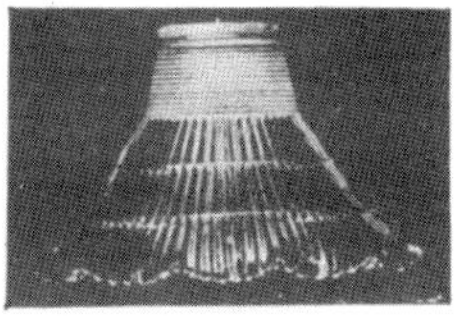

No. 9633

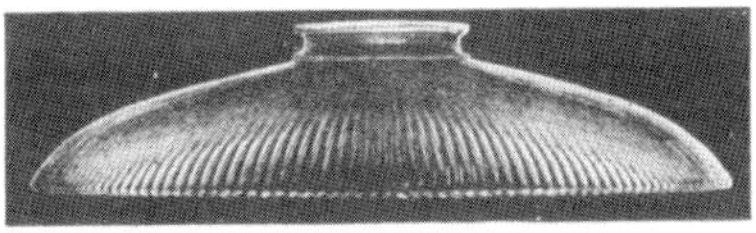

No. 2522

No.	Neck.	Width.	Height.	Lamps Recommended.	Std. Pkg.	List Price per 100
9623	2¼	6⅜	3⅞	16 c. p.	70	$ 83.00
9633	2¼	6¼	4	16 c. p.	70	83.00
†9651	2¼	9⅜	5	50 c. p.	20	158.00
†9673	2¼	7½	4¼	32 c. p.	50	100 00
9097	2¼	7¼	2¾	16 c. p.	70	113.00
x9000	2¼	7	3	8 to 16 c. p.	70	75.00
9004	2¼	7	3¼	8 to 16 c. p.	70	75.00
§2505	...	6½	4	10 to 32 c. p.	80	83 00
2506	...	6	4½	10 to 32 c. p.	80	83 00
o7301	2¼	5¾	3¼	8 to 16 c. p.	70	95.00
7381	2¼	6¼	4⅞	8 to 16 c. p.	30	122.00
o7391	2¼	7¼	5¾	16 to 32 c. p.	30	182.00
††2552	3¼	9¼	2½	Cluster	30	167.00
						Price each
††2562	4	12¾	3¼	Cluster	10	2.50
2522	4	16	4	Cluster	10	5.00
††9024	4	19¼	3½	Cluster	10	10.00

† Design similar to 9623. †† Design similar to 2522. o Design similar to 7381. x Plain edge of 9004 § Plain edge of 2506

Order by Catalogue numbers

HOLOPHANE GLOBES

Electric

These Globes are designed for use on light chandeliers and sidewall brackets where excessive weight is to be avoided. They should be carefully chosen to harmonize with the design of fixture on which they are to be fitted.

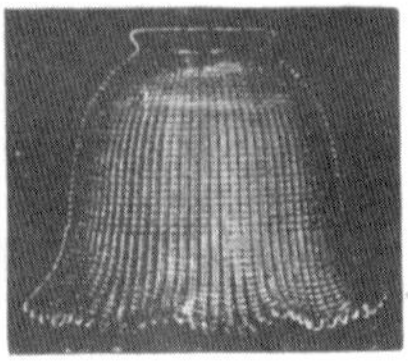

No. 2450. Pendant Open Globes

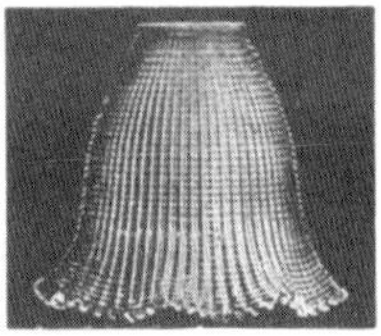

No. 2705. Pendant Open Globes

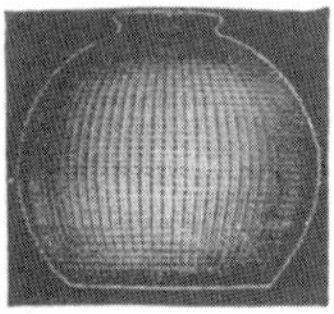

No. 2150. Pendant Open Globes

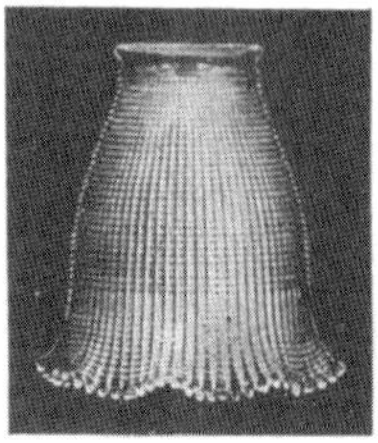

No. 2250. Pendant Open Globes

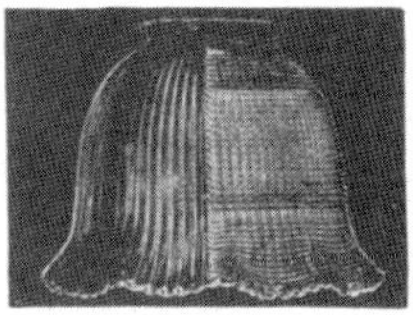

No. 245. Pendant Open Globes

Prices and Data on Pendant and Open Globes

No.	Class	Neck	Width	Height	Lamps Recommended	Std. pkg.	List Price per 100
***2150**	B	1⅝	4¼	4	8 to 16 c. p.	80	$100.00
2250	B	2¼	4¾	4¾	10 to 16 c. p.	90	75.00
***2705**	B	1⅝	4½	4¼	8 to 16 c. p.	100	71.00
2450	B	2¼	5½	4	10 to 16 c. p.	70	92.00
245	Special	2¼	5½	4	10 to 16 c. p.	70	92 00

* Price includes holder.

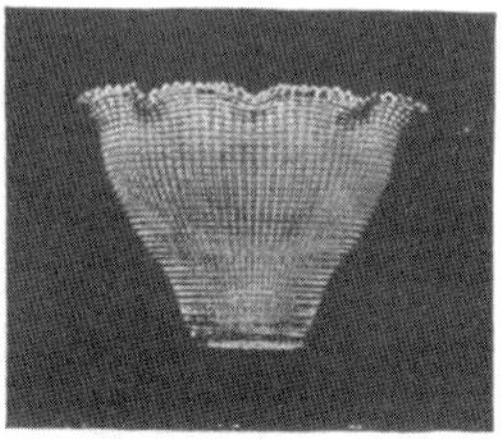

No. 1385. Upright Open Globes

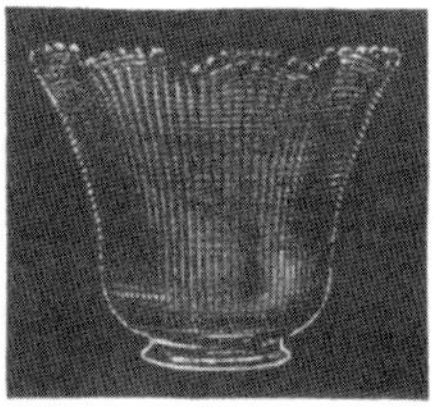

No. 2805. Upright Open Globes

Upright Open Globes

No.	Class	Neck	Width	Height	Lamps Recommended	Std. pkg.	List Price per 100
1385	A	2¼	6	4¼	8 to 16 c. p.	80	$92.00
2805	B	2¼	5½	4½	10 to 16 c. p.	60	92.00
***2451**	B	2¼	4¾	4½	8 to 16 c. p.	60	92.00
†2205	B	2¼	4½	4½	8 to 16 c. p.	90	75.00

*** Design similar to 2150. † Design similar to 2250.**

Order by Catalogue numbers

HOLOPHANE BALLS AND STALACTITES

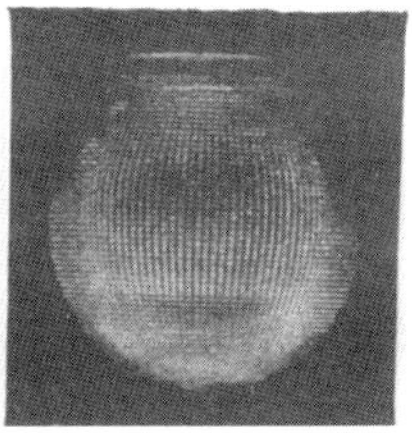

No. 3154

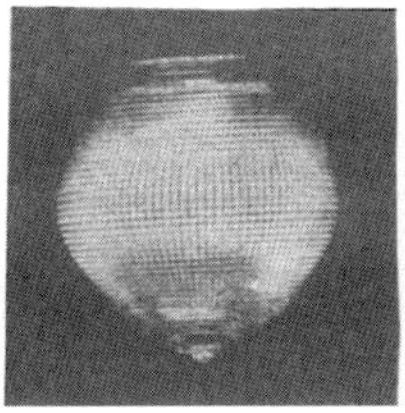

No. 3350

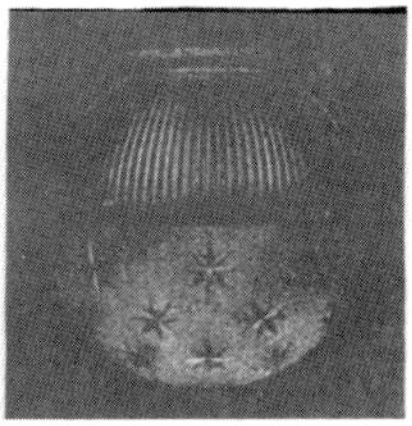

No. 9136J

Prices and Data on Pendant Electric Balls

No.	Class.	Holder.	Diameter.	Lamps Recommended.	Std. Pkg.	List Price per 100
3050	B	3¼	5½	10 to 16 c. p.	30	$142.00
3063	B	3¼	6	16 to 20 c. p.	30	183.00
3064	B	4	6	16 to 32 c. p.	30	183.00
3155	B	3¼	6½	16 to 20 c. p.	20	225.00
3154	B	4	6½	16 to 32 c. p.	20	225.00
3550	B	4	8	24 to 32 c. p.	10	400.00
3555	B	5	8	32 to 50 c. p.	10	400.00
3556	B	6	8	32 to 50 c. p.	10	400.00

Upright Electric Balls

No.	Class.	Holder.	Diameter.	Lamps Recommended.	Std. Pkg.	List Price per 100
3405	B	3¼	5½	10 to 16 c. p.	30	$142.00
3105	B	3¼	6½	16 to 20 c. p.	20	225 00
3145	B	4	6½	16 to 32 c. p.	20	225.00
3500	B	4	8	24 to 32 c. p.	10	400.00
3505	B	5	8	32 to 50 c. p.	10	400.00
3506	B	6	8	32 to 50 c. p.	10	400.00

Short Stalactites

No.	Class.	Holder.	Width.	Height.	Lamps Recommended.	Std. Pkg.	List Price per 100
3383	A	3¼	4¼	4½	4 to 10 c. p.	80	$ 83.00
3353	A	3¼	4½	5	10 to 16 c: p.	60	100.00
3358	B	3¼	4¾	5	10 to 16 c. p.	60	100.00
3363	A	3¼	5	5	16 to 20 c. p.	60	117.00
3350	A	3¼	6	6	16 to 20 c. p.	30	183.00
3354	A	4	6	6	16 to 32 c. p.	30	183.00

Medium Length Stalactites

No.	Class.	Holder.	Width	Height	Lamps Recommended	Std. Pkg.	List Price per 100
3343	B	3¼	3½	4¾	4 to 10 c. p.	100	$ 67.00
3158	B	3¼	3½	5¼	8 to 16 c. p.	80	75 00
3150	B	3¼	4¼	6¼	10 to 16 c. p.	60	108.00
3250	B	4	5½	8½	24 to 32 c. p.	20	200.00
5000	C	4	7¼	10	32 c. p.	10	400.00
5005	C	5	7¼	10	32 to 50 c. p.	10	400.00
5006	C	6	7¼	10	32 to 50 c. p.	10	400.00

Reflector Balls

No.	Holder.	Diameter.	Lamps Recommended.	Std. Pkg.	List Price per 100
***9136**	3¼	6	10 to 16 c. p.	20	$300.00
***9137**	3¼	7	16 to 20 c. p.	10	400.00
***9148**	4	8	16 to 32 c. p.	10	600.00

NOTE.—F, G, H, J represent patterns cut in ground glass bottoms. Illustrations of special cuttings sent on requste

* Extra price for special cutting: F, $1.00; G, H, J, $1.25 net for each globe.

Order by Catalogue numbers

HOLOPHANE FIXTURES

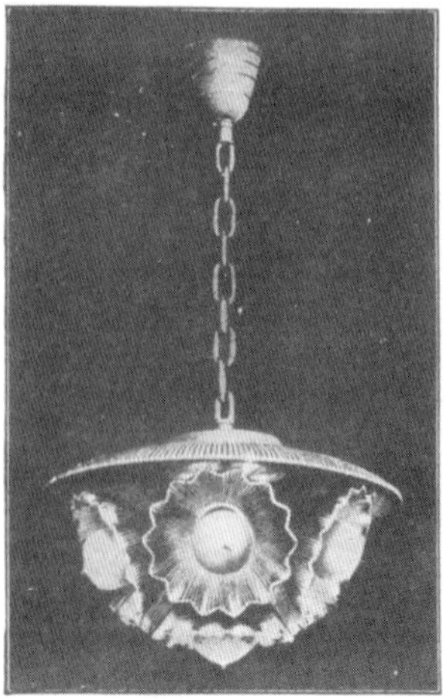

No. 66Z. Arc

Chain suspension with crowfoot

Type.	No. Lamps.	Length Over all, Inches.	Standard Finish.	List Price Each Clear Reflectors.	List Price Each Satin Finish Reflectors.
64Z	4	33	Black	$22.00	$23.50
65Z	5	33	"	23.70	25.30
66Z	6	33	"	25.40	27.10
74Z	4	32	"	16.15	17.10
75Z	5	32	"	17.60	18.60
76Z	6	32	"	19.05	20 15
84Z	4	33	"	16.40	17.35
86Z	6	33	"	19 30	20.40
94Z	4	34	"	29 60	31.85
95Z	5	34	"	31.85	34.25
96Z	6	34	"	34.10	36.65
64W	4	33	Brush brass	24.30	25.80
65W	5	33	"	26.00	27.60
66W	6	33	"	27.70	29.40
74W	4	32	"	18.45	19.40
75W	5	32	"	19.90	20.90
76W	6	32	"	21.35	22.45
94W	4	34	"	31.90	34.15
95W	5	34	"	34.15	36 55
96W	6	34	"	36.40	38.95

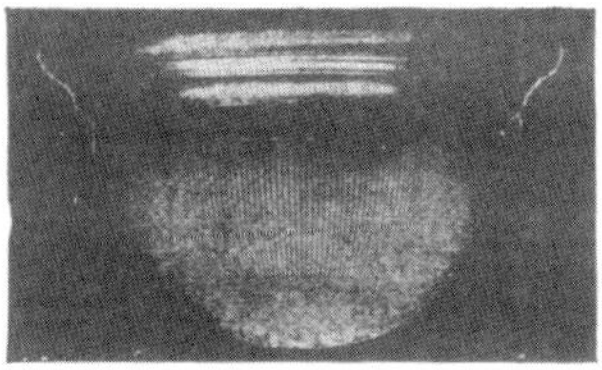

Type K

Type.	Size.	No. Lights.	Diameter at Ceiling, Inches.	Depth of Holder, Inches.	Standard Finish.	List Price Each.
G	7	1	10½	3⅛	Brush brass	$11.00
G	8	1	11	2⅛	"	12.20
G	9	1	15	4¾	"	16.70
G	10	1	16	4½	"	19.25
K	10	3	13⅛	2¾	"	14.90
G	12	1	18	4½	"	22.10
K	12	3	15⅞	2¾	"	18.50
G	14	1	20	4½	"	28.55
K	14	4	17⅞	3	"	25.85
G	16	1	22	4½	"	36.65
K	16	5	19¾	3	"	34.10
G	20	3	27	6½	"	89.60
K	20	6	24¾	3	"	81.00

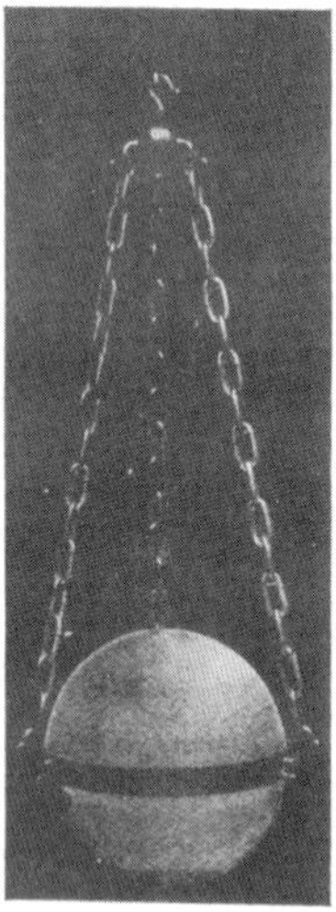

Type N and M

Type.	Size.	No. Lights.	Length Over All.	Standard Finish.	List Price Each.
N	10	1	3 feet, 1 inch	Brush brass	$32.00
M	10	3	3 feet, 1 inch	"	33.60
N	12	1	3 feet, 2 inches	"	37.60
M	12	3	3 feet, 2 inches	"	39.00
N	14	1	3 feet, 5 inches	"	50.40
M	14	4	3 feet, 5 inches	"	52.40
N	16	1	3 feet, 8 inches	"	62.60
M	16	5	3 feet, 8 inches	"	65.50
N	20	3	4 feet	"	142.00
M	20	6	4 feet	"	140.00

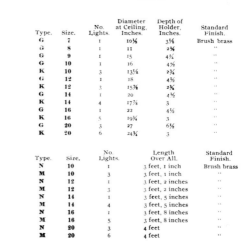

No standard package discount

Order by Catalogue numbers

FEDERAL INDOOR CLUSTERS

For Use with Tungsten Lamps

List Prices No. F752 Cluster

	20-inch.	18-inch
2-light	$6.40	$5.35
3 "	6.70	5.65
4 "	7.00	5.95
5 "	7.30	6.25
6 "	7.60	....

Four-light cluster furnished unless otherwise specified. Prices do not include lamps

Length of cluster over all, 23 inches

The cluster is furnished with a porcelain glass reflector, and the center disk in which the sockets are placed is made of white porcelain enameled steel. This arrangement gives an excellent reflecting surface. Any cluster will be wired with sockets on two circuits without extra charge, if division is specified in ordering.

No. F752. 20-inch Cluster

List Prices No. F753 Cluster

This cluster is similar to No. 752 with the addition of a diffuser. The general dimensions are the same as No. 752

	20-inch.	18-inch.
2-socket	$8.05	$7.10
4 "	8.35	7.40
4 "	8.65	7.70
5 "	8.95	8.00
6 "	9.25	....

Four-light 20-inch cluster furnished unless otherwise specified. Prices do not include lamps

Length of cluster over all, 28 inches

No. F753. Cluster

List Prices No. F764 Cluster

2-socket	$7.80
3 "	8.10
4 "	8.40
5 "	8.70
6 "	9.00

Four-light cluster furnished unless otherwise specified. Prices do not include lamps

Length of cluster over all, 26 inches

No. F764. Cluster

All fixtures provided with crowfoot. Insulating joints extra. Standard finish brushed brass sent unless otherwise specified. Polished brass or bauer barff without extra charge. Oxidized copper, brass or nickel, 15 per cent extra. Prices on other finishes on application

Order by Catalogue numbers

FEDERAL FIXTURES

List Prices No. F501 Inverted Cone Clusters

A	**B**	**C**	
Without sockets or wiring	With sockets and wiring	With sockets, wiring, husks and holders, but without shades	

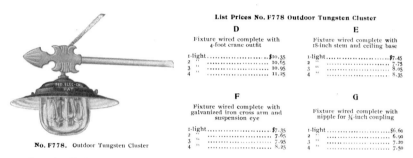

15-inch

1-light $8.00

20-inch

4-light . . . .$ 9.90	4-light $11.30	4-light $13.25
5 " 9.95	5 " 12.15	5 " 14.30
6 " 10.00	6 " 13.00	6 " 15.20
7 " 10.05	7 " 13.85	7 " 16.20
8 " 10.10	8 " 14.70	8 " 17.25
9 " 10.15	9 " 15.55	9 " 18.15

25-inch

4-light $19.95	4-light $21.90	4-light $23.50
5 " 20.00	5 " 22.65	5 " 24.65
6 " 20.05	6 " 23.35	6 " 25.80
7 " 20.10	7 " 24.05	7 " 26.95
8 " 20.15	8 " 25.15	8 " 28.10
9 " 20.20	9 " 25.43	9 " 29.25

No. F501. 20-inch

List Prices No. F778 Outdoor Tungsten Cluster

D	**E**
Fixture wired complete with 4-foot crane outfit	Fixture wired complete with 18-inch stem and ceiling base
1-light $10.35	1-light $7.45
2 " 10.65	2 " 7.75
3 " 10.95	3 " 8.05
4 " 11.25	4 " 8.35

No. F778. Outdoor Tungsten Cluster

F	**G**
Fixture wired complete with galvanized iron cross arm and suspension eye	Fixture wired complete with nipple for ¾-inch coupling
1-light $7.35	1-light $6.60
2 " 7.65	2 " 6.90
3 " 7.95	3 " 7.20
4 " 8.25	4 " 7.50

Cluster adapted for lamps as large as 100-watt. Domes of different sizes furnished for different sized lamps. Four-light combination D with dome for 60-watt lamps furnished unless otherwise specified. Double braid wire furnished sufficient for length of crane or stem ordered.

For this cluster equipped with large series incandescent sockets add $2.70 per socket to the list price of the cluster desired.

Prices do not include lamps.

F404 List price $7.10

Lamp not included

The standard bracket can be used as a piano, reading, bed, wall or decorative fixture.

Extras

Special red silk hexagonal lamp shade, with 2-inch silver bead fringe. . . . . .list, $5.00

Slightly different in shape from that shown in opposite cut.

For oxidized silver, bronze or oxidized copper finishes, $1.00 list extra.

No. F404. Couch Bracket

Order by Catalogue numbers

CURRENT VALUES

The current values in this book should be used only as a guide. They are not intended to set prices, which vary from one section of the country to another. Auction prices as well as dealer prices vary greatly and are affected by condition as well as demand. Neither the author nor the publisher assumes responsibility for any losses that might be incurred as a result of consulting this guide.

All prices in this book are for all units in restored condition without shades, except those units noted as * complete; ** w/ candles and bobaches; and *** butler silver.

All desk and table lamps are priced with shades shown.

PRICE GUIDE

Page	Item #	Price
8	7840	225.00 – 250.00
9	7870	225.00 – 250.00
10	7872	215.00 – 235.00
11	7873	225.00 – 250.00
12	7874	250.00 – 285.00
13	7875	285.00 – 315.00
14	7876	300.00 – 365.00
15	7877	325.00 – 385.00
16	7798	335.00 – 365.00
17	7878	340.00 – 390.00
18	7879	350.00 – 390.00
19	7880*	300.00 – 350.00
20	7881	325.00 – 375.00
21	7848	300.00 – 385.00
22	7882	215.00 – 250.00
	6977*	275.00 – 400.00
23	7883*	250.00 – 350.00
24	7784	375.00 – 450.00
25	7885*	450.00 – 875.00
26	7886	350.00 – 425.00
	7533	335.00 – 400.00
27	7887	525.00 – 700.00
28	7888	225.00 – 425.00
29	7812	285.00 – 335.00
30	7816	300.00 – 350.00
31	7814	350.00 – 425.00
32	7813	350.00 – 435.00
33	7811	365.00 – 450.00
34	7889	275.00 – 325.00
35	7890	285.00 – 350.00
36	7891	425.00 – 650.00
37	7847	385.00 – 500.00
38	7787	350.00 – 475.00
39	7708*	400.00 – 650.00
	7817*	425.00 – 600.00
40	7893*	450.00 – 680.00
	7819*	425.00 – 525.00
41	7850*	650.00 – 900.00
42	7894	700.00 – 900.00
43	7818*	700.00 – 825.00
44	7863	750.00 – 900.00
45	7932	700.00 – 850.00
46	7895*	1,000.00 +
47	7896	1,000.00+
48	7917*	1,500.00+
49	7918	650.00 – 850.00
50	7920	1,250.00+
51	7921	1,250.00+
52	7898*	900.00 – 1,500.00
	7899*	650.00 – 850.00
	6842*	225.00 – 335.00
53	6843*	225.00 – 325.00
	7901*	585.00 – 750.00
	7900*	750.00 – 1,000.00
54	7902	675.00 – 900.00
55	7903*	700.00 – 1,000.00
56	7904*	600.00 – 700.00
57	7905	800.00 – 1,000.00
58	7906	150.00 – 200.00
	7907	225.00 – 300.00
59	7908	225.00 – 300.00
60	7909	150.00 – 200.00
61	7910	300.00 – 400.00
62	7911	275.00 – 325.00
63	7912	250.00 – 300.00
64	7913	375.00 – 475.00
65	7915	400.00 – 500.00
66	7916	400.00 – 550.00
67	7338	200.00 – 250.00

68	7340	225.00 – 300.00
69	7341	250.00 – 350.00
70	7342	300.00 – 365.00
71	7343	375.00 – 450.00
72	7344	750.00 – 1,000.00
73	7345	1,000.00+
74	7346	350.00 – 400.00
75	7347	700.00 – 900.00
76	7348	325.00 – 400.00
77	7349	375.00 – 475.00
78	7029	500.00+
	7028	500.00+
79	7025	650.00+
	7027	525.00+
	7026	500.00+
80	6978	100.00 – 150.00
	7012*	175.00 – 225.00
	6976	135.00 – 175.00
81	6986	65.00 – 85.00
	6987	100.00 – 150.00
	6988*	150.00 – 225.00
82	7009	100.00 – 150.00
	7010	100.00 – 125.00
	7011	100.00 – 135.00
83	6967*	300.00 – 350.00
	6990	85.00 – 125.00
	6973*	275.00 – 350.00
84	6994*	100.00 – 125.00
	6992*	200.00 – 285.00
	6991*	135.00 – 185.00
	6993	85.00 – 115.00
85	7810	200.00 – 265.00
	6998	215.00 – 275.00
86	6999*	450.00+
87	6920*	125.00 – 185.00
	6919*	150.00 – 200.00
	6922*	150.00 – 200.00
	7433*	50.00 – 125.00
	7438*	50.00 – 125.00

	7437*	65.00 – 125.00
88	6941*	150.00 – 250.00
	6476*	50.00 – 100.00
	6475*	50.00 – 100.00
	6942*	150.00 – 200.00
89	7503*	135.00 – 185.00
	7504*	135.00 – 185.00
	7505*	115.00 – 150.00
	7507*	140.00 – 185.00
	7506*	115.00 – 150.00
	7508*	125.00 – 165.00
90	7509*	450.00 – 650.00
	7510*	135.00 – 185.00
	7511	35.00 – 50.00
	7512*	100.00 – 180.00
91	7513*	750.00+
	7383	50.00 – 75.00
	7550	200.00 – 250.00
	7357	65.00 – 85.00
92	7514*	375.00 – 400.00
	7541	425.00 – 575.00
93	7488	50.00 – 65.00
	7353*	150.00 – 200.00
	7466	300.00 – 450.00
	7352	35.00 – 50.00
	7354*	135.00 – 200.00
	7397	50.00 – 65.00
94	7517*	450.00+
	7518*	150.00 – 280.00
	7474	300.00 – 350.00
	7543	325.00 – 365.00
	7453	300.00 – 365.00
95	7522	35.00 – 50.00
	7519	50.00 – 65.00
	7521	25.00 – 30.00
	7544*	200.00 – 275.00
	7523	35.00 – 50.00
	7520	35.00 – 50.00
	7467	100.00 – 125.00

96	7524	250.00 – 300.00
	7525	700.00+
97	7526	600.00+
	7527	800.00+
98	7528	385.00 – 450.00
	7484	325.00 – 400.00
99	7545	900.00+
	7529*	700.00+
100	7530	350.00 – 450.00
101	7531	425.00 – 500.00
102	7365	450.00 – 500.00
103	7374	285.00 – 350.00
	7372*	350.00 – 500.00
104	7532*	300.00 – 400.00
105	6500	20.00 – 30.00
	6501	20.00 – 30.00
	6502	25.00 – 35.00
	6503	25.00 – 35.00
	6504	25.00 – 35.00
	6505	25.00 – 35.00
106	6506	50.00 – 100.00
	6507	25.00 – 35.00
	6508	25.00 – 35.00
	6509	85.00 – 115.00
	6468	35.00 – 45.00
	6510	25.00 – 30.00
107	6571	85.00 – 125.00
	6467	85.00 – 125.00
	6511	25.00 – 45.00
	6473	50.00 – 75.00
	6465	50.00 – 75.00
	6568	50.00 – 75.00
	6559	35.00 – 45.00
108	6569	65.00 – 85.00
	6515	85.00 – 100.00
	6513	85.00 – 100.00
	6660	85.00 – 125.00
	6572	100.00 – 125.00
	6512	65.00 – 100.00
	6514	40.00 – 65.00
	6661	85.00 – 125.00
109	6520*	145.00 – 175.00
	6519	100.00 – 145.00
	6518	85.00 – 125.00
	6486*	165.00 – 235.00
	6516	75.00 – 100.00
	6517	50.00 – 75.00
110	6523	140.00 – 185.00
	6524*	165.00 – 225.00
	6521*	150.00 – 200.00
	6522*	150.00 – 200.00
111	6529*	165.00 – 225.00
	6526*	185.00 – 225.00
	6525*	165.00 – 225.00
	6528*	100.00 – 200.00
112	6570	85.00 – 100.00
	6530	75.00 – 100.00
	6532	75.00 – 125.00
	6696*	150.00 – 285.00
	6531	85.00 – 125.00
113	6453	85.00 – 100.00
	6455	50.00 – 85.00
	6456	150.00 – 200.00
	6454	65.00 – 100.00
	6488	75.00 – 100.00
	6470	85.00 – 125.00
114	6585	50.00 – 100.00
	6578	85.00 – 100.00
	6576	85.00 – 100.00
	6582	100.00 – 150.00
	6574	100.00 – 150.00
	6581	100.00 – 150.00
	6579	150.00 – 185.00
	6580	175.00 – 285.00
115	6457	125.00 – 165.00
	6458	150.00 – 225.00
	6853	50.00 – 85.00
	6671	115.00 – 190.00

116	6459	115.00 – 200.00
	6460	100.00 – 150.00
	6669	150.00 – 200.00
	6670	165.00 – 235.00
117	6494*	200.00 – 300.00
	6484*	200.00 – 325.00
	6489	100.00 – 150.00
	6686	150.00 – 200.00
	6683	150.00 – 225.00
118	6461*	225.00 – 350.00
	6695*	200.00 – 300.00
	6682	150.00 – 250.00
	6474	65.00 – 90.00
119	6689	135.00 – 185.00
	6690	150.00 – 225.00
	6687*	265.00 – 350.00
120	6497	300.00 – 385.00
	6491	175.00 – 285.00
	6401*	price open
	6463	150.00 – 200.00
121	6402	150.00 – 200.00
	6403	100.00 – 150.00
	6404	100.00 – 115.00
122	6405	150.00 – 200.00
	6406	135.00 – 185.00
	6408	100.00 – 135.00
123	6409	175.00 – 225.00
	6410	75.00 – 100.00
	6411	75.00 – 100.00
124	7264*	200.00 – 300.00
	6417*	300.00 – 450.00
	6414*	300.00 – 450.00
	7552*	450.00 – 550.00
	6415*	200.00 – 300.00
125	No. 5	100.00 – 185.00
	No. 37	50.00 – 80.00
	No. 20	125.00 – 175.00
	No. 52	100.00 – 185.00
	No. 4	65.00 – 100.00

	No. 15	100.00 – 135.00
	No. 3	60.00 – 85.00
	No. 12	165.00 – 225.00
	No. 2	40.00 – 60.00
	No. 14	40.00 – 60.00
126	7721	6,500.00+
127	7614	5,500.00+
128	7718	5,000.00+
129	6742*	300.00 – 435.00
	6743*	400.00 – 575.00
130	6745*	350.00 – 485.00
	6744*	350.00 – 525.00
131	6746*	385.00 – 500.00
	6747*	350.00 – 450.00
132	6800*	75.00 – 90.00
	6801*	200.00 – 275.00
	6898*	250.00 – 325.00
133	6803*	225.00 – 350.00
	6748*	225.00 – 350.00
	6804*	300.00 – 400.00
	6802*	350.00 – 475.00
134	6805*	400.00 – 500.00
	6749*	350.00 – 420.00
	6806*	350.00 – 450.00
135	6808*	400.00 – 650.00
	6807*	325.00 – 400.00
136	7260	125.00 – 185.00
	6809*	400.00 – 550.00
	6750*	950.00+
	7261	50.00 – 75.00
137	6810*	150.00 – 235.00
	6811*	165.00 – 250.00
	7263	45.00 – 75.00
	6838*	250.00 – 350.00
	7262	50.00 – 85.00
	6812*	225.00 – 300.00
	6815*	185.00 – 285.00
	6813*	325.00 – 500.00
138	6839*	350.00 – 450.00

174	9561* ....650.00 – 850.00
	9562** ....500.00 – 650.00
175	9563* ....675.00 – 800.00
	9564* ....500.00 – 650.00
176	9565* ....500.00 – 650.00
	9566** ....550.00 – 650.00
177	9542** ....300.00 – 425.00
178	9543* ....650.00 – 800.00
179	9570* ....800.00 – 1,000.00
180	9567* ....700.00 – 900.00
181	9545*....................1,000.00+
182	9514*....................1,250.00+
183	9547*......................900.00+
184	9548*......................950.00+
185	9549*....................1,500.00+
186	9568*....................1,250.00+
187	9550 ....1,250.00+
188	9571*....................1,250.00+
189	9572*....................1,200.00+
190	8722.............325.00 – 365.00
	8708.............285.00 – 335.00
191	8717.............500.00 – 600.00
192	8718.............550.00 – 675.00
193	8721**..........400.00 – 485.00
194	8719.............500.00 – 625.00
195	8720.............800.00 – 900.00
196	8879**..........125.00 – 185.00
	8809.............100.00 – 165.00
197	8876**..........140.00 – 185.00
	8868**..........140.00 – 185.00
198	8881.............150.00 – 225.00
	8880**..........175.00 – 250.00
199	8882**..........160.00 – 200.00
	8883.............250.00 – 300.00
200	8885.............200.00 – 300.00
	8884**..........250.00 – 325.00
201	8886**..........235.00 – 300.00
	8887.............235.00 – 300.00
202	8865* ....400.00 – 650.00

203	8890**..........150.00 – 235.00
	8888**..........185.00 – 275.00
	8889* ....185.00 – 275.00
204	8891* ....225.00 – 275.00
	8892**..........200.00 – 275.00
	8893* ....250.00 – 350.00
205	8894* ....325.00 – 450.00
	8895* ....185.00 – 250.00
206	8896* ....200.00 – 250.00
	8897* ....175.00 – 225.00
207	9033* ....385.00 – 450.00
	9035**..........400.00 – 500.00
	9034* ....400.00 – 475.00
208	9037.............200.00 – 300.00
	9036.............425.00– 475.00
209	493 ....price open
	495 ....price open
	496 ....500.00+
	497 ....price open
210	8493**..........140.00 – 200.00
	8465**..........140.00 – 190.00
	8470**..........150.00 – 210.00
	8468**..........150.00 – 210.00
211	8466**..........200.00 – 300.00
	8473**..........200.00 – 300.00
	8474**..........160.00 – 185.00
	8469**..........160.00 – 185.00
212	8444**..........335.00 – 400.00
	8480**..........300.00 – 375.00
	8481.............250.00 – 300.00
213	8458**..........175.00 – 225.00
	8455**..........150.00 – 200.00
	8453* ....235.00 – 300.00
	8456**..........150.00 – 200.00
214	8460**..........165.00 – 225.00
	8449* ....235.00 – 300.00
	8471**..........150.00 – 200.00
	8457**..........200.00 – 275.00
215	8482* ....200.00 – 285.00

	8451*	225.00 – 300.00
	8484**	185.00 – 250.00
	8485	165.00 – 240.00
216	8486**	165.00 – 225.00
	8487**	175.00 – 225.00
	8490**	100.00 – 150.00
	8489**	150.00 – 225.00
	8488* w/beveled glass panels	175.00 – 285.00
217	9551**	8,500.00+
218	9552	6,500.00+
219	9553**	6,800.00+
220	7548	325.00 – 365.00
	7006	50.00 – 75.00
	6698	40.00 – 65.00
221	7007	75.00 – 115.00
	6699	65.00 – 100.00
	7549	350.00 – 450.00
222	holophane fixture*	400.00 – 500.00
	7551	300.00 – 385.00
224	E401*	100.00 – 130.00
	E402*	200.00 – 250.00
	E315*	120.00 – 140.00
	E300*	60.00 – 75.00
	E305*	60.00 – 75.00
	E310*	100.00 – 150.00

Art Dome Shades

225	15100	1,300.00+
	15101	1,200.00+
	15102	1,150.00+
	15103	1,000.00+
	15104	1,000.00+
	15105	500.00 – 600.00
226	15106	1,000.00+
	15107	1,200.00+
	15108	900.00+
	15109	900.00+

	15110	800.00+
	15111	850.00+
	15112	800.00+
	15113	500.00 – 600.00
227	15116	500.00 – 650.00
	15121 w/fringe	300.00 – 500.00
	15120 w/fringe	450.00 – 650.00
	15118	350.00 – 500.00
	15117	400.00 – 650.00
	15119	450.00 – 600.00
	15124	300.00 – 400.00
	15123	150.00+
228	15115	450.00+
	15114	650.00+
	15114½	850.00+
	15165	1,200.00+
	15166	1,300.00+
229	15163	1,200.00+
	15164	1,200.00+
230	7922	1,300.00+
231	7546	800.00+
	7926*	1,100.00+
232	7929*	1,250.00+
233	7547	850.00+
	7930*	1,350.00+
	7931*	1,350.00+

Bent Art Glass

234	44-211	75.00 – 135.00
	43-543	100.00 – 175.00
	42-542	125.00 – 200.00
	48-548	185.00+
	51-212	175.00 – 225.00
	50-210	200.00+
	49-230	225.00+
	41-541	325.00+
	40-540	150.00 – 225.00

38-211 ....75.00 – 100.00

235 39-539

w/fringe.......200.00 – 235.00

46-546 ....225.00+

45-232 ....300.00+

21-521 ....150.00 – 175.00

22-522 ....85.00 – 110.00

23-523 ....100.00+

1440 w/fringe ..200.00 – 235.00

30-530 ....225.00 – 265.00

31-531 ....85.00 – 115.00

24-201 ....125.00 – 150.00

26-526 ....150.00 – 185.00

27-203 ....100.00 – 140.00

28-236 ....125.00 – 185.00

29-205 ....135.00 – 150.00

236 34-222 ....135.00 – 160.00

35-535 ....75.00 – 100.00

36-536 ....140.00 – 160.00

37-537 ....160.00 – 175.00

32-532 ....140.00 – 150.00

33-533 ....225.00 – 260.00

18-518 ....300.00+

1898..................25.00 – 50.00

4-14 ....30.00 – 60.00

1245 w/fringe ..150.00 – 185.00

430.....................20.00 – 30.00

14......................15.00 – 25.00

48 celluloid ....40.00 – 65.00

No. 6 ....2.00 – 5.00

No. 30 ....5.00 – 10.00

No. 19 ....5.00 – 10.00

No. 20 ....7.00 – 10.00

No. 26 ....7.00 – 10.00

Teplitz Glass

237 6907..............125.00 – 150.00

7054..............125.00 – 150.00

7591................90.00 – 125.00

7588..............100.00 – 130.00

7595..............100.00 – 130.00

7594..............100.00 – 130.00

7589..............100.00 – 130.00

7590..............125.00 – 150.00

7596..............125.00 – 150.00

7598................90.00 – 120.00

6098 ....125.00+

6909 ....135.00+

7052 ....150.00+

7065 ....150.00+

238 7110 ....165.00+

7066 ....150.00+

2026 ....165.00+

7067 ....150.00+

7063 ....165.00+

7034 ....135.00+

7027 ....150.00+

403 ....175.00+

404 ....175.00+

239 5823...............85.00 – 120.00

2040 ....150.00+

6517 ....100.00+

5823½.............65.00 – 100.00

2040½ ....100.00+

6517½...............65.00 – 90.00

413 ....150.00+

513 ....175.00+

95.................100.00 – 125.00

413½ ....100.00+

513½ ....100.00+

95½...................65.00 – 85.00

93½ ....100.00+

94½.................75.00 – 100.00

3453½...............70.00 – 90.00

240 6716..............100.00 – 160.00

6878..............120.00 – 165.00

1090..............135.00 – 175.00

6716................65.00 – 100.00

	6878½	85.00 – 120.00
	1090½	85.00 – 120.00
	287	150.00 – 185.00
	325	165.00 – 200.00
	9112	200.00+
	287½	90.00 – 120.00
	325½	100.00 – 120.00
	9112½	150.00+
	6715	175.00+
	6715½	120.00+
	799	150.00+
241	2423	75.00 – 100.00
	413T	145.00+
	6620½	50.00 – 65.00
	4920½	40.00 – 60.00
	2423½	50.00 – 65.00
	413½	100.00+
	433	100.00 – 150.00
	433½	100.00 – 175.00
	430	125.00 – 160.00
	430½T	145.00 – 185.00
	4892	125.00 – 200.00
	5209	200.00+
	6652	40.00 – 65.00
242	2160	85.00 – 150.00
	427	125.00 – 200.00
	2057	135.00 – 225.00
	311	200.00+
	509 crystal	40.00 – 65.00
	509 colors	225.00+
	512 crystal	65.00 – 85.00
	512 colors	235.00+
	132	100.00 – 150.00
	6095 rare	225.00+
	3632 rare	200.00 – 225.00
	9243 rare	235.00+
	505	200.00+
	2158	190.00+
	5622	200.00+

	4518	200.00+
	5862	125.00 – 200.00
243	8518	60.00 – 75.00
	8516	40.00 –55.00
	8517	40.00 – 55.00
	8515	65.00 – 85.00
	470	70.00 – 90.00
	115	50.00 – 100.00
	511	100.00 – 145.00
	114	35.00 – 50.00
	514	50.00 – 100.00
	113	65.00 – 100.00
	113½	65.00 – 100.00
	434	145.00 – 185.00
	309	120.00 – 145.00
244	6859	50.00 – 100.00
	7037	50.00+
	1832 red	50.00+
	crystal	35.00 – 50.00
	amber	40.00 – 65.00
	two colors	50.00+
	1801	45.00 – 65.00
	467	3.00 – 8.00
	451	3.00 – 8.00
	452	3.00 – 8.00
	449	10.00+
	450	10.00+
	447	5.00+
	448	5.00+
	451	3.00 – 8.00
	37	3.00 – 8.00
	38	3.00 – 8.00
	445	10.00+
	446	10.00+
	459	10.00+
	460	10.00+

Holders only, No. 6, No. 1, No. 7,
No. 2, No. 5 ....2.00 – 5.00
No. 40 ....5.00 – 12.00

Opal Glassware

	Item	Price
	102	25.00 – 35.00
	110	35.00 – 45.00
	103	20.00 – 40.00
	432	30.00 – 50.00
	107	30.00 – 50.00
	806½	65.00 – 100.00
259	9189	40.00 – 50.00
	1864	45.00 – 60.00
	1865	50.00 – 60.00
	9191	25.00 – 35.00
	9910	45.00 – 65.00
	9972½	35.00 – 45.00
	9589½	35.00 – 50.00
	2540	35.00 – 55.00
	9590	30.00 – 40.00
	4501½	30.00 – 40.00
	2536	30.00 – 40.00
	9836½	50.00 – 65.00
260	9815½ crystal roughed inside	35.00 – 45.00
	10069½	30.00 – 40.00
	238	45.00 – 60.00
	194S	55.00 – 75.00
	180B	60.00 – 80.00
	10018½	30.00 – 40.00
	10090	35.00 – 50.00
	8884½	30.00 – 45.00
	4780	30.00 – 40.00
	9999½	35.00 – 45.00
	9896½	35.00 – 40.00
261	7017	125.00 – 165.00
	8656	100.00 – 125.00
	4083	160.00 – 225.00
	8656½	50.00 – 65.00
	9175	180.00 – 250.00
	9368	125.00 – 150.00
	9367½	30.00 – 40.00
	9368½	35.00 – 45.00
	8950½	35.00 – 45.00
	9115½	40.00 – 50.00
262	6578	50.00 – 100.00
	870C	85.00 – 120.00
	9086	35.00 – 60.00
	9082	50.00 – 75.00
	292	40.00 – 65.00
	8780	3500 – 50.00
	9083	40.00 – 50.00
	4081	40.00 – 65.00
	8770	25.00 –40.00
263	10139	50.00 – 65.00
	9170	140.00 – 175.00
	9917½	35.00 – 45.00
	10111½	40.00 – 50.00
	10141	40.00 – 50.00

Colonial Prisms

	Item	Price
	No. 0448½	25.00 – 50.00
	No. 0448	5.00 – 15.00

Holophanes

	Item	Price
265	extensive type	40.00+
	intensive type	45.00+
	focusing type	40.00+
	Form S	25.00+
266	2481, Class A	50.00+
	2811, Class B	45.00+
	2711, Class C	60.00+
	2621	25.00+
	2631	25.00+
	holders	3.00 – 5.00 ea.
267	9004	40.00 – 45.00
	2506	75.00+
	9097	40.00+
	9623	45.00+
	7381	40.00+
	9633	40.00+

	2522	35.00+
268	2450	45.00 – 55.00
	2705, 1⅝"	
	neck	40.00 – 45.00
	2150, 1⅝"	
	neck	40.00 – 50.00
	2250	50.00 – 55.00
	245	65.00+
	1385	50.00 – 60.00
	2805	45.00 – 55.00
269	3154	75.00+
	3350	75.00 – 100.00
	9136J	65.00 – 80.00
270	66Z	450.00+
	Type K	125.00+

| | Type N&M | 175.00+ |

Federal Indoor Clusters

271	F752	100.00 – 125.00
	F753	125.00 – 185.00
	F764	65.00 – 100.00
272	F501, no shades	250.00+
	F778*	175.00+
	F404*	200.00 – 300.00

COLLECTOR BOOKS

Informing Today's Collector

For over two decades we have been keeping collectors informed on trends and values in all fields of antiques and collectibles.

COLLECTOR BOOKS
Informing Today's Collector

HATPINS, WATCHES & PURSES

1712 Antique and Collectible **Thimbles** and Accessories, Mathis $19.95

1748 Antique **Purses**, Revised Second Ed., Holiner ..$19.95

1278 Art Nouveau & Art Deco **Jewelry**, Baker $9.95

4850 Collectible **Costume Jewelry**, Simonds $24.95

3875 Collecting Antique **Stickpins**, Kerins $16.95

3722 Collector's Ency. of **Compacts, Carryalls & Face Powder Boxes**, Mueller $24.95

4854 Collector's Ency. of **Compacts, Carryalls & Face Powder Boxes**, Vol. II, Mueller........................$24.95

4940 **Costume Jewelry**, Rezazadeh $24.95

1716 Fifty Years of Collectible **Fashion Jewelry**, 1925 – 1975, Baker $19.95

1424 **Hatpins** & Hatpin Holders, Baker $9.95

4729 **Sewing Tools** & Trinkets, Thompson...............$24.95

4878 Vintage & Contemporary **Purse Accessories** $24.95

3830 Vintage **Vanity Bags & Purses**, Gerson $24.95

INDIANS, GUNS, KNIVES, TOOLS, PRIMITIVES

1868 Antique **Tools**, Our American Heritage, McNerney $9.95

4943 **Flint Arrowheads & Knives**, Tully $9.95

2279 **Indian Artifacts** of the Midwest, Hothem $14.95

3885 **Indian Artifacts** of the Midwest, Book II, Hothem..$16.95

4870 **Indian Artifacts** of the Midwest, Book III, Hothem..$18.95

5162 Modern **Guns**, Identification & Values, 12th Ed., Quertermous..$12.95

5166 Standard Guide to **Razors**, 2nd Ed., Ritchie & Stewart $9.95

4730 Standard **Knife** Collector's Guide, 3rd Ed., Ritchie & Stewart $12.95

PAPER COLLECTIBLES & BOOKS

4633 **Big Little Books**, Jacobs $18.95

4710 Collector's Guide to **Children's Books**, Jones ..$18.95

5153 Collector's Guide to **Children's Books**, Vol. II Jones $19.95

1441 Collector's Guide to **Post Cards**, Wood $9.95

2081 Guide to Collecting **Cookbooks**, Allen...............$14.95

2080 Price Guide to **Cookbooks & Recipe Leaflets**, Dickinson $9.95

4654 **Victorian Trade Cards**, Cheadle $19.95

4733 **Whitman Juvenile Books**, Brown $17.95

OTHER COLLECTIBLES

4704 Antique & Collectible **Buttons**, Wisniewski.......$19.95

2269 Antique **Brass & Copper** Collectibles, Gaston ..$16.95

3872 Antique **Tins**, Book I, Dodge............................$24.95

5030 Antique **Tins**, Book II, Dodge $29.95

5251 Antique **Tins**, Book III, Dodge $29.95

4845 Antique **Typewriters & Office Collectibles**, Rehr $19.95

5154 B.J. Summers' Guide to **Coca-Cola**, 2nd Ed. $19.95

5033 **Beatles, The**, Ref. and Value Guide, 2nd Ed., Crawford, Lamon & Stern $19.95

1128 **Bottle** Pricing Guide, 3rd Ed., Cleveland.............$7.95

3718 Collectible **Aluminum**, Grist $16.95

4560 Collectible **Cats**, An Identification & Value Guide, Book II, Fyke..$19.95

4852 Collectible **Compact Disc** Price Guide 2, Cooper $17.95

3430 Collector's Encyclopedia of **Granite Ware**, Book II, Greguire $24.95

4705 Collector's Guide to **Antique Radios**, 4th Ed., Bunis $18.95

This is only a partial listing of the books on antiques that are available from Collector Books. All books are well illustrated and contain current values. Most of these books are available from your local bookseller, antique dealer, or public library. If you are unable to locate certain titles in your area, you may order by mail from COLLECTOR BOOKS, P.O. Box 3009, Paducah, KY 42002-3009. Customers with Visa or MasterCard may phone in orders from 7:00–5:00 CST, Monday–Friday, Toll Free 1-800-626-5420. Add $3.00 for postage for the first book ordered and $0.40 for each additional book. Include item number, title, and price when ordering. Allow 14 to 21 days for delivery.